Whitm

Donald R. McCoy

Coming of Age

The United States
during
the 1920's and 1930's

Penguin Books

Penguin Books Ltd, Harmondsworth, Middlesex, England
Penguin Books Inc, 7110 Ambassador Road, Baltimore, Maryland 21207, U.S.A.
Penguin Books Australia Ltd, Ringwood, Victoria, Australia

———

Published simultaneously in a hard-cover edition by Penguin Books Inc

———

———

Printed in the United States of America

For Arthur A. Ekirch, Jr., friend and teacher

Preface

EVERY generation in the history of the United States has been a time of considerable change. Therefore, to call the decades between the two world wars a period of change is to label nothing unique in America's past. What was different was the rapidity of change between the wars, in the direction of a more highly integrated government, economy, and society.

This volume emphasizes the political, economic, and diplomatic developments of the 1920's and 1930's, although it is also concerned with cultural and social trends that affected the lives of Americans. The goal is to provide broad coverage within an interpretive framework that recognizes conflict, though as a force that, far more often than not, accelerated rather than reversed long-term trends. And make no mistake: A high degree of continuity in change chiefly characterized the interwar decades, despite the dramatic contrast between the prosperity of the 1920's and the depression of the 1930's. It is hoped that by showing the continuing and hastened trends of the two decades, as well as the differences, a clearer understanding of the entire period will emerge.

I want to take this opportunity to thank, for their encouragement and help, Robert A. Divine, of the University of Texas; Bernard Rogers, of Henry Ford Community College; and Dean George R. Waggoner, W. Stitt Robinson, and William M. Tuttle, Jr., of the University of Kansas.

DONALD R. MCCOY

University of Kansas
1972

Contents

[1]
America and Its People, 1920

MANY students of the 1920's and 1930's have treated these decades as periods during which one set of conditions and ideas dominated the United States. Observers have also viewed America as though a great chasm separated the two decades. Neither characterization is accurate. The prosperity of the 1920's did not spread to all the people, just as the depression of the 1930's was not disastrous for all Americans. Government in the former decade was less unrealistic and conservative than usually portrayed, and government in the latter decade less radical and effective. Both periods were marked by diversity, not only in a sharp struggle between the ideas of the past, the present, and, unknowingly, the future, but also in the status and thought of the nation's economic and social classes and its individual citizens.

In effect, the United States of the 1920's and 1930's was an island of time somewhat separated from the past and the future by the titanic storms of the two world wars. It was an island of diverse people and forces struggling both to escape and preserve the past and to find and evade the future, in a time and place sufficiently isolated so that none of these desires could be accomplished effectively. America was coming of age. What it did not know was what "coming of age" meant.

The United States in 1920 was a huge landmass of 3,022,000 square miles, with an empire embracing almost 713,000 square miles, which included the Philippine Islands, Guam, American Samoa, the Hawaiian Islands, Alaska, Puerto Rico, the Virgin Islands, the Panama Canal Zone, Guantánamo Bay, the Corn Islands, and miscellaneous small islands in the Pacific. In terms of population 105,711,000 people lived in the continental United States and another 12,280,000 in its overseas holdings, an overall increase of 40 percent since 1900. The proportion of foreign-born persons in the United States had reached a peak of one out of eight Americans; one out of three was either foreign-born or had one or both parents of foreign birth. The Negro population numbered 10,463,000, and there were at least 500,000 Mexican-Americans, 244,000 Indians, and 173,000 Orientals, mainly of Japanese and Chinese origin. There were at least 3,000,000 Jews, and the largest single religious group was the Catholic church, which had almost 18,000,000 communicants.

Most Americans lived in the Northeast or in the states bordering the Great Lakes, but the population continued to fan out to the West and the Southwest. For the first time in the nation's history, a majority of people was classified as residing in urban places. Indeed the increase since 1910 was impressive, as urban dwellers jumped by over 30 percent, whereas rural Americans grew by only 3 percent. Migration continued to be a constant part of American life, with only 77.4 percent of the native population living in the states of their birth. The population was also growing older on the average, continuing a long-established trend in American history, from age 22.9 to age 25.3 between 1900 and 1920. The impact of better health practices and care was seen in the rise in the rate of life expectancy at birth from 47.6 years for whites and 33.0 for nonwhites in 1900 to 54.9 and 45.3 respectively in 1920.

Attainment of an eighth-grade education for all Americans came closer as a result of compulsory schooling laws. Indeed a new goal was being established, that of a secondary-school education, as 311,000 people graduated from high school in 1920, compared with 156,000 in 1910. The rise in school enrollments also affected non-

white Americans as the percentage of them enrolled in
school climbed from 44.8 to 1910 to 53.5 in 1920, compared with an increase of from 61.3 to 65.7 for whites.
This was partly reflected during these years in the
increase of Negroes in skilled and semiskilled jobs from
15.5 percent to 21.0, although whites at the same time
rose from 60.5 to 67.0 percent in these categories. The
number of college degrees granted in America had
mounted from 40,000 in 1910 to almost 54,000 in 1920,
an increase considerably greater than that in the nation's
population. The colleges had also grown in their numbers, in the greater variety of courses offered, and in the
increasing establishment of graduate schools, which produced instructors who were better trained in their
specialties.

There were great changes in occupational trends.
Women played a larger role in the economy, their number in the labor force mounting from 4,999,000 to
8,229,000 between 1900 and 1920. Moreover, a wider
range of jobs was open to them as they made their ways
increasingly into offices, shops, factories, and even pro-
fessions. The great expansion of schools and telephone
operations accounted for a considerable part of the new
economic opportunities for women, and during World
War I they proved that they could satisfactorily take
over jobs, even in industry, previously held only by men.
Although the greatest numerical jump in occupational
categories among Americans between 1900 and 1920 was
in manual labor, the increase in white-collar and professional workers was proportionately more dramatic. Manual workers rose by about 60 percent, whereas those in
the latter fields grew by almost 110 percent.

The economy had boomed. The gross national product
had soared from $37,100,000,000 to $73,300,000,000 (1929
prices) between 1901 and 1920. The average manufacturing workweek declined from 51 hours in 1909 to 46.3
hours in 1919. Trade-union membership skyrocketed

between 1910 and 1920, by almost 150 percent, to some 5,000,000. The index of manufacturing productivity per man-hour rose from 36.6 to 42.1 between 1909 and 1919, and the index of farm productivity per worker increased from 57.3 to 70.1. Agriculture saw the dawn of power mechanization, as mirrored in the growth of tractors in use from 1,000 in 1910 to 246,000 in 1920. A similar development in automobiles and trucks had taken place, with the number of motor-vehicle registrations rising from 468,000 in 1910 to 9,239,000 in 1920. Other configurations of modern America could be seen. The amount of life insurance in force grew from about $15,000,000,000 to $40,000,000,000 between 1910 and 1920. Somewhat more startling was the growth of government in the United States. The expenditures of state and local governments shot up from $1,100,000,000 in 1902 to $5,600,000,000 by 1922. Federal budget expenditures increased from less than $500,000,000 in 1902 to $5,000,000,000 in 1921.

The rise of industrialism and commercialism in nineteenth-century America had posed great problems. Instability and inequity had marked the nation's economy to the end of the century. Small, unregulated operations in a booming economy had easily led to poor price-fixing and wage-setting practices, overproduction, and a dog-eat-dog competition. The consequences had been severe price and wage fluctuations and periods of great unemployment. By the turn of the century it was clear that something had to be done to stabilize the economy without rendering it stagnant. The cures chiefly contemplated were public regulation and consolidation of industry. This led to the rearing of state regulatory bodies and nationally to the expansion of the Interstate Commerce Commission and the establishment of the Tariff Commission, the Federal Reserve System, and the Federal Trade Commission. Attempts were also made within industries to rid themselves of or to control the least stable elements, usually through agreements and consolidation. Consequently, it was plain by 1920 that the nation had adopted two ways, public regulation and private consolidation, to stabilize business and that they were often at odds with each other. As the movement toward regulation faltered, consolidation marched steadily onward. By 1920 the top 5 percent of America's corporations, some seventeen thousand firms, received 79 percent of the country's corporate income. It was also clear by 1920 that the efforts to stabilize business were not satisfactory to many Americans, as most businessmen were restive under whatever government regulation there was, and many other Americans were nervous as to what the power of the growing industrial combines could do to business competition, labor, and farmers.

As for agriculture, little had been done to stabilize it. Farming basically continued to be uncoordinated economically either from within or from without its ranks. Therefore, it was subject to the caprices of markets with which individual farmers could not effectively cope. Labor had done better with the formation of some unions that could bargain from positions of strength in seeking higher wages, better working conditions, and fewer hours of work. Nevertheless the workingman's best protection was still supply and demand, for unions had organized only a minority of workers and were far from potent in extracting concessions from management.

Culturally, America also had a long way to go. Although native art had a long list of significant nineteenth-century figures, including Mary Cassatt, Thomas Eakins, Winslow Homer, Albert Ryder, and James Whistler, it was generally something puzzled over or even derided among Americans, and despite the nation's artistic tradition and the growing strength, vitality, and daring of its art, it was neither as well respected nor as popular as music. The tradition in serious music, however, was weak. The number of American composers of any merit was small, virtually limited to Edward MacDowell, a superb imitator of European music who had died in 1908, and to Charles Ives, whose genius was not yet recognized. A handful of respectable symphony orchestras was well established, including the New York Philharmonic, the Boston Symphony, the Philadelphia Orchestra, and the Chicago Symphony. The Metropolitan Opera and the Chicago Opera were the only opera companies worthy of international reputations.

Popular music, band music, and church music were the main supports of musical America. Music, often charitably called so, was an important part of most church services. Band music had been popularized by John Philip Sousa, among others. Ragtime and its copiers and offspring had made popular music widespread in performance if not yet in respectability, just as the waltz and the square dance had been the opening wedges in making social dancing popular with the upper and middle classes. The phonograph reinforced interest in music and dancing, and its portability made dancing possible for any young person who wished to dance, with or without parental approval. The dance as an art form, however, was in its infancy, both in reproducing European ballet and in developing an indigenous form.

The glory of American culture was literature. During the nineteenth century a legion of serious authors developed in the United States. Samuel Clemens, Emily Dickinson, Nathaniel Hawthorne, Edgar Allen Poe, and Walt Whitman were a few among those talented men and women who had built a national literature worthy of admiration in a remarkably short period of time. These superb writers of novels, poems, and short stories were complemented by a noteworthy group of philosophers and historians, including Ralph Waldo Emerson, Henry David Thoreau, William James, George Bancroft, and Francis Parkman. Given the nation's literary heritage and its vigor, it is not surprising that James

Branch Cabell, F. Scott Fitzgerald, and Sinclair Lewis burst on the American scene during and immediately after World War I.

A less pleasant fact of American life in 1920 was the severe antagonisms among the various groups that composed the nation's people. The adjustment of groups to one another is always difficult, and the mixing of peoples in America was extreme. The great flow of immigration during the nineteenth and early twentieth centuries had brought large numbers of people of differing national, religious, language, and skills backgrounds to the United States, and serious social conflict was one result. It was not just the old settlers against the newcomers, the English against the Irish, or the Scandinavians against the Italians; nor was it only Protestants against Catholics, and both of them against the Jews and those of the Orthodox churches. There was also a complex problem of communication. Language was a sizable barrier for many immigrants to surmount with both English-speaking Americans and people in other foreign-language groups. Even when immigrants learned the English language, their grasp of it was usually deficient enough to make for gibes and other irritations. And as they received, so they often gave to later comers to the United States. The folkways and religious loyalties that immigrants brought with them further hampered communication and perception as well as acceptance by other groups who might be vexed by the "strange" ways of people outside their own circles. And these circles could be drawn tightly, as testified to by the conflicts among Catholics, Jews, and even Protestants who came from different European backgrounds.

This exclusiveness meant that although American society had a porous economic class system, it had a tight social class system, based in part on the date of arrival of one's family in the New World. Loosely speaking, those who had Colonial antecedents ranked first, those

whose ancestors immigrated before the Civil War were
next, then came those whose parents arrived after the
war, and last were those who were born abroad. There
were other social status factors, of course. In terms of
national origins the English, Scottish, Scotch-Irish, and
Dutch were on top, followed by other northern and
western Europeans, followed in turn by those from southern and eastern Europe. Along religious lines, the order
of status was Protestants, Catholics, and Jews and Greek
and Russian Orthodox. There were, of course, local var-
iations, but these patterns roughly fitted the ethnic
groups that composed most of America's population. What
traditionally released Americans from the bonds of this
status system was accomplishment, and in America that
usually meant economic or political success. With money
or power one could gain prestige, education, respectability, associations with higher-status groups, and even
intermarriage. It was already clear by 1920 that most
first-generation Protestant Americans had achieved a
modicum of respectability. Even many Catholics and
some Jews had made considerable progress toward that
goal. For more recent comers and their young, more
time was needed to scale the walls of status in America.

There were other groups in American society who,
despite their family's date of arrival, remained at the
bottom. These were the racial minorities. Most Indians
were confined to the wastelands of the government reservations provided for them. They were permitted to
leave the reservations, of course, but the opportunities
awaiting them outside were few, and they had been ill
prepared to take advantage of them. Moreover, most
Indians were not allowed to vote, and they had little
voice in the governance of the reservations. Off the reservation they were segregated and sorely discriminated
against in most areas. The exceptions were those few
who had taken advantage of the scant opportunities
available to Indians and those who had intermarried. Of

these, however, most prospered only in places like Oklahoma where the Indians had retained a considerable amount of integrity and power or in areas where Indians were a rarity and therefore did not automatically encounter prejudice.

Oriental-Americans and nearly all Mexican-Americans suffered the triple disadvantage of belonging to a low-status religion, of being recent immigrants, and of having skin colors different from those of most other Americans. Discrimination and segregation were their lot, although some breakthroughs had been made. Industrious, thrifty Chinese- and Japanese-Americans had in many cases made a modest competence for themselves, and a few Mexican-Americans had settled in the North and Midwest during World War I and found economic opportunities somewhat superior to those in the Southwest.

Blacks formed the largest of America's racial minorities. By 1920 Negroes were tightly segregated in housing, schooling, and the use of public accommodations. Most lacked political representation, and few of them were permitted to exercise their constitutional right to vote. Education and health care had improved for Negroes, but it was vastly inferior in both quality and quantity to that received by whites. Their economic status had improved, too, but not enough to touch the poverty of the great majority of black Americans. Most of them lived in the South, where their role was one of obsequiousness unless they wanted to face the terror or violence visited upon "uppity niggers." In the South it was usually "Darkie, don't let the sun set on you in this town" and to get off the sidewalk with hat in hand when passing a white. The North and West provided resident blacks with some economic opportunity, the right to vote, better schooling, and a slight relaxation of segregation, discrimination, and intimidation. Those sections were not the promised land, but they were better. Nevertheless, what it boiled down to was that the one in every ten Americans who was black had few tribunes at home and no consuls from abroad to speak out for him.

Discussion of long-term trends does not give the full flavor of life in America in 1920. More immediate events had contributed to shaping the state of the Union then. Specifically, World War I and postwar conditions had struck the United States with earthquake force. Millions of men had been plucked from their homes for military service. Many of them did not come back, some because they did not survive and a much greater number because they had discovered or were seeking a new life. Those soldiers and sailors who did come home often returned with more liberated attitudes toward family, sex, and regimentation. Millions of civilians migrated to the cities to take advantage of wartime job opportunities. Others who remained at home found new occupations. All this in part accounts for the rise in urban dwellers by 1920, the larger number of women at work, and the slightly improved economic position of black Americans. The needs of war also contributed to the spurt in mechanization and industrialization in the United States. This in turn accelerated the growth of professional management and of the legions of white-collar workers and service personnel in the nation. Businessmen and industrialists gained new prestige, for they were credited with loyally raising the money and producing the goods necessary to victory.

Family ties were also weakened during the war. Many more Americans were now on their own, and most of them found it acceptable, for the challenge was stimulating and the new freedom exhilarating. A relaxation of morals accompanied this. Young men away from home were under less restraint in their social behavior, and many a young woman agreed that Johnny should have a good time before he went overseas. Indeed some consented to the proposition that they should give their all to him before he risked his everything. The search for a good time and the relaxation of sexual patterns did not pass with the coming of peace. Too many people had eaten from the apple and found it sweet. Although postwar America was far from being libertine, courtship patterns and social relationships were not to revert to the stricter prewar norms.

The war also exacerbated tensions among ethnic and racial groups. Many German-Americans were caught by the declaration of war in 1917 with divided sympathies, and they generally became targets of suspicion and even of hate during the war. Most Irish-Americans were unhappy with America's wartime alliance with Great Britain, which they saw as oppressing Ireland. The situation remained heated after the war's end as ethnic groups looked to the United States to champion the claims, often conflicting, of one homeland after another. Racial conflict increased with the greater migration of Negroes, largely because of the competition with whites for jobs and housing. These tensions, in the unstable postwar job market, were to break out in race riots in a number of cities. Partly because of the rise of world bolshevism, wartime political conformity was perpetuated in bitterly hostile attitudes toward left-wing groups. Spurred by a wave of strikes in 1919, similar attitudes were directed toward organized labor, sometimes because unions were viewed as being Red-tinged, sometimes because it was easy to picture disruption of production as unpatriotic. The excitements of war and of wartime superpatriotism were not to end with the armistice, any more than adjustments to shifting economic and social circumstances were easily made. These factors and traditional forms of prejudice contributed largely to the Red Scare of 1919–1920 and the reinvigoration of the Ku Klux Klan, which enlisted hundreds of thousands of men in a crusade to intimidate racial, religious, political, and ethnic minorities.

As superpatriotism was slowly unwinding, skepticism grew about the war and the reasons for fighting it. It was becoming clear in America that World War I had been conducted at a terrible cost. Twenty-seven nations had taken part in the conflict. Some 65,000,000 men had been mobilized, of whom 37,500,000 had been casualties, including 8,500,000 dead. The immediate cost of the war had been $360,000,000,000. Although the United States had suffered only 117,000 dead and 204,000 wounded, she mourned them grievously. Then, too, there was America's war cost, $36,000,000,000, most of which had yet to be paid. Paying the war debt and caring for disabled veterans would never be far from the nation's thoughts during the coming years. The natural question of Americans was, For what was all this given? They had marched off to war in order "to end all wars" and "to make the world safe for democracy." And why not, for they believed in the inevitability of progress and in themselves as an instrument of progress. The war itself was damaging enough, but that would have been acceptable had America's allies been as noble as they had been portrayed and had the chief war aims been attained. Certain goals were achieved, of course. The Central Powers were defeated. More important, empires disintegrated, and democracies or something like democracies often sprouted in their places. Most of the areas involved in the war in Europe experienced a lessening of social distinctions and an expansion of the social-service state, but this was not enough for Americans. They had fought for the whole loaf. The emergence of strife-torn entities of dubious political pedigree out of the old Ottoman empire, the rearing of the Bolshevik state in Russia, and the threats of Communism in Hungary and Germany were not what Americans desired or expected. As for the struggle "to end all wars," the continued fighting in eastern Europe and in the Near East confounded that. The revelations of secret treaties and the postwar scramble for annexations and reparations among the Allies were even more damaging. The bickering at Versailles and the compromises that President Woodrow Wilson had to make in forging the peace treaty also added to the increasing mood of skepticism about the war and the intentions of other nations. To a considerable extent this skepticism was to shape America's relations with the rest of the world for the next twenty years.

There were sources of skepticism on the domestic front, too. Some Americans could not reconcile wartime persecutions, the rise of racial tensions, and the Red Scare with a crusade for world democracy and perpetual peace. There were also disillusioning scandals about wartime production contracts and the liquidation of surplus government property. A wartime prohibition act, which Wilson signed into law after the armistice, to be effective July 1, 1919, irritated many Americans. The necessity for this after the horse was back in the barn was unclear. Moreover, it was rapidly followed by the ratification in 1919 of the Eighteenth Amendment, which banned intoxicating beverages from the country. Most soldiers thought this no fitting reward for their services. No one found the postwar bickering between President and Congress edifying, especially the fight over the ratification of the Versailles Treaty in which Wilson, who had compromised so artfully at Paris, refused to budge one inch at home. The Senate Republicans, now in a majority, having not been consulted by Wilson before or during peace negotiations, would not accept a treaty without reservations, and the President, having already given so much, would not accept a treaty with reservations.

The government's lack of planning for postwar reconstruction was another source of friction. Although some administration officials proposed that action be taken to ease the country back into peacetime, Wilson rejected the idea, because people would "go their own way."

Since Congress was in no mood to act, Americans had no choice but to "go their own way." Indeed, wartime regulatory machinery was quickly dismantled and federal war contracts rapidly canceled, which left industry all tooled up but with no place to go. Fortunately for the economy, wartime agricultural price supports were to continue until 1920. The results were nevertheless unpleasant. Without controls the cost of living spiraled upward; in New York City, for example, it rose by 28 percent between 1919 and 1920. Industrial production dropped, as did employment, during the first half of 1919, and although economic activity climbed to new highs the latter half of the year, considerable hardship resulted from the vast shifting of jobs during the year. In 1920 the government finally acted to reduce the high cost of living. The Federal Reserve Board raised the rediscount rate and curtailed credit in an effort to discourage economic expansion. Farm price supports expired, as did many American loans to Europe, which had been bolstering much of America's foreign agricultural market. Taxes were also raised. Consequently, prices broke, and not only inflation but the postwar prosperity quickly faded. The turn came after July, 1920, when the cost of living stood at 104.5 percent above the 1914 level. The skid was spectacular, with the cost of living falling to 68.7 percent above 1914 by March, 1921. Employment also broke rapidly, and there were four million jobless by March, 1921. President Wilson had done nothing, being preoccupied with foreign affairs until his stroke in September, 1919, after which government affairs drifted largely without coordination from the White House. It is small wonder that large numbers of Americans were disillusioned with Wilson and his administration.

The election of 1920 was fought in the context of the attitudes and forces thus far discussed. This election is usually portrayed as a turning point, one in which the voters repudiated the maintenance of world peace through collective security and the continuation of the various movements labeled progressivism. Actually, the election was a confirmation of decisions already made to change the course of government policies. Progressivism, which had been flagging by 1916, had been sidetracked during America's participation in World War I and had not become a significant movement in the immediate postwar period. With Theodore Roosevelt dead, Woodrow Wilson increasingly discredited, and Robert La Follette still suffering from the stigma of supposed wartime disloyalty, there was no one behind whom progressives could unite. Even had there been a strong leader available, it was plain that the interests of the former progressives had become diffused, partly because their earlier successes had siphoned off support for additional action, partly because of their varying emphases on what should be postwar goals, partly because of the bitterness between Democratic and Republican progressives, and partly because some progressives had been disillusioned by the results of big-government action. Whatever the reason, progressivism had disintegrated as a political force in America. Consequently, there would be neither a progressive major-party nominee nor platform in 1920.

The questions of the treaty of Versailles and the League of Nations had largely been settled for America, thanks to the intransigence of Wilson and the Senate. It was clear by the spring of 1920 that the Senate and the people would not accept the treaty whole. The question was, What parts of the Versailles agreement would the United States recognize? The issue during the 1920 election was not whether the nation should follow either prewar or wartime ideas, but what ingredients would be taken from them to determine America's postwar course in foreign relations. It was to be a mixture of both, with the added component of reaction to postwar circumstances. In short, the election was to be a referendum on who should do the mixing and how.

As to whom, the presidential nominees, the situation was confused. Former major-party nominees, including Wilson, were not really in contention. Neither the Wilson government nor the Democratic state administrations had produced a commanding figure. Although many Democrats were willing to receive their party's nomination, most were unwilling to seek it aggressively as long as the President did not deny that he wanted renomination. The fact that most Republicans felt assured of resuming their status as the majority party led to an abundance of candidates for the Republican nomination.

The Republican convention met first, in Chicago in early June. The keynote speaker was Wilson's nemesis in the Senate, Henry Cabot Lodge, who urged the Republicans to make Wilson and the League of Nations the main issues of the election campaign. From the clash between the party's pro- and anti-League forces emerged a plank that condemned the covenant of the Versailles Treaty and proposed instead the formation of an international association pledged to the development of international law and to securing an "instant and general international conference" to deal with threats to peace. The overriding Republican platform promise was "to end executive autocracy and restore to the people their constitutional government." Farmers were promised facilitation of agricultural marketing and a better system of credits. The party recognized labor's right to collective bargaining but pledged to reduce the frequency of strikes. Also among the high points in the Republican platform were demands for economy in government, a protective tariff, and encouragement of business.

The contest for nomination initially revolved around three front-running candidates: Theodore Roosevelt's close friend, General Leonard Wood; Roosevelt's running mate on the 1912 Progressive ticket, Senator Hiram Johnson; and the highly respected governor of Illinois, Frank O. Lowden. Eight other candidates trailed these three in the initial balloting. For the first eight ballots neither Wood, Johnson, nor Lowden could come close to a majority of delegate votes, and the convention was prepared to look to another quarter. On the ninth ballot Senator Warren G. Harding, of Ohio, gained the lead and on the next ballot swept easily to a majority and nomination. With effective organization the Ohio dark horse had garnered sufficient second- and third-choice support to assure victory when it was clear that the prime candidates could not succeed. Harding's moderation and geniality clinched the affair. If few admired him, almost everybody could get along with him as the party's chief spokesman. Harding seemed safe and sane, if not inspiring. For his running mate the Republicans chose Calvin Coolidge, the moderate, able governor of Massachusetts.

The Democratic delegates met in San Francisco late in June. The party stood for ratification of the Versailles Treaty "without reservations which would impair its essential integrity." The Democratic convention, too, wanted economy in government but sought tariff revisions "for revenue only." It also wanted to aid farmers in marketing their produce and recognized labor's right to bargain collectively but without strife that would disrupt industrial production. What really differentiated the major-party platforms, besides treaty and tariff policies, was that the Democrats were less happy with businessmen and proposed a somewhat higher level of government activity than the Republicans. Yet nothing could have documented the passing of progressivism more than the conservatism of the two parties' platforms compared with their past several platforms.

Fourteen men were formally placed in candidacy for

the Democratic presidential nomination, and several
others were added as the balloting proceeded. There was
no doubt that the gang was all there and that the Democrats would have difficulty choosing their standard-
bearer. The leading candidates were Wilson's son-in-law,
former Secretary of the Treasury William Gibbs Mc-
Adoo, Attorney General A. Mitchell Palmer, and Governor James Cox, of Ohio. The problem was that administration elements were divided between McAdoo and
Palmer and that the Palmer and Cox groups could agree
only that McAdoo should not be nominated. Ballot after
ballot the three men remained in contention but with
not enough strength even to gain a majority much less
the two-thirds of the delegate votes needed for nomination. On the thirty-eighth ballot Palmer, who had usually
trailed, released his delegates, and Cox slowly advanced
until he received a majority on the forty-third ballot.
That was a sufficient show of strength, and on the next
and final ballot the Ohio governor received the nomination. Like the Republicans, the Democrats had chosen
a compromise candidate. Cox, a mild reformer, a mild
League man, and a mild antiprohibitionist, was a per-
sonable man who had made few enemies and was not
connected with the Wilson Administration. Cox and
the administration were able to agree on the nomination of Assistant Secretary of the Navy Franklin D.
Roosevelt for Vice-President, thus balancing the ticket
with a young, energetic easterner.

Although the political action of 1920 was largely supplied by the Democratic and Republican parties, there
were nominees of other parties in the field. They included those of traditional minor parties—the Socialists,
Prohibitionists, and Socialist Laborites—as well as tickets
presented by the new Single Tax, American, and Farmer-
Labor parties. Of these, the largest and most significant
were the Socialist and the Farmer-Labor parties. The So-

cialists renominated their doughty perennial presidential candidate, Eugene V. Debs, who in 1920 was serving a term in Atlanta federal penitentiary for sedition. The Socialist party was a shell of what it had been before the war, because of divisions over whether to approve the war, wartime and postwar repressions, and defections to the Communist Third International. Yet Debs, campaigning from prison, put color and vigor into the politics of 1920 with his salty observations on the state of the Union and the need for a socialist republic. The Farmer-Laborite nominee was Parley P. Christensen, an obscure lawyer for the Industrial Workers of the World. Christensen depicted the major parties as wings of one huge reactionary combine. The future belonged, he asserted, to a government that would democratically nationalize key industries, give massive assistance to farmers, and strive for decent wages and working conditions for workers. Like the Socialists, the Farmer-Laborites condemned the treaty of Versailles.

The Democratic and Republican nominees, however, commanded most of the nation's attention. Harding ran an astute campaign. Well financed, well organized, and well publicized, the Republican campaign emphasized the need for a return to stability, to "normalcy." The government, under Harding, would no longer be big brother, but ostensibly the impartial mediator of national disputes whose goal was to allow the ravaged economy to heal so that it could provide bountifully for all Americans—businessmen, farmers, and workers alike. Republicans insisted that a Harding Administration would take care of the nation's traditional concerns efficiently and economically. It would not embark on crusades abroad or launch spectacular idealistic programs at home. America would extend the hand of peace and friendship overseas but would not become involved in foreign rivalries.

The Republican effort was clearly aimed at impressing the voters with their nominee's equanimity and dignity. Harding spent most of the campaign on his front porch in Marion, Ohio, talking to delegations of voters. The party, through the widespread use of speakers and publicity, reinforced his operations. It was a hardworking campaign that concealed most of the energy behind it. The Democratic effort was more plainly aggressive, not only in tone but also in the extraordinary amount of traveling and speaking that Cox did.

Cox stressed three issues. He favored the entry of the United States into the League of Nations and the initiation of federal programs to aid in the development of natural resources and education, to better industrial working conditions, and to assist farmers. The Democratic nominee also opposed what he called the attempt on the part of "selfish, greedy" interests to buy the election for the Republicans in order to repress labor, exploit agriculture, shift the tax load to the average man, and make "the Federal Reserve System an annex to big business." What it all came down to was that the Democrats were proposing a slightly higher level of government activity than the Republicans, and the Republicans were championing the need for more business activity.

The major issue between the two parties, however, was the League of Nations. Cox was stuck with the League, for he could not repudiate it without splitting his party and losing Wilson's backing. The League was also Harding's Achilles' heel, for there was a substantial group of League supporters among Republicans and independents. Harding had to find a position that would satisfy both the Republican and the independent opponents and proponents of the League; Cox sought to put a wedge between the two conflicting groups in the hope that the pro-League elements would come to him. As it turned out, the respective goals of the two men were exceedingly difficult to attain. Harding had the more difficult task. He wobbled about, now flirting with the League, now rejecting it, and in doing so he irritated both the anti- and the pro-League groups. Finally he came up with the assertion that Senate approval of the League covenant could not be secured if Article X was in it, the section under which League members could be called out to defend recognized national boundaries. Harding declared that what was needed was a world association, perhaps even a revised League, based on justice instead of force. This position was satisfactory to the anti-League forces, who saw no harm in such talk, and to most League advocates among the Republicans, who saw a glimmer of hope for eventual American entry into the League. Cox's response was to say that he was flexible on the League. Indeed late in October he declared that he would do whatever was necessary to reach agreement with the Senate on ratification of the treaty of Versailles. Thus, ironically, both nominees wound up breaching their own campaign consistency on the League of Nations. The victor, however, was Harding, who was substantially able to retain both his pro- and his anti-League support.

November 2, 1920, was Harding's fifty-fifth birthday, and the voters gave him a most welcome birthday present: overwhelming election as President of the United States. The popular vote ran 16,000,000 for the Republicans to only 9,000,000 for the Democrats, the most lopsided presidential election of the twentieth century. The Socialists polled 920,000 votes, only a few more than in 1912 when the electorate was much smaller. The Farmer-Laborites attracted 265,000, and the combined vote for the other minor parties was only slightly more.

The Harding victory was attributable to several factors. Many German-Americans, Irish-Americans, and other hyphenated Americans abandoned the Democrats.

Large numbers of workingmen and farmers swung to the Republicans. Only in the South did a majority of voters stand by the Democrats. Elsewhere Stephen Early's report from South Dakota to Franklin Roosevelt was borne out: "The bitterness toward Wilson is evident everywhere and deeply rooted. He hasn't a friend." That bitterness not only hurt the Cox-Roosevelt ticket but was also mirrored in congressional elections: The number of Republican seats rose from 240 to 303 in the House of Representatives and from 49 to 59 in the Senate.

Harding and Coolidge had been able to get large numbers of voters to identify with them as small-town men who had made good. The Republican party had benefited from the calming, dignified images they had projected, which contrasted with the world-beating aggressiveness of their opponents. More significant, the Republicans had been the beneficiaries of adverse reaction to the coldness and stubbornness of Woodrow Wilson, of the identification of the Democratic party with liquor at a time of high-dry sentiment, of the outrage of nationalists and ethnic groups with Wilson's foreign policies, and of what historian Arthur S. Link has called "the fragmentation of the progressive movement." The combination of inflation and then recession after the war had further motivated voters to seek a change. The heartfelt Republican promise of lower taxes, less government interference, and more frugal government was attractive to businessmen, small and large. It is probable that workingmen were willing to punish the Democrats for their lack of sympathy even if it meant voting for a man, Harding, who consorted with business leaders. Moreover, the dependence of many ethnic groups on manufacturing for a livelihood pushed them toward accepting the Republican party's high-tariff and sound-money panaceas. Their lot could not be worse, many of them believed, than it had been during the immediate postwar period. Certainly, Cox and Roosevelt did not persuade them otherwise. In short, the Republicans owed their triumph to Wilson's failure to achieve the better nation and better world of which he so often spoke and to their own ability to conjure up an appealing picture of the "normalcy" to which they would return the nation.

Foreign Affairs of the 1920's

THE voters of America had unknowingly elected two Presidents in 1920, for in less than three years Warren Harding would be dead, and his running mate, Calvin Coolidge, would succeed to the Presidency. Few Presidents of the United States could have been more different in their personalities, methods, and backgrounds.

Warren Gamaliel Harding was born in the Ohio village of Blooming Grove in 1865. He was the first of six surviving children, whose father was a veterinarian who later became a homeopathic physician. The family later moved to Marion, the small city usually identified as Warren Harding's hometown. In 1882 he was graduated from Ohio Central College, a nearby normal school, but soon decided that teaching was not for him. He found his calling when in 1884 he, along with two other young men, purchased the dilapidated Marion *Star*. Soon the *Star* was the town's leading newspaper, and Harding was its sole owner. If far from brilliant, he was gregarious, ambitious, and sufficiently diligent to develop his newspaper and a reputation as a publicist for Marion. Harding became widely involved in the town's affairs, and politics eventually became one of his chief activities. Using Marion County as his power base, he was elected to the state senate in 1899 and reelected two years later, when he was also chosen floor leader. Proven loyal to the party and effective at the art of political conciliation, he was elected lieutenant governor in 1903. Later, in 1910, Harding ran unsuccessfully for governor, and in 1912 he was selected by President William Howard Taft to place him in nomination at the Republican national convention. In 1914, with a shifting of the political tide to more conservative Republicans, Harding was able to draw on the pool of goodwill that he had accumulated over the years to be elected United States senator. His Senate career, however, was mediocre. His attendance record was poor, and no significant legislative proposals or enactments carried his name. In no way was he looked to for leadership in the Senate. Nevertheless, genial, go-along Harding was well liked, he offended few people, and he was befriended by many. When the time came, he was available for bigger things.

Calvin Coolidge was born on July 4, 1872, in the crossroads settlement of Plymouth Notch, Vermont, of the backwoods branch of a distinguished New England family. His father was a small merchant and farmer and a perennial server in minor political offices. Coolidge, unlike Harding, was born into a small family, one that numbered only his father and himself with the early death of his mother and sister. Also unlike Harding, he teethed on the virtues of silence, hard work, and responsibility. Coolidge was graduated from Amherst College in 1895. He then read law in Northampton, Massachusetts, becoming a member of the bar in 1897. Although his law practice was never very successful, by dint of hard work and reliability, he slowly became a Republican party worthy. He passed up the political ladder, rung by rung, rarely being out of office. Coolidge entered the Massachusetts senate in 1912 and became senate president in 1914 and lieutenant governor two years later. Building on his reputation for steadiness and moderation, he attained the governorship in 1919. He performed competently in that post, although he gained fame only for his part in quelling the Boston police strike. It was that, and particularly his widely publicized telegram to Samuel Gompers, president of the American Federation of Labor, stating that "there is no right to strike against public safety by anybody, anywhere, any time," that brought Calvin Coolidge to national prominence.

Different as Harding's and Coolidge's backgrounds were, their administrations' personnel and policies were remarkably similar. There was considerable continuity in their cabinets, with Treasury Secretary Andrew Mellon, Commerce Secretary Herbert Hoover, Postmaster General Harry New, Interior Secretary Hubert Work, and Labor Secretary James Davis remaining on to the end or almost to the end of the Coolidge Presidency. Those who left did so either voluntarily, under outside pressure, or through death or illness. Harding and Coolidge had been elected on the same platform, to which they adhered to a high degree. Coolidge not only inherited and championed most of those platform policies but appeared to be even more comfortable with them than Harding had been. The policies of the two administrations were, however, more consistent than they were successful. This is well seen in the foreign policies of the two Presidents.

Harding, in his March, 1921, inaugural address, declared that he would avoid "entangling alliances" and subjecting decisions on American affairs "to any other than our own authority." Although thereby rejecting the League of Nations, the President said that the United States should be willing to confer with other countries on the maintenance of peace and the achievement of disarmament. Harding repeated these sentiments in April, adding that America should make peace with its former enemies and assist the economic recovery of Europe.

Harding had to step warily because of the Senate's determination to maintain the supremacy in foreign relations that it had seized from President Wilson. In selecting Charles Evans Hughes to be Secretary of State, Harding helped himself immensely in charting a safe passage between the Charybdis of problems abroad and the Scylla of Senate jealousy. Hughes, a former Republican presidential nominee and Supreme Court justice, had the prestige to steer clear of the dangerous shoals of foreign policy. He had the skill to do so, too. A master of detail and public relations, Hughes was a faithful servant and generally a wise counselor. Thanks also largely to him, America's representation abroad was of a high caliber, certainly several notches above that of the Wilson years.

Although Hughes looked favorably upon the League of Nations and was given virtually a free hand by Harding, he was trapped by the strong anti-League sentiment in the United States. He was a realist, however, and was under orders from the President not to stir a repetition of the fierce battle between the White House and the Senate that had taken place in 1919–1920. He prodded Harding and gently the Senate to go as far as possible in maintaining America's world influence, but he stopped short of reviving "the old controversy." There was no chance for American membership in the League, and he knew it. This meant that the administration would have to find alternative paths to conclude peace with its wartime enemies, to maintain that peace, and to attain other foreign-policy aims.

The first objective was to end the state of war with the Central Powers that still technically existed. This was done in part by the Knox-Porter resolution which simply declared the war to be over and reserved to the United States the rights stipulated in the treaty of Versailles. Hughes then negotiated treaties with Germany, Austria, and Hungary based on the Knox-Porter resolution to which were added the applicable parts of the Allied peace treaties with those countries. In Germany's case a disclaimer regarding the League covenant and the United States was added. The Senate Foreign Relations Committee attached a further reservation that there could be no representation of or participation by the United States in any organization authorized under the Versailles Treaty unless provided for by Congress. Even with that, Senate debate on the Hughes peace treaties was spirited. Finally, in October, 1921, the treaties were ratified, and the following month President Harding declared the war officially ended.

Meanwhile, something infinitely more important was developing: a concerted effort to reduce naval armaments and to bring accord in the Far East among the interested powers. After the end of the war, pressures built up in Great Britain, Japan, and the United States for naval expansion. Not only did this threaten the economy movement in America, but it also highlighted the possibility of another war should the United States come into conflict with either of the other two nations, which were bound to each other in an alliance. Senator William E. Borah, of Idaho, seized the initiative with his legislative proposals in 1920–1921 for a joint Anglo-Japanese-American effort to cut naval expenditures. Harding approached the problem more cautiously. Soon after his election, he discussed the idea of an international disarmament conference and later mentioned it in his inaugural address. He was not, however, willing to sacrifice American naval development until effective international action was taken.

In 1921 public opinion for a disarmament meeting grew rapidly, and the British pondered international action that might allow them to retain the benefits of their alliance with Japan without facing the possibility of war with the United States in the future. While Borah's resolution for a conference of Britain, Japan, and America on naval disarmament was moving to a vote, the Harding Administration began making inquiries abroad about disarmament questions. When, early in the summer of 1921, it became clear that Congress would adopt the Borah resolution, the administration decided to act.

On July 8, while the American ambassador in London was notifying Secretary Hughes of British interest in a conference on Far Eastern affairs, Hughes was dispatching cables to London, Paris, Rome, and Tokyo to seek responses on a proposed disarmament meeting. After Hughes read of the British proposal that evening, he cabled to ask if Great Britain would agree to a conference on both disarmament and Far Eastern questions. The Secretary of State, upon receiving a favorable reply from London, issued invitations to attend an international conference that far exceeded in scope that contemplated by Senator Borah. The meeting would include nations other than England, Japan, and America, it would discuss Far Eastern issues, and it could conceivably discuss armaments other than naval.

The conference was carefully staged by Hughes. Not only Britain, France, Italy, and Japan but also Belgium, China, the Netherlands, and Portugal were asked to attend. Russia was pointedly not invited, for the activities of the conference were somewhat motivated by fear of the Bolshevist state. Secretary Hughes led the American delegation, which also included Senator Henry Cabot Lodge, the chairman of the Foreign Relations Committee, and Senator Oscar Underwood, the Senate minority leader. On the first day of the Washington Conference, November 12, 1921, Hughes asked dramatically that England, Japan, and America scrap a total of 1,878,043 tons of capital ships, more than half of what they had built or were building. He also proposed that no new keels be laid down for ten years, that no capital ship displace more than 35,000 tons or be replaced until it was twenty years old, and that the total allowable replacement tonnage for battleships and cruisers be 500,000 each for the United States and the United Kingdom, 300,000 for Japan, and 175,000 each for France and Italy. He urged that similar agreements be negotiated for smaller vessels. Hughes's address was unexpectedly far-reaching, and its impact was sensational. As one observer remarked, "Hughes sank in thirty-five minutes more ships than all the admirals of the world have sunk in a cycle of centuries."

The conference took up Secretary Hughes's challenge. It met for three months and in the end agreed upon a Five-Power Treaty that fixed capital ship tonnages at 558,950 for Britain, 525,850 for America, 301,320 for Japan, 221,170 for France, and 182,800 for Italy, thereby scrapping almost exactly what Hughes had called for. The replacement tonnage ratios were set at 5:5:3:1.75: 1.75, as he had recommended, and the powers accepted the ten-year building holiday and the 35,000-ton limit on the size of battleships. Among other restrictions were the maximum tonnages pegged for aircraft carriers, of 135,000 each for England and the United States, 81,000 for Japan, and 60,000 each for France and Italy, with no single carrier to exceed 27,000 tons' displacement. America, Britain, and Japan also agreed to maintain the status quo on fortifications in their insular possessions in the Pacific.

Limitations on naval armaments were not all that came out of the Washington Conference of 1921–1922. There was a provision prohibiting the use of poison gas. More significant was the treaty among England, France, Japan, and the United States that was in effect to replace the Anglo-Japanese alliance and eliminate the possibility of war between Great Britain and America. This Four-Power Treaty bound the signatories to respect one another's rights regarding their Pacific "insular possessions and dominions" and in the event of dispute to confer to compose the differences involved. In case of threats to their Pacific territories from any outside power —for example, Russia—they agreed to consult with one another on the action to be taken. This treaty was to be effective for ten years. There was also the Nine-Power Treaty by which the nations participating in the conference pledged to honor the territorial integrity and sovereignty of China, to seek no special rights there, and to maintain the "open-door" concept. In exchange, China agreed not to discriminate against the legitimate actions of foreign citizens. Also deriving from the conference, Japan decided to negotiate the restoration of the Shantung peninsula to China and to initiate the withdrawal of her troops from eastern Siberia.

As could be expected, the treaties underwent searching debate in the Senate, especially the Four-Power Treaty, which had been secretly negotiated. Nevertheless, Henry Cabot Lodge, well supported by public opinion and by the administration, ably steered the treaty through the Foreign Relations Committee and the Senate with only one reservation, which was that America was committed to no use of "armed force, no alliance, no obligation to join in any defense." Even then, the final margin of victory was only four votes. The other treaties, however, were quickly ratified in 1922 after this flexing of the Senate's muscles.

Although the Washington Conference was not the "turning point" in the history of mankind that its champions claimed it to be, neither was it insignificant. In effect, an "association of nations," which Harding had promised during the 1920 election campaign, had met and come to agreement on a number of crucial issues. The Five-Power Treaty had turned the developing naval-arms race into a disarmament marathon and set a precedent for further joint reductions of armaments. The Four-Power Treaty had provided a vehicle for easier international communication on Pacific affairs and allowed England, to the relief of both itself and America, to slip out of its alliance with Japan. The bases for the relaxation of tensions in China had been laid as a result of the conference. And it cannot be overlooked that the naval agreement permitted tremendous cuts in the American arms budget and those of other states at a time when government economy held a high

priority. As William Allen White wrote, "Hats Off to
Warren G." He had brought "home the bacon." If Japan
did not later fully abide by the provisions of the various
Washington treaties, it did for several years. The blame
for treaty violations lay not with the conference but
with the failure of the participants to attach enforcement provisions, or at least to undertake adequate intelligence surveillance and make diplomatic protests. The
Washington treaties realistically could not serve for a
millennium, but they did serve well for the time being,
and little more can be expected of any agreements
among states.

There were, of course, endeavors to build upon the
work of the Washington Conference. President Coolidge
urged further international arms reductions. For him,
arms limitation was a bulwark not only to the maintenance of peace and the reduction of expenditures but
also to the development of international business prosperity, which he believed to be the most effective hedge
against war. His encouragement of a comprehensive
international disarmament conference in 1924 served to
support the efforts of the League of Nations in that
direction. His next opportunity came in 1927. Although
public feeling for arms limitation remained high, the
League's work proceeded slowly. There were some indi-
cations that now some other major powers were ready
for another disarmament meeting with the United States.
When the Coolidge Administration showed its willingness to discuss extending the Washington Conference
ratios to all types of naval vessels, the response from
abroad seemed favorable. The President and Frank B.
Kellogg, who had succeeded Hughes as Secretary of
State in 1925, proposed another naval conference with
England, France, Italy, and Japan.

Preparations were made for the conference to meet in
Geneva, Switzerland. The conference, however, which

opened June 20, 1927, seemed ill-fated from the beginning. Italy and France declined to participate, and it became plain that Japan, the United Kingdom, and the United States did not see eye to eye on what further naval limitations should be imposed. Coolidge was optimistic that the three powers represented at Geneva would come to agreement and that France and Italy would later adhere. His optimism was not gratified. The diplomats and naval officers at the conference did not view matters in the same light, and armaments interests were pressing the delegates to scuttle the talks. The most important problem was the inability of Britain and America to agree on cruiser tonnages. Despite some concessions, the two powers never came close to agreement. Japan allowed the two English-speaking nations to fight it out, and that they did until the naval conference slipped beneath the waves in August, with its tattered flags flying.

Coolidge's favorite hope for maintaining peace had been blasted. His disappointment mounted in 1927–1928 as other countries entered into discussions of naval limitations aimed at permitting them to construct what they wanted while sharply restricting the classes of vessels in which America was interested. He made it clear in his 1928 Armistice Day speech that he would have no part of this, for it meant that the "principle of limitations would be virtually abandoned" for all nations except the United States. The President's response was to return to Harding's initial plans to keep the navy strong in the absence of genuine disarmament. Within the restrictions imposed by the Five-Power Treaty, he recommended to Congress in December, 1927, the appropriation of funds to begin a nine-year, billion-dollar naval development program. If further naval disarmament was impossible, at least Coolidge would keep the nation's sea defenses in adequate condition. There was also the possibility that heightened American naval expenditure would bring the leading powers around the conference table again.

It should be observed that while the United States sought international disarmament during the 1920's, it also kept its armed forces at a higher level of strength than in the period before World War I. The officers and men in the army, navy, and marines numbered almost 252,000 in 1925, compared with 139,000 in 1910. The army general staff was given administrative as well as advisory duties within the War Department, thereby strengthening the authority of uniformed personnel. The wartime citizens' military training camps were continued, and the reserve officers' training corps was expanded, allowing for a growth of reserve army forces. Presidents Harding and Coolidge kept the navy at maximum treaty strength, and the Washington Conference had resulted only in the scrapping of the navy's overage ships and those still under construction. Moreover, the navy, with some success, sought development of craft in unrestricted classes of vessels and reorganized and modernized the fleet. Harding had sponsored or approved most of these policies, and Coolidge saw no reason to change them as long as other nations showed little desire to pare their armed forces proportionately to the level of the United States military services.

Although world peace was fragile and the ways of maintaining it difficult, Americans quested down other paths that gave promise of skirting the maw of war in the future. It was clear as President Harding took office in 1921 that the United States not only would not join the League of Nations but would have nothing to do with it or its agencies. Indeed, when Hughes became Secretary of State, he did not reply to communications from the League for almost four months, and then only to acknowledge their receipt. By 1922, however, the situation had thawed slightly, and Hughes started to open channels of communication between the United States and the League. Later that year the government began to send unofficial observers to the meetings of certain League agencies, and by the end of his Presidency, Harding had approved American participation in the work of four minor organizations of the League. This trend continued under Coolidge, who was able to secure funds from Congress to underwrite American participation in the League's Preparatory Commission for the Disarmament Conference. By the end of the decade the United States had taken part in forty League conferences and had five permanent unofficial observers in Geneva. Of course, no President during the 1920's could work to bring America into the League, for as Democrat Cordell Hull noted, "the League of Nations [was] almost a byword for ridicule with many millions." Yet by the time of Herbert Hoover's Presidency, the United States was in effect an unofficial member of the League.

Being an unofficial member was not enough, however, just as almost achieving naval disarmament was not enough. Another path was sought. That was the perfection of international law and its enforcement through the decisions of a world court. Harding had discussed this during the 1920 election campaign and in his inaugural address. The problem was that the existing Court of International Justice was affiliated with the League, which was a stigma for large numbers of American citizens and congressmen. Nevertheless in 1923 Harding asked the Senate to approve America's membership on the court, with reservations to insure that thereby no legal relationship between the United States and the League would be established. Despite fierce senatorial opposition, Harding and Secretary of State Hughes stood by this position as a necessary way to promote the adjudication of international disputes. Public opinion rallied around the administration, despite the efforts of influen-

tial senators such as William E. Borah who wanted a
world court but not the League's world court. Before
his death, however, Harding aided his opponents by
indicating that he would accept further reservations
that would make the court a real "world court and not
a League court."

It was this divided position that Calvin Coolidge inherited. Nevertheless he rejected the advice of those who
told him to abandon the issue. In his first message to
Congress Coolidge resurrected Harding's earlier proposal
to the Senate. The new President's aides also secured
endorsement of the world-court proposal from the 1924
Republican national convention. Perhaps because Coolidge knew that he would be damned regardless of what he
did, he took his election in 1924 as approval by the voters of membership on the world court. He repeatedly
brought the issue to the attention of Congress and the
people. Yet, by Harding's and even Coolidge's willingness to accept reservations that would keep American
membership on the court clear of contact with the
League, the government was voluntarily yielding too
much to the opposition, for reservations might make
America's membership repugnant to the countries that
were already members.

Finally in late 1925 and early 1926 the Senate took
up the world-court question. On January 26 the Senate
voted seventy-six to seventeen for United States membership on the court, although with five reservations. A
complicating factor was the stipulation that the reservations had to be accepted individually by each of the
court's forty-eight members. Unfortunately for the cause
of American membership on the court, Coolidge just sat
and waited for the approval of the member states, and he
seemed offended when any of those nations raised questions about the reservations. Yet they accepted the four
reservations divorcing the United States from contact
with the League in the court's operations. What the

court members could not accept was the stipulation that the United States would not be bound by the court's advisory decisions rendered without America's consent, even though the countries on the League's Council enjoyed that privilege. When Coolidge rejected the offer of a number of court members to negotiate this reservation, American adherence to the world court became a dead issue.

Adherence to the world court had fallen through, progress on disarmament was flagging, and America's contacts with the League were growing too slowly. Only one other path appeared to remain, the outlawing of war. The American Committee for the Outlawry of War had been founded by Chicago businessman Salmon O. Levinson in 1921. Rejecting the idea of collective security, because it was based on force, the outlawrists sought an international law that would forbid the use of force between and among nations. On that basis, the outlawrists believed, not only could the nations assure the continuance of world peace, but they could fashion a comprehensive body of world law and establish an effective world court to enforce it. Nothing could be more idealistic, and nothing promised to be less effective, than outlawry. Yet, through constant agitation, Levinson was able to rally prominent and influential Americans, including Senator Borah, to his cause. The outlawrists got nowhere with Warren Harding, and Coolidge initially evaded them with generalizations even greater than their own. Coolidge's campaign for American adherence to the International Court of Justice did not discourage them, for he went out of his way not to alienate them. The President was astute enough to pick opportunities when they came, and when one failed, he would take up another. Outlawry's day was to come.

By 1927 Professor James T. Shotwell, of Columbia University, had brought the outlawry idea to the attention of French Foreign Minister Aristide Briand, who saw in it a way to reduce ill will between France and America and perhaps to secure an American guarantee of existing national boundaries in Europe. At least, should the two nations agree to outlaw war, France would have the moral right to call upon the United States to help defend *la patrie* in case of attack by another nation. In any event, France could not lose by making a gesture. Therefore, on the tenth anniversary of America's entry into World War I, Briand publicly pledged France's readiness "to subscribe, with the United States, to any mutual engagement tending, as between those two countries, to 'outlaw war.'"

Both President Coolidge and Secretary of State Kellogg were displeased with the French Foreign Minister, but they could not ignore his proposal, especially because the idea had well-organized support in the United States. Also to be considered was the rise in good feelings between America and France following Charles A. Lindbergh's spectacular flight to Paris. Therefore, Coolidge left the door open for study of the proposal. The French soon sent a draft treaty declaring that the two nations "condemn recourse to war and renounce it, respectively, as an instrument of their national policy towards each other." It was additionally provided that all disputes that might arise between France and America would be settled by "pacific means."

Neither Coolidge nor Kellogg was impressed with the proposed pact, which resembled France's recent defensive treaties with other European countries and which therefore could be considered offensive to Germany. The administration procrastinated, hoping that public interest would subside. There were just too many implications to the draft pact and particularly ones that might involve the United States in France's intrigues on the Continent. Moreover, Coolidge believed that there was a good chance that the Senate, "a very curious body," would not ratify a Franco-American outlawry treaty, because by its terms Congress would lose its power to declare war on France. The President also knew, as he told a press conference, "There isn't any shortcut to peace."

Yet public and even Senate interest in Briand's draft treaty did not recede. By December, 1927, Coolidge decided to authorize official discussions on the proposal, assuming that a better formula than Briand's would be found. That formula was one suggested by Senator Borah, which was that the outlawry of war be made multilateral. When Kellogg discussed this approach with the President, Coolidge replied, "We can do that, can we not?" And do that they did.

On December 28 Secretary of State Kellogg wrote Briand that France and America "might make a more signal contribution to world peace by joining in an effort to obtain the adherence of all the principal powers of the world to a declaration renouncing war as an instrument of national policy." Kellogg had outmaneuvered Briand. His counterproposal, if implemented, not only would retain America's freedom of action in case of hostilities between France and any other nation but would also make any warlike action by France embarrassing. Moreover, Briand had become too well identified with outlawry to abandon the project forthwith.

While the French Foreign Minister waited to see what the international reaction would be, Kellogg enthusiastically circulated his proposal among the leading powers and found that it was acceptable. On August 27, 1928, the Kellogg-Briand Treaty, as it had become popularly known, was signed in Paris by the representatives of fifteen nations, including France, Germany, Great Britain, Italy, Japan, Poland, and the United States. The Senate, by an overwhelming vote, ratified the pact without qualification on January 15, 1929.

Although many other countries later adhered to its principles of banning "recourse to war" and settling disputes by peaceful means, the Kellogg-Briand Treaty proved a swordless sheath. The best that can be said for the pact is that it was a magnificent gesture and as such supplied a standard toward which men of goodwill would strive. As Coolidge had observed, the treaty's effectiveness relied upon public opinion. That turned out to be a frail reed upon which to lean, with the revival of militant nationalism in the world during the following decade.

Nipping at the heels of the nations during the 1920's were the questions of repayment of the Allies' war debts and the payment of reparations by the defeated powers for damages they inflicted during the war. Harding, in his first message to Congress, emphasized the need for an orderly liquidation of the debts other countries owed the United States. Wilson had established America's position, making it clear that the debts were to be paid in full and without reference to the debts and reparations that other countries owed America's debtors. Both Harding and Coolidge generally adhered to this policy. Although the wartime and postwar loans overseas had stimulated the country's economy and had been lent at 5-percent interest, other nations accepted the conditions, and neither the American Government nor taxpayers were prepared to discharge the debt. Moreover, the debt, almost twelve billion dollars large, would probably wreak havoc with America's economy if it was not repaid. No question of the 1920's and early 1930's caused more unhappiness in relations between the United States and other countries.

The Harding Administration was willing to be somewhat flexible because of the varying abilities of America's debtors to pay. Congress was less so, and in February, 1922, it created the Debt Funding Commission to make settlements on the basis that the maximum deadline for payment would be 1947 and that the minimum adjusted-interest rate would be 4.25 percent. The passage of the Debt Funding Act led to widespread grumbling among

America's former allies. Great Britain and France wanted cancellation of the debts, not mild concessions on interest and the time of payment. France flatly declared that it could not abide by the restrictions of the legislation. After months of delay and negotiation, England and America in January, 1923, agreed to payment of the former's $4,600,000,000 debt over a period of sixty-two years and at an average interest rate of 3.3 percent. Unhappy though Congress was with this evasion of its guidelines, it accepted the agreement. This action was crucial to breaking the resistance of other countries to debt negotiations, and during the five years of its operations the Debt Funding Commission concluded agreements with fifteen nations. The debts involved were some $11,600,000,000, with interest rates varying between 0.3 and 3.3 percent and payment running for sixty-two years.

Although the United States would not concur, there was an undeniable relationship between the war debts and the reparations imposed upon the former enemy powers. The German reparations were set at the staggering amount of $33,000,000,000 under the Versailles Treaty. Germany, not surprisingly, defaulted almost immediately. When threats of force were unavailing, there was pressure, particularly from Great Britain, for cancellation of all war debts and reparations. The United States would not agree to this. Indeed, its government played blind to the deteriorating state of the German economy and the mounting antagonisms in Europe over the issue. Not only did America avoid involvement, but its government took the position that Germany's inability to pay reparations, which America had renounced for herself, had no bearing on other nations' ability to pay their just debts to the United States.

In January, 1923, French and Belgian troops occupied the Ruhr in retaliation for Germany's default, and the German economy was flying to pieces. This double crisis led to a change in America's attitude. Secretary of State

Hughes suggested formation of a European payments commission to straighten out the situation. He added that Americans would be willing to serve on the commission. Making the arrangements took time, but in November, 1923, an international financial commission was established, to be chaired by an American, Charles Dawes. The Dawes committee, as it was known, studied the situation and devised a plan for dealing with the German reparations. It was arranged in 1924 that American bankers would lend the funds necessary to permit Germany to put its finances in order and to resume reparations payments. This was made easier by substantially reducing the amount of reparations and spreading their payment over a long period of time. As long as there was prosperity this system worked to keep Germany paying reparations and the former allies paying their debts to America. The system broke down, however, with the arrival of the international depression in the 1930's.

In addition to supporting the Dawes plan, the American government during the 1920's encouraged private loans to foreign countries and businesses on the theory that this would help to stabilize the world's finances and promote a prosperous international economy. American dollars poured overseas, with the nation's private investments abroad leaping from $7,000,000,000 in 1919 to $17,200,000,000 by 1930. Perhaps it would have worked had the world's economy been in sounder condition or had American loans been made more judiciously. The international economy, however, was anemic during the 1920's, and there was no effective government regulation of American loans. Consequently, dollars traveled abroad and helped build a flimsy facade of prosperity for the world. Ill-advised investments weakened the world's economy by supporting unsound enterprises, and many of the loans, good and bad alike, were lost with the coming of the depression of the 1930's.

The greatest investment fiasco was the lending of funds to shore up Germany. The $2,500,000,000 lent to Germany under the Dawes plan corresponded to the amount that the Germans paid in reparations, and that in turn corresponded to the debt payments that the American government received from its former allies. In effect, the United States was supporting the whole debt-payments and reparations structure, while congratulating itself on the progress made in reducing those burdens. The Dawes plan and massive private American investments abroad not only allowed Europe to avoid coming to grips with reparations and war debts but, as historian Hajo Holborn has written, "made it possible to postpone the adjustment to the structural changes of the world economy produced by the war."

Complicating the situation was the intense international economic rivalry of the 1920's. The economic upheaval caused by the war was awesome. The prewar pattern of markets and exchange was upset. New industries were born, the reliance of various countries on imports was substantially raised or lowered, new economic controls were established, new creditor and new debtor nations emerged, and economic expectations were heightened. During the war Americans and Japanese seized many of the markets that Europeans, more deeply involved in the war, could not supply with goods or funds. One major power, Russia, created an entirely new economic system, and another, Italy, would soon considerably reshape its economy. Large-scale emigration, which had in the past helped to relieve economic pressures, was no longer possible. Moreover, colonization was less a possibility than before in opening up new markets and supply sources. Every country struggled to maintain its wartime economic expansion. This was justified not only by popular expectation for economic progress but also by the intense desire for increased self-sufficiency, so that in the case of another war the various nations would not be so reliant upon foreign supplies. In Europe and the Near East the situation was aggravated by the establishment of small, new states where empires had previously existed, small countries that lurched onto the economic scene guided more by nationalistic pride than economic wisdom. In Asia, China and India strove with some success to develop large industries to reduce their dependence on finished goods from overseas. Similar developments occurred in Latin America. The upshot was that economic nationalism swept the world as the nations, with a common degree of derangement, sought simultaneously to gain new markets abroad while trying to reserve their home markets to themselves.

The curtailment of immigration was part of the story, and the United States was not alone in restricting it. Indeed Great Britain had come to control immigration as early as 1905. Cheap labor had been welcome in many countries as long as it could be put to work. In that way immigration would not only provide the manpower necessary to keep the engines of the economy expanding, but it would also supply a new market at home as well as keep workers' wages low because of competition for jobs. Several factors, however, worked against continued large-scale migration to industrialized countries. One was the rise of democratic movements whereby native labor's protests at being underemployed and underpaid became increasingly effective. Another was a growing lack of confidence, especially after the war, that the economy could expand enough to absorb new labor. A third was the rise of xenophobia, which had been encouraged by the hatreds unleashed by the war. All this was bolstered by the ease with which people could usually make targets of the outlanders who competed for jobs.

All of these forces were present in the United States after the war, and they were intensified by the great number and variety of immigrant peoples in America.

The result was the dramatic heightening of the anti-immigrant movement in the immediate postwar years. It was easy for native Americans to conclude that the flood of immigration had depressed wages, debased morals, contributed to urban corruption, increased welfare rolls, exacerbated antagonisms among groups, and introduced disloyal and radical groups. It was not surprising that ever larger numbers of native Americans became unsympathetic to the problems of newcomers and demanded that the door be shut to further mass immigration. Both the Democratic and the Republican platforms in 1920 favored restriction of immigration. Before Harding became President, Congress passed an emergency quota bill, which would have limited annual European immigration to 3 percent of any country's nationals resident in the United States in 1910. The measure died, however, when Wilson failed to sign it. The bill was reintroduced and overwhelmingly approved by the new Congress in 1921. Because of the new statute, immigration in 1921–1922 was reduced from the expected 1,500,000 to 309,556, which helped relieve competition in the then depressed labor market. It also changed the complexion of immigration, as a majority of immigrants now came from northern and western Europe, a result desired by those restrictionists who viewed people from elsewhere as being a supremely corrupting influence. The law was generally hailed as a great success and in 1922 was extended for two additional years.

Anti-immigration feeling did not subsequently weaken. Harding had indicated that he favored further restriction, and so did Coolidge when he became President, saying that "those who do not want to be partakers of the American spirit ought not to settle in America. . . . America must be kept American." That was a popular sentiment and motivated new legislation in 1924 to curtail immigration. The administration's only reservation was over the measure's provision to ban the immigration of Japanese. President Coolidge and Secretary Hughes fought vigorously for an annual quota of 250 Japanese immigrants in the hope of not offending Japan. Congress would have none of it, as the great majority of both Democrats and Republicans passed the National Origins Act of 1924 without a Japanese quota. This mean and shortsighted action contributed to Japan's feeling of vexation with the United States.

The 1924 act was the law of the land. Under it, immigration was to be scaled down until by 1927 it would be limited to a maximum of 150,000 a year, with quotas based mainly on the national origins in Europe of the American people in 1920. The law was so complicated that quotas could not be established until 1929, and then rather arbitrarily. The net result was plain, however. In addition to barring most people with dark skins from immigration, the proportion of immigrants from northern and western Europe was increased, and the number of immigrants permitted annually was further slashed. This 1924 legislation would be the nation's basic immigration law for over a quarter of a century. It helped cut America's rate of population growth and reduce the diversity of the people and some of the antagonisms among them. It also probably aggravated Europe's economic and political problems, since the United States had been the world's largest prewar market for surplus people. No one can question that the United States had the sovereign right to restrict immigration. Moreover, although immigration limitation did not accomplish all that was claimed for it, there can be little doubt that it eased internal problems of labor competition and intergroup antagonisms. What little it did by way of increasing America's isolation from the world was probably offset by slowly reducing divided loyalties over the years. In the long run, though, the chief legitimate criticism of the immigration legislation of the 1920's has been of its

discrimination against non-Europeans and among different types of Europeans. Here America's prejudices
were displayed for all to see.

There was yet another issue of the 1920's that had
serious ramifications, both foreign and domestic. That
was America's tariff policy. Most Republicans viewed
the imposition of higher tariffs as a domestic matter,
as a way to protect American producers from excessive
competition from abroad. One of the first measures
considered by Congress under Harding was the tariff,
under the spur of the Farm Bloc. This was the Emergency Tariff Act, passed in May, 1921, which increased
duties on corn, meat, sugar, wheat, and wool. In 1922,
in the Fordney-McCumber Act, Congress substantially
raised the average level of duties on imports. Indeed
farm duties shot up to the highest level to that point
in the nation's history. In an effort to vest the act with a
measure of flexibility, however, Congress authorized the
President to increase or reduce item imposts by a maximum of 5 percent if conditions called for a change.
Splendid in theory, the provision was seldom used in
practice.

During the 1920's the high tariff pleased most Americans, for it helped keep internal taxes low and seemed
to protect ailing and not-so-ailing domestic business. Yet
it was an unwise and shortsighted policy. Many Americans lost with the rise in the prices of foreign goods
marketed in the United States. The high tariff was also
used to justify the further erection of trade barriers
abroad, not only tariffs but also devices seldom used by
America, such as import licenses, commodity quotas,
and quality controls. It would be too much to say that
there was a great deal of retaliation against American
tariffs, though, for many foreign countries were just as
eager as the United States to protect their home markets. What was lamentable was that the United States, in
the enactment and implementation of the Fordney-

McCumber tariff, threw away the opportunity to bargain effectively for the reduction of trade barriers. The result was that American exports, an important basis of prosperity for an expanding economy, did not rise as rapidly as they could have. Between 1922 and 1929 the manufacturing production of the United States rose by 50 percent, while exports increased by only 38 percent. Moreover, imports rose at an even slower rate than exports, with a surplus of eleven billion dollars of exports over imports accumulating between 1921 and 1929. It is axiomatic that nations cannot sell effectively if they do not buy sufficiently, and there was a limit to the extent to which American loans abroad could make up the difference between its exports and imports. There was also the question of foreign debts to the United States. Debts cannot be paid without money or acceptable surplus goods. No nation had enough surplus goods that America would accept in payment of debts, and none had a favorable enough balance of trade to raise easily the cash or gold necessary to repay the United States.

America's intentions were generally good, but its knowledge was defective. The Harding and Coolidge administrations tried to contribute to world stability through their loan and disarmament policies and by easing the payment of debts, but that was insufficient. Not only did the tariff aggravate the situation, but it was complicated by the policies of other countries. Their officials and peoples were as incautious about borrowing and spending as Americans were about lending, and most were highly nationalistic about developing their economies and heightening trade barriers. Moreover, some foreign nations were not playing fair. No European state was in such poor condition throughout the 1920's that it could not have improved its payment of foreign debts. Of course, no creditor nation was in such bad condition that it could not have further reduced the burdens of its debtors. Although well-considered tariff decreases by the United States could have aided the world's economy, the high tariff was only one strand in the composition of the crazy-quilt international economy. The war had produced new economic yarns for the world, and no nation knew nor was eager to learn how to weave them into a durable fabric.

Other situations were to arise to test America's mettle during the 1920's. With one country, Communist Russia, there was no test. The policy of nonrecognition set by President Wilson was continued by Harding, Coolidge, and Hoover. The Communists stood for more than the Americans could tolerate. Not only had they removed Russia from the Allied side during the war, but the bloodiness of the revolution and the following civil war, talk of world revolution, constant propaganda against the United States and capitalism, the loss of American lives during their occupation of Archangel and Vladivostok, the Bolsheviks' support of atheism, and their unwillingness to repay Russia's debts were among the factors that made Americans unwilling to establish diplomatic relations. Although the United States carried on a widespread relief program in Russia during the Harding Administration, financed with $48,000,000 equally supplied by private and government sources, this did not weaken the general attitude of distrust nor lead to recognition that Russians had grievances against America. Russia was willing to negotiate on concessions, but the United States declined to do so unless the Bolsheviks made concessions before the commencement of negotiations, which they were unwilling to do. Thus the question of recognition remained in abeyance.

China represented another problem. Seeking to restore full sovereign rights over its vast territory, China was undergoing upheavals of world significance. The nation was gripped by civil war among the forces of the north, the south, and various warlords. Many different foreign interests, ranging from American missionaries to Russian

Communists, were giving support to one side or another. And the country was being racked by waves of anti-foreign sentiment, much of it aimed at having foreign powers keep the promises they had made during the world war and at the Washington Conference about revision of the tariff and extraterritorial treaties. The official American position was to remain impartial among the contestants for power within China and sympathetic to Chinese demands for fuller control over their own affairs. Indeed, by 1925, the United States insisted that Britain and Japan undertake the promised treaty revisions as a way to help stabilize conditions in China. This eventually led to tariff autonomy for China and the substantial reduction of foreign extraterritoriality rights. These actions, however, ended neither China's troubles nor antiforeignism there. President Coolidge hoped to avoid inflaming the situation further, refusing to make a display of force or to join with other powers in protecting foreigners resident in China. If this policy did not settle unrest in China, it had the merit of preventing unnecessary aggravation of Chinese affairs.

The only other foreign situation of prime concern to the United States was in South America. The Harding and Coolidge policies there can be described as the dawn of the Good Neighbor Policy. Under Harding the United States endeavored to show its concern for the welfare and independence of its Latin American neighbors. One of the administration's first actions, in 1921, was a treaty that allocated $25,000,000 to Colombia as a form of penance for America's role in wrenching Panama away from that country in 1903. This action materially benefited the United States, which soon more than recovered the cost of the Colombian grant in profits from expanded American operations in Colombia's oil fields. The Harding Administration then stepped into the boundary dispute between Costa Rica and Panama, forcing its satellite to accept an international arbitral award in favor of Costa Rica. During the 1920's the United States also gave more support than ever before to facilitating cooperative advances in economics, transportation, health, and the settlement of disputes among western hemisphere nations.

More pressing, however, were America's relations with its immediate neighbors to the south. Wilson's policies of nonrecognition and military intervention had left bitterness and suspicion between Mexico and the United States. When Álvaro Obregón and Harding became presidents of their countries within a few months of each other, the signs were propitious for restoration of good relations. Obregón diluted Mexico's confiscatory policies toward American business, yet he would not concede to Secretary Hughes's demands for compensation of all American losses in Mexico since 1910 and for stricter guarantees of the rights of Americans there. Progress continued on both sides, however. Mexico further softened its regulation of foreign interests, and Harding declared that his government was willing to discuss the differences between the two states and extend recognition even before further Mexican moves. In 1923 negotiations began that soon led to the recognition of Mexico and the exchange of ambassadors.

Widespread rebellion in Mexico posed another problem, because of the possibility of the overthrow of a friendly government there. Therefore, President Coolidge lifted the embargo on arms sales to Mexico in 1924 and permitted American financiers to extend credits to the Mexican Government for the purchase of a "few muskets and a few rounds of ammunition." Obregón's successor, Plutarco Calles, however, did not feel as friendly toward the United States, despite Coolidge's action, and subsequently Mexico placed new restrictions upon foreign economic activity. The situation was further complicated by open and sometimes violent conflict between church and state in Mexico, which outraged American Catholics. Despite mounting pressures for intervention, Coolidge hewed to the line of negotiating differences. Another complication arose, however, when Mexico and the United States chose opposite sides in the bloody Nicaraguan civil war of 1926–1927. Matters got out of hand after the United States sent marines to Nicaragua. Congress became perturbed, and Mexican-American relations speedily deteriorated. Alarmed, Coolidge dispatched former Secretary of War Henry L. Stimson to Nicaragua to seek a settlement. Stimson negotiated a truce between the stalemated forces there, one that led to a coalition government and elections and that provided for the withdrawal of most American forces by 1931.

Coolidge also encouraged the work of private citizens working toward rapprochement with Mexico, and President Calles indicated his wish for reestablishment of good relations between Mexico and the United States. When the bitter-ender American ambassador to Mexico, James R. Sheffield, resigned, Coolidge had his chance to better relations. Choosing his Amherst College classmate Dwight Morrow as the new ambassador in 1927 was a brilliant stroke. Morrow, showing himself a skillful negotiator, plunged into a love affair with Mexico. His feelings were soon reciprocated, with the result that armistices were negotiated between officials and capitalists and between church and state in Mexico. Tensions quickly subsided, and by the end of the 1920's the basis had been laid for the good relations between the two neighboring countries that were to endure for decades.

Accompanying all this during the decade was the reduction of official American involvement in Central America and the Caribbean. Marines were removed from Cuba and the Dominican Republic and reduced in Nicaragua. The policy was eventually to withdraw all American marines from the area's countries, reversing thereby the practice of intervention begun a generation earlier. The efforts of Harding and Coolidge and similar actions by Hoover represented the beginnings of an era of harmony among the American republics, an era that was to flower during Franklin D. Roosevelt's administration. Indeed it was probably the finest hour in the foreign relations of Harding and Coolidge. It paid dividends even during the 1920's in increased friendliness between the United States and Latin America and led to tangible benefits in the form of smaller budgets for so-called peace-keeping activities in countries to the south and increased business investments.

Of course, this is only a survey of the peaks of the foreign relations of the United States during the 1920's. Worth mentioning as the last pinnacle in this overview, however, is the creation of commercial opportunities. That American businessmen took advantage of these opportunities is plain. Private investors poured their capital into overseas projects, as their investments jumped from $7,000,000,000 in 1919 to $17,200,000,000 in 1930. Even foreign investments in the United States rose markedly, from $3,300,000,000 in 1919 to $8,400,000,000 in 1930. Although American exports did not expand enough to rid the nation of its mounting surplus production, nor imports rise sufficiently to permit America's customers to develop enough exchange to keep the trade going, the growth was impressive. From 1922 to 1929 exports increased from $3,900,000,000 to almost $5,400,000,000 and imports from $3,200,000,000 to $4,500,000,000. Moreover, the United States was not just confining itself to traditional markets, for its greatest export increases were to Africa and South America, to which its exports grew by 130 percent between 1922 and 1929. Clearly, despite its occasional blunders, America was more than ever a trader nation. That dictated the character of much of its relations with other countries.

Although the 1920's have traditionally been viewed as an "isolationist" interlude for America, this is an "isolationist" observation in itself, predicated on an ignorance of many of the facts and especially of what other countries were doing at the time. What happened was partly a return to prewar foreign-relations viewpoints, partly a reaction to the war and Versailles, and partly an adjustment to the facts of international affairs during the 1920's. Plainly America's foreign relations represented a change from prewar attitudes and actions as well as from Wilsonian doctrines. Although Americans sought to avoid entangling alliances and pressed for debt payment, they also extended the branches of friendship and goodwill. The United States aggressively sought further business expansion while joining in the insanity of so many nations in raising trade barriers. But America also, in its quest for trade and goodwill, extended loans that other nations eagerly accepted. The country lessened its interference in Latin American affairs and sought, however bumblingly, stability everywhere, as any classical trading nation would. America's efforts for peace during the decade were no more successful than Wilson's, and for the same reason. There was in them more idealism than realism, more the search for shortcuts than the hard work needed to make them work. This was true whether it involved the League of Nations idea, disarmament based on goodwill, or the outlawing of war based on public opinion. Similarly, the lending policy of the United States was based on the idea that prosperity would continue indefinitely and that therefore the loans would not be defaulted. This was an appealing notion and one that also underlay part of post–World War II American policy, except that then the United States was better prepared to accept financial losses. In short, during the 1920's American foreign policy was no less internationalist than the foreign policies of most other nations, and no more selfish, nor wiser. It certainly shared the mutual weakness of being far from effective in the long run.

[3]
Harding at Home

CLASS in America has never been monolithic. During the first two decades of the twentieth century there were at least two politically active middle classes. One had crusaded for reform of national institutions and had been the backbone of the various progressive movements. The other wanted little if any part of uplifting crusades and sought chiefly to be left alone, to ward off government regulation of its affairs. The first group had sought to use government to strike a balance among the classes and interests. The second had been content to have balance come out of the interplay among individuals and groups, to allow each man to take advantage of opportunities as they arose. What the two middle classes had in common was their quest for power. Before World War I power had favored the first group, but the other middle class seized the initiative during the postwar period when a majority of Americans was weary of crusades at home and abroad.

Warren G. Harding was the chief political beneficiary of the second middle class and, to a considerable extent, was representative of it. Gregarious and hearty, he took pride in being a self-made man and in getting along with other people. He championed no crusade, for he basically wanted what would get the most votes for his candidacies. The best ways to accomplish this goal, he believed, were to do his constituents' will and be loyal to those with whom he worked. Progress was inevitable if one took care to avert violent conflict among people and kept one's temper. Harding liked his pleasures, too, and he meant to enjoy them. Yet he took his job as

President seriously. Harding was far from the most intelligent or best educated of chief executives, but he tried diligently to make up for his shortcomings by working harder: Few presidents had accepted such long working days. He also had a big heart. If he did not understand people in the abstract, he was not outstripped by any President in understanding and sympathizing with the feelings and foibles of the average man.

Warren Harding took the oath of office as President on March 4, 1921, and set out the guidelines, in his inaugural address, for his administration's domestic policies. In government the watchwords were to be efficiency and economy as the nation strove to resume its "onward, normal way." The government's role was to promote economic prosperity for all and comity among business, agriculture, and labor. One way to accomplish this was to eliminate unnecessary government interference in business affairs. There were to be, as he had written in an article published the previous November, "Less Government in Business and More Business in Government."

This did not mean that Harding was going to ignore the nation's economy; far from it. That this was true was highlighted in the President's first message to Congress, on April 11. He called not only for lower taxes and for ways to achieve more efficient operation of government but also for lower railway rates, improvement of highways and the merchant marine, encouragement of civil and military aviation, regulation and development of radio, expansion of hospital facilities, and creation of a veterans' bureau and a department of public welfare. Harding had outlined a sensible if not breathtaking program. He had made it clear that he was not going to sit back and merely let Congress pass laws of its own choosing for his signature and administration. He was going to tell the lawmakers what ought to be done. What Harding was not going to do, however, was press Congress hard for enactment of his program, which explains why much of it was not enacted or was not passed the way he wanted.

Yet the President's program was popular with broad strata of American business. With this great amount of business favor he could count on considerable assistance in the enactment and implementation of his program. Moreover, one proposal, reducing the cost of government, found favor with almost all Americans. Not only were the number of government employees and the amount of federal expenditures well above prewar levels, but because of the war, the national debt had leaped from about $1,200,000,000 in 1914 to almost $25,500,000,000 in 1919. This meant that the interest on the debt was almost as large in 1919 as the debt itself had been five years earlier.

One way to attack this, and inefficiency as well, was the establishment of a system to regularize and chop the fat off the budget requests of government agencies. Traditionally the President had little control over the budget requests that the agencies transmitted to Congress. He also had little power over the spending of appropriated funds. Wilson had asked for a federal budget system but could not agree with Congress on the plan it devised in 1920. In the spring of 1921, however, Harding was able to secure the Budget and Accounting Act, which gave the President full authority over budget matters. He called in a tough Chicago banker and a talented wartime supply tactician, Charles Dawes, to take command of the new Bureau of the Budget. During the year Dawes headed the bureau he bullied and negotiated his way to greatly reduced current expenditures and budget requests. A new era had started in federal budgeting and spending. Now agency heads were responsible to the President for their budgets, which meant that the White House could coordinate the preparation of those budgets as well as have considerable control over expenditures. During their administrations Harding and

Coolidge used this authority to slash federal spending drastically and to keep it down. Expenditures dropped from $5,116,000,000 in 1921 to $3,373,000,000 in 1922 and remained somewhat below that amount until 1930.

Economy, however, did not stand by itself as a goal. The reduction of expenditures was essential to the attainment of two other objectives, decreasing federal taxes and the national debt. The key figure here was Secretary of the Treasury Andrew Mellon. One of the country's richest men and an expert juggler of figures and funds, he contrasted greatly to Charles Dawes, the boisterous and evangelical budget-cutter. Frail and quiet, even timid, Mellon reminded one reporter of "a tired double-entry bookkeeper who is afraid of losing his job." Yet he effectively supported Harding's fiscal policies, serving as the devoted acolyte at the altar of government economy. The prayed-for results reduced the tax load of all Americans, but particularly of those, the wealthy, who paid the most. With tax reduction more money was available from the rich for economic expansion and from the less well endowed for consumer spending. In the Mellon philosophy increased private expenditures would benefit all Americans, thanks to the additional flow of funds available for profits and wages. It also meant, the administration reasoned, that the government had less money to waste, especially on activities that might disrupt the economy. With debt reduction, taxes could eventually be reduced more as the interest obligation was pared.

In the summer of 1921 Congress began hearings on a new tax law. Secretary Mellon recommended repeal of the excess-profits tax and the halving of the maximum surtax on incomes, effective retroactively at the beginning of 1921. After fierce congressional debates, an act emerged that was considerably different from what Mellon wanted, but the measure allowed the administration to say that it had been faithful to its promise of tax reduction. The new law repealed the excess-profits tax, commencing January, 1922, raised corporation taxes to make up for the prospective loss of revenue, reduced the maximum surtax by almost one-fourth, and raised exemptions, which especially benefited the least wealthy taxpayers. Although no one was completely satisfied with the law, it reduced individual tax burdens and eliminated thousands of potential taxpayers. The taxpayers' savings totaled about $800,000,000 in 1922, which left a large amount of revenue available for cutting the national debt. The mounting revenue surplus encouraged Mellon to press for further reduction of levies on the rich. Harding blocked this move, however, because he thought that future tax cuts should benefit all taxpayers. Therefore, there was no new tax legislation until after his death.

There were, of course, other ways of promoting prosperity. The President was eager to have Herbert Hoover in his Cabinet, either to spur the development of natural resources as Interior Secretary or to help stimulate business as Commerce Secretary. Hoover had distinguished himself in overseas relief activities and as chief of the wartime Food Administration. A master of all trades, he knew how to apply efficiency to what he was doing; a self-made millionaire and a good humanitarian, he was wedded to the principle that business was the goose that would lay the golden egg that would nourish all Americans. His choice was to be Secretary of Commerce.

Hoover took what normally has been among the least significant portfolios in American government and vesting it with his drive, knowledge, and intelligence, made it into the most dynamic of the executive positions under Presidents Harding and Coolidge. He was in effect Secretary of Commerce and "assistant secretary of everything else." Hoover's personal influence extended to operations in the Departments of Labor, Interior, and War. He was listened to respectfully on policies of international trade, agriculture, postal affairs, and finance. If Hoover was not the nation's first minister, he had more impact on government and business in America than any other Cabinet member, if for no other reason than that he was the champion of positive and coordinated assistance to business development.

After Harding was inaugurated, no department was put into gear more quickly than Hoover's. The new secretary pushed out political time-servers and recruited efficient administrative personnel. He reorganized the Commerce Department and stimulated the issuance of great streams of information and propaganda. Hoover established an advisory committee of business, farm, and labor leaders, not only to gain advice but also to cement relations between the department and the leading sectors of the economy. His was one agency during the days of slender appropriations that grew both in personnel and in budget. He was also an empire builder, acquiring bureaus from the Interior and Treasury departments and creating new divisions to supervise the growth of radio and civil aviation. He employed experts to produce special studies and to improve and expand the collection and distribution of economic statistics. Hoover reared his own foreign office in the Bureau of Foreign and Domestic Commerce in order to make American industry and agriculture more conscious of trade opportunities abroad and to assist the exploitation of foreign materials and markets. He was also the prime advocate of trade associations to provide better coordination of economic activities within industries, although he took care to emphasize the need for fair and honest trade and price practices. The Bureau of Standards was converted into one of America's foremost research organizations in Hoover's pursuit of greater business and industrial efficiency through standardization and modernization. His end goal was simple: prosperity for all through the development of efficient, consumer-serving, and cost-conscious business. Hoover progressed toward that objective to a remarkable extent during the 1920's, as the range of available and reliable products and services vastly increased, prices remained stable, wages increased, and even trade and labor antagonisms slowly declined.

Yet, as Herbert Hoover knew, there were sectors of the economy other than business. To get them into harness proved difficult. Dealing with organized labor was a great problem, partly because of the inbred hostility between most unions and the business-oriented government leaders and partly because of labor's small bargaining power. Although the unions had reached an all-time-high membership during the war, it fell off rapidly during the postwar decade. Moreover, even at the point of the unions' highest membership, most American workers were unorganized. Labor's influence was further undercut by the fact that a majority of workers had freely joined in the great voting shift to Harding and the Republicans in 1920. In any event, business was the favored one and intended not to be hindered in achieving its goals by the whims of labor. Business believed that it knew best, and it had the power to do what it wanted, regardless of what the unions said.

Yet the Harding Administration usually was not intentionally antagonistic to the labor unions or to workingmen. As a publisher Harding had done well by his own employees and believed that that was what all employers should do. It was easy for him to transfer this belief to the management of national affairs. After all, no one could travel safely in the ship of state if the crew was malnourished and rebellious. One of Harding's gestures was to appoint as Secretary of Labor James J. Davis, a former union official who had later become a small-time politician and an organizer for the Loyal Order of Moose. Secretary Davis was somewhat effective as an apostle of labor peace through negotiation, and he commanded the attention and affection of some union leaders and members, particularly those in craft unions who were or expected to become prosperous artisans. Harding also attempted to enlist the support of Samuel Gompers, the president of the American Federation of Labor. The chief executive often invited the A.F.L. leader to the White House and told him bluntly, "Mr. Gompers, I want your help." Gompers seldom accepted the presidential invitations, however, and would have no part of Harding's plan to persuade workers to accept wage reductions in order to match lowered prices and encourage business revival. Moreover, Gompers made plain his personal dislike of the administration. The result was that organized labor lost its chance to communicate effectively with the White House.

Trouble was bound to come, since the country had already entered into depression by the time Harding took office. Although the administration's main objective was to resuscitate business, it refused to follow tradition and ignore the plight of the unemployed. Hoover took the lead here when by the summer of 1921 unemployment continued to remain around four million. He recommended that cities and counties start their building projects immediately instead of waiting until the following spring, the usual construction time. The administration also suggested that business forgo its normal fall layoffs of workers. These steps were clearly not enough, however. On Hoover's recommendation Harding called an unemployment conference to meet in September to encourage the development of new local and private work projects and spreading employment around. While relief from local and private projects was growing, in January, 1922, the federal government began to do its share. The President directed all federal agencies to start their building and repair projects as soon as possible in order to swell the number of jobs available. The results, although not phenomenal, helped reverse the tide of unemployment. The number of jobless had reached almost 5,500,000, but then began to dip, running contrary to the usual winter expansion of unemployment. From the spring of 1922 onward, the rolls of the jobless declined rapidly.

The administration's sharpest labor crisis came to a head during the spring and summer of 1922, with the coal and railway strikes, which had been in the offing since the waning days of the Wilson period. One of the few successful postwar strikes had been in the coal industry, when in 1920 the United Mine Workers received a 17-percent wage raise. That agreement was to expire April 1, 1922. Mineowners had meanwhile decided against a general wage agreement and against one that would even maintain wage levels. John L. Lewis, president of the U.M.W., pulled the coal miners out on strike to force industry-wide negotiations of a new contract. That spring Secretaries Hoover and Davis worked to bring the mineowners and the miners to the bargaining table, but without success. After violence erupted in June in Herrin, Illinois, where twenty-one strikers and strikebreakers were killed, the government intensified its actions. Soon, under direct pressure from Harding, the opposing sides were negotiating, but to no avail. The President then asked the mineowners to return the mines to production, under state protection. That won him widespread congratulations and also demands that he take over the mines and force the miners back to work. He refused to do that because of his conviction, as his secretary wrote, that "every man in America has the unquestioned right to work or to decline work as he himself believes." So the situation continued, with the miners still striking and the owners therefore able to produce little coal. By August the possibility of a winter coal shortage appeared high.

Another strike situation had meanwhile blazed across the land. Business and agriculture had demanded a sharp reduction of the high railway rates, which would require a concomitant lowering of the wages of railway-men. The workers, despite a general decline in prices, were not going to accept wage reductions without resistance. Nevertheless the Railroad Labor Board decreed a 12.5-percent cut in wages in 1921. That decision was declared unacceptable by both the unions and the carriers, the former who thought it harsh and the latter who thought it too small a reduction. The Railway Brotherhoods scheduled a strike for October but called it off when the Railroad Labor Board announced that there would be no further wage cuts for at least six months and that consideration would be given to revising work rules. In May, 1922, the board announced some work-rule changes favorable to labor but also further slashed wages for railway employees because the Interstate Commerce Commission had reduced agricultural-freight rates by 16.5 percent. In response the railway shopmen declared a strike, to begin July 1. Efforts at conciliation were unsuccessful, although other railroad unions stayed at work for the time being.

Harding was not unsympathetic to the workers, knowing that the railroads had been far from faithful in obeying the orders of the Railroad Labor Board and that labor had legitimate grievances. He tried strenuously but unsuccessfully to bring the employers and men back together in negotiations. Consequently, the President took a more forceful stand in both the railway and the coal conflicts, for they threatened to disrupt the national economy and to bring civil strife. On August 18, 1922, Harding asked Congress for authority to appoint a coal commission and to approve the administration's plans to mine and distribute coal should the strikes continue. He also publicly condemned both the railway workers and the carriers for failing the country. Congress soon gave the President what he had requested. Facing a November election, the legislators then left the strikes to Harding to handle, while the public became increasingly unhappy, tending to blame labor more than business for the crisis.

The President and his Cabinet spent hours in late August discussing the situation. The results are unclear, but within a few days, on September 1, Attorney General Harry Daugherty procured a court order enjoining workers from interfering with the functioning of the railroads. Moreover, the court order forbade anyone connected with the strike to take any action that would continue the strike. Harding had apparently backed his Attorney General without being fully aware of the sweeping nature of the injunction, the stiffest in American history. The Cabinet was divided, labor outraged, and management delighted by the order. The press applauded the injunction but often with reservations about its harshness. Harding directed Daugherty to secure recision of its most extreme provisions, but basically the order stood to prevent the hampering of railroad operations. Agreements were subsequently made in which the striking shopmen lost considerably in organizational and seniority rights. All railway workers felt forced to accept the wage cuts ordered by the Railroad Labor Board.

Even before the railway injunction, negotiations had begun on the coal dispute. By early September the mineowners and the United Mine Workers agreed to extend existing wage levels well into 1923, and commissions were established to investigate future ways of negotiating to the best advantage of all concerned. In the case of coal the federal government's urgings and pressures had greater effect in getting labor and management to reach agreement than with the railroads. Whatever the trouble, the labor front had been pacified by the end of the summer of 1922. Labor had gained a black eye with the public, although management seemed in little better position because of its intransigence. The lesson was that labor had best not overextend itself soon, although it must not be overlooked that the unions' stiff fight had discouraged further wage reductions.

Despite the unpleasant repercussions of the coal and rail strikes and the administration's apparent antilabor stand, Harding's aim was to gain industrial peace in a way favorable to both workers and employers. One evidence of this had been the government's endeavors to stem unemployment. Another was Harding's and Hoover's efforts to get the steel industry to abolish the twelve-hour workday, which could easily be the basis for a great steel strike. In April, 1922, the President wrote to Elbert Gary, of United States Steel, making that request. When that did not work, Harding invited a group of leading steel executives to dinner at the White House to discuss the question, which led to the formation of a study committee. The committee studied but did not act until May, 1923, when it rejected the President's request as being too expensive to implement. The administration persisted, and public opinion grew more favorable, however, and the steel operators took up the question again. In late June they announced that the twelve-hour day would be abandoned, and beginning in August the steel industry shifted over to an eight-hour workday. Thus was largely eliminated one of the country's worst labor practices, for few other industries working their employees more than eight hours a day could continue doing so much longer. But this action, the government's concern for unemployment, and increased federal mediation of labor disputes were insufficient to make organized labor happy with Harding.

The other large economic sector that the administration had to contend with was agriculture. Farmers were better heard than workers by the administration, partly because of their traditional support for Republicans and partly because of their greater representation in Congress. Although a farmer was not selected to be Secretary of Agriculture, Henry C. Wallace, Harding's choice, was closer to being a farmer than James J. Davis was to being a workingman. Wallace was born of a farm family and had farmed for five years. After that he went into teaching and then into agricultural journalism. He founded *Wallace's Farmer* and developed it into one of the nation's leading farm journals and himself into one of the farmers' most vigorous spokesmen.

Yet Wallace's appointment and the existence of a strong Farm Bloc in Congress did not insure that farmers would receive satisfaction from the new administration. That was largely because agricultural problems were so severe and because farmers were not of one mind as to what to do about them. During the war too many farmers had incurred too much debt, and the disastrous break in prices in 1920–1921 made it difficult for them to pay off their debts. The ten leading crops had fallen in value per acre from $35.74 in 1919 to $14.45 in 1921. Although prices generally fell in all economic sectors, the ratio of prices received by farmers to those that they paid dropped from 110 to 80. To complicate the situation, farmers' income remained low throughout the 1920's, and their taxes rose by about 150 percent over prewar rates.

The cause of the trouble was plain. Farmers were producing more than the market would take. They had not adjusted their production to demand. Foreign markets had given abundant evidence before the war that they would require less American agricultural production. The average of American farm exports for the years 1908–1912 compared with the period 1895–1899 had declined by more than half in wheat, three-fifths in cattle, and two-thirds in corn and hogs. Inflated wartime needs had apparently led farmers to disregard these trends. Moreover, consumption trends at home had taken a downward turn as the per capita domestic consumption of potatoes, meat, and wheat flour declined between

1910 and 1920. All this was happening as the acreage under cultivation increased and hourly manpower productivity rose, thanks largely to the expanding mechanization of farm operations. By 1921 farmers were eager for a solution, though not one that would lead them to change their ways significantly.

During Harding's Presidency the federal government responded quickly, if not always wisely, to farm needs. Secretary of Agriculture Wallace urged massive assistance for farmers. While he was trying to lead Harding forward, political pressure was being applied from behind by the congressional Farm Bloc and the American Farm Bureau Federation, which sought better farm financing, freight-rate reductions, tariff increases, stimulation of cooperatives, and greater regulation of meat-packers. Hoover and Mellon saw the farmers as a grasping special-interest group that could disrupt federal finances and the national economy, but Harding generally went along with Wallace and the Farm Bloc.

The federal farm program moved forward quickly. In 1921 and 1922 Congress raised the tariff against competing foreign produce, and the Interstate Commerce Commission cut freight rates. The President pressed the I.C.C. for further reductions, and he appealed to the heads of the largest railroads for voluntary rate reductions. In May, 1922, the commission announced a decrease of 10 percent in freight tariffs. Although the order did not apply to rates already reduced on farm commodities, it did affect some agricultural products not yet covered and goods that farmers had to buy.

The year 1921 saw other government action on farm issues. Harding cooperated with the Farm Bloc and the American Farm Bureau Federation in pressing for five pieces of legislation that they particularly wanted. Four of the measures were easily steered through Congress. The Future Trading Act provided for prohibitive taxes on market speculation in grains and regulated dealers in contract markets. The Packers and Stockyards Act forbade unfair practices, the manipulation of prices, and restraints in trade among interstate packers, and regulated stockyard rates. One amendment to the Farm Loan Act increased the funds of land banks and the possible size of farm loans, and another amendment made private investments in farm-loan bonds more attractive by raising the interest rates. The Emergency Agricultural Credits Act was more difficult to enact. It was the administration's substitute for a broader measure sponsored by Senator George Norris, of Nebraska, and as such it divided farm forces in Congress. Moreover, the progressive Republicans were offended by the sharp tactics employed by the administration to gain consideration of its bill. Yet, despite spirited opposition from Norris and his allies, the measure was finally carried. To facilitate farm sales, the act authorized the War Finance Corporation to lend funds to farm cooperatives, exporters, foreign buyers, and banks. The corporation could also lend money for the raising and marketing of livestock and buy the paper of rural banks that was secured by farm commodities. The results were not only the increased flow of credit to farmers and farm-related groups but also the salvation of many rural banks whose resources had become strained. The amendments to the Farm Loan Act also expanded credit for agriculture, and the Future Trading and Packers and Stockyards laws put restraints on those who would squeeze farmers and consumers by manipulating rates and prices. Although the farmers congratulated themselves for these advances, the administration's role was crucial in devising a good deal of the legislation and seeing it through Congress.

Among the greatest problems facing farmers, legislators, and government officials was lack of knowledge and planning. Congress tried to compensate for this in June, 1921, with the creation of the Joint Commission on Agricultural Inquiry, a group of senators and represent-

atives appointed by the President. The commission suggested expanded farm credit, reduced freight rates, increased help for farm cooperatives, better farm-to-market
roads, improved and supervised terminal facilities for
the wholesaling of perishables, additional agricultural
research, and improved grades and standards for products. There was also the National Agricultural Conference called by Secretary Wallace at the end of 1921.
The conference largely endorsed the commission's recommendations, but it went a bit further. It asked Congress
and the President to "take such steps as will immediately
reestablish a fair exchange value for all farm products
with that of all other commodities." The conference also
recommended that farm organizations advise their members, as Harding had asked, of the probable demand for
products and to suggest measures to limit the acreage of
surplus commodities. Further suggested for study were
government guarantees of farm prices and the development of crop insurance.

The Harding Administration could accept much of
this. Indeed, in 1922, it vigorously pressed for enactment
of some of the agricultural conference's recommendations. This contributed to the passage of the Capper-
Volstead Act, which exempted farm associations, especially cooperatives, from antitrust laws. Congress also
agreed to the further extension of the War Finance
Corporation's authority to provide farm loans and approved the Grain Futures Act to take the place of the
Future Trading Act of 1921, which had been invalidated
by the Supreme Court. This replacement statute authorized the licensing of exchanges that handled futures markets and the supervision of trading in futures to prevent
unfair manipulation of prices. In addition, the scientific
and research work of the Department of Agriculture
was expanded and improved and its results more widely
disseminated.

During its first eighteen months in office the Harding

Administration had done as much for farmers as any preceding administration, but it was not enough to meet the farmers' demands. Farm prices remained low; by 1923 business and labor were well ahead of agriculture in marching out of the swamp of depression. Farmers called for more help, and Harding responded by backing legislation extending additional credits on more liberal terms. Loans, however, were not going to solve the problem any more than efficiency in cultivation and marketing could. Generally refusing to alter production to demand, farmers expected the government to find panaceas to restore their prosperity. Already by 1923 attention was being given to the idea of federal subsidization of agricultural operations, especially the plan of George N. Peek and Hugh S. Johnson to support marketing of farm surpluses overseas at low prices in order to raise domestic produce prices. This concept, however, would not come to a head until another President occupied the White House.

Harding had additional problems to worry about. An important area of concern for him was the treatment of Negroes. He had promised to work for an antilynching law and to give black Americans a better share of government jobs. They also hoped for a relaxation of segregation in government offices by the Republican administration, for their votes, as a result of recent large-scale Negro migration from the South, were becoming increasingly important. In 1921 the President asked Congress "to rid the stain of barbaric lynching from the banner of a free and orderly representative democracy." In a speech later that year in Birmingham he urged, "Let the black man vote when he is fit to vote." Yet, although Harding wanted the gradual amalgamation of Negroes into American politics and hoped to subdue racial conflict, black citizens had little to show for his sentiments. The political color line was not breached in the South. Segregation continued to be the rule in Wash-

ington and in government service. Although the number
of Negro civil servants grew, they were largely confined
to menial labor, and few additional patronage appointments were made. The Dyer antilynching bill was passed
by the House of Representatives, but southern Democrats talked it to death in the Senate. Admittedly Harding did more for black Americans than had Wilson, and
he had been willing to discuss their problems publicly.
That was not enough, however, in terms of humanity,
the Constitution, or good political tactics. Perhaps Harding could excuse himself because of the times, but in the
judgment of history he, and for that matter Coolidge
and Hoover, who did no more if as much, did not
measure up to the task or the opportunities.

Harding was the first of four presidents to encounter
the push by World War I veterans for a bonus for their
services. In 1921 it was enough that he opposed such
legislation in order to repulse veterans' pressures. The
following year, however, Republican legislative leaders,
with eyes cocked toward the fall congressional elections,
ordered consideration of a bonus. Despite stiff presidential opposition, Congress approved a measure authorizing issuance of service certificates to veterans that could
be redeemed immediately or held for twenty years at
vastly increased value. Harding refused to change his
position and vetoed the bill in September as special-
interest legislation that would boost the national debt
by one-sixth. Congress was unable to override his veto.
In 1924 President Coolidge vetoed a measure providing
veterans with paid-up insurance and allowing them to
borrow up to 25 percent of its value. This time the
errand boys of the American Legion were able to secure
enough votes to override the veto. The usual postwar
raid on the treasury had begun by the veterans, despite
the generous appropriations approved by the federal
government for the care of disabled veterans.

If Harding's position on further compensation to

veterans was successful only as a holding action, he was more successful in furthering joint state-federal action. Although his proposal to create a public-welfare department to coordinate and improve the country's programs of health, education, recreation, and child welfare was not enacted, he was able to gain passage of the Sheppard-Towner Act. This 1921 legislation authorized cooperative state-federal action to combat the high infant mortality rate and to promote better hygiene among women and children. Better funded and more popular was Harding's endeavor to heighten federal participation in road construction and planning in cooperation with the states. Under the Federal Highway Act of 1921, a network of key roads was planned so that federal and state funds could be spent intelligently. The money appropriated by Congress, $75,000,000, was almost four times the amount spent in 1920. It was, however, only a suggestion of the vast amount of federal funds that was to be allocated in the future to assist the development of good highways that would carry the nation's burgeoning number of automobiles and trucks.

Harding was also serious about government efficiency. The initial efforts to develop selection, promotion, and retention procedures in the foreign service under the Rogers Act came during his administration. This was substantially to improve the caliber of American representation abroad. Harding encouraged his Cabinet members to reorganize their departments for greater efficiency, and with some success, most notably in the Post Office, Commerce, and Agriculture departments. Indeed the President espoused an overall government plan of reorganization that, among other things, would have expanded the Post Office Department into a communications department, combined the War and Navy departments into a defense department, and added a new education and welfare department. Moreover, he wanted a great shift of bureaus so that they would be placed in the department most akin to their functions, for example, the transfer of the Forestry Division from the Agriculture Department to the Interior Department. These proposals were modified in the Cabinet; nevertheless Harding still had a massive reorganization of the executive branch planned for congressional consideration in 1924. But 1924 never came for Harding, and the reorganization scheme never came to Congress. There were piecemeal accomplishments, of course, one being the Budget and Accounting Act and another the Government Classification Act of 1923, which not only gave civil servants a needed pay raise, but for the first time provided for standardized compensation rates, improved personnel practices, and job specifications. These were tools that succeeding administrations would use to make for a more effective civil service.

One of Harding's greatest opportunities to reshape the nation came in his appointments to the Supreme Court. During his short tenure as President he appointed William Howard Taft as Chief Justice and George Sutherland, Pierce Butler, and Edward T. Sanford as associate justices. These four, along with the several economic conservatives already on the Court, assured that the judicial view of economic matters would be conservative not only in the 1920's but well into the 1930's. As early as 1921 the Court showed its teeth to labor in *Truax v. Corrigan,* in which the justices backed Taft's opinion curtailing a union's use of picketing. In *Adkins v. Children's Hospital* in 1923 the Court, although with Taft dissenting, invalidated a minimum-wage law for women in the District of Columbia. In other cases the Court held unions liable to the issuance of injunctions against many of their activities and declared unconstitutional the regulation of child labor through the taxing power. If the Court was generally antilabor, it was equally probusiness. Although the justices held that railways were subject to federal regulation, they usually invalidated state laws that regulated business. It was plain, thanks considerably to Harding's appointments, that the Supreme Court had returned to the doctrine of economic laissez-faire.

Harding is frequently rated the worst President of the United States. This is partly because his probusiness activities were seen as deplorable by the following generation, which found business guilty of causing the depression of the 1930's and wrote off the Republican chief executives of the 1920's as accomplices in the crime. Harding's reputation is also badly scarred because the scandals of his administration have been somewhat exaggerated and his accomplishments largely overlooked. Of course, Harding believed that business development would lead to prosperity for all and that it was the government's role therefore to encourage enterprise. That did not mean, however, that he was viciously anti-labor or insensitive to the plight of the farmers. He was sometimes unsure of himself on such complicated matters as international debt and domestic fiscal policies, but he was far from uninformed on most government affairs. Even though he was not the Senate's master, he was not its tool. Moreover, in his proposed policies, Harding was well aware of the desirability of highway, aviation, and water development, radio regulation, further government welfare work, and additional reclamation and conservation projects. If he had among his official family Harry Daugherty, Edwin Denby, and Albert Fall, he also had Hoover, Hughes, and Wallace. Perhaps Harding's greatest problem for his reputation's sake was that he did not have sufficient time to try to complete his program. Also to be considered is the Congress with which he had to deal, composed as it was of warring factions and made even more difficult by Republican losses in the 1922 congressional elections, largely a response to the President's inability to take the country far enough along the road to prosperity. Nevertheless

Harding had done much of what he had promised during the 1920 election, and he was still personally popular. He had represented the noncrusading middle class well and had done it without too much harm to labor and agriculture. For better and worse, he had laid the bases for much of what was to come later in the 1920's.

[4]
Coolidge Is President

On June 20, 1923, President Harding set out on a tour
to learn more about the nation and to explain government policies to the voters. It was to be a "voyage to
understanding." Talks to the people, conversations with
regional leaders, and participation in local rituals were
to be mixed with occasional stops for pleasure. He
crossed the country in two weeks, getting increasingly
good responses from the crowds, and then sailed to
Alaska for a vacation. By the time he returned toward
the end of July, he was ill, reportedly from eating
tainted seafood. His speaking engagements in Portland,
Oregon, were canceled, and his train sped to San Francisco where he was treated for cardiac collapse. Harding's condition seemed to improve, so much so that
by the afternoon of August 2 he was considered out of
danger. That night, however, he had a relapse and died
suddenly. When Senator Henry Cabot Lodge was told
the news, he exclaimed, "My God! That means Coolidge
is President!"

Calvin Coolidge was indeed President, and the personal contrast with his predecessor was startling. He was
thrifty, shy, and cautious. Reliability, not good fellow-
ship, was his hallmark. He was slow to judge and unlikely to prejudge. He appeared to have the knowledge,
intelligence, and tough-mindedness needed to operate
the government, taking problems as they came, though
not seeking them out to the extent that Harding had.
Yet Coolidge was like Harding in that he was dedicated
to the Republican platform of 1920 and that he, too,
believed in fattening the golden goose of big business

so that it might produce abundantly for all Americans. Also like Harding, he wanted to do right by all men and urged others to do likewise. The presidential style would change drastically, but the policies would remain largely the same.

In keeping with his image of simplicity, Coolidge, who was vacationing in Vermont, was sworn in by his father, a notary public, early in the morning of August 3 by the pale light of an oil lamp. After finishing his night's sleep, the new President rushed to Washington to take up his duties. There he helped arrange Harding's funeral and settled down to get to know his job. Except for Secretary of War John W. Weeks, who was also from Massachusetts, the Cabinet members and their deputies knew very little of their new chief, but Coolidge moved swiftly to get to know them and the problems of their departments. As he intended to follow Harding's policies, so he felt obligated to retain his appointees. Coolidge's designation of an astute southern Republican leader, C. Bascom Slemp, as his secretary, was taken as a sign that he planned to seek election to the Presidency in his own right. He also moved to make life in the White House as dignified and as solemn as it had been under Wilson and McKinley, as different from the Harding days, Alice Roosevelt Longworth observed, "as a New England front parlor is from a back room in a speakeasy." Yet Coolidge was not aloof from the people. He addressed them as often as any President, indeed more than most. He went out of his way so that people might see him and even shake his hand. And he directed his staff to give special attention to letters from those who had grievances against the government. It was clear, however, that he would have little to do with know-it-alls and name-droppers. Most seekers after special privilege found themselves better off talking with one of the President's secretaries. Even his closest friends were reluctant to give him advice unless he asked for it.

He did seek assistance, of course, and not only from
government officials. Coolidge also looked to Samuel
Gompers, who warmed more to him than he had to
Harding, and to other labor, farm, and business leaders,
to publishers, lobbyists, and educators, and to Democrats
as well as Republicans. Yet the new President depended
basically on his Cabinet officers for assistance in running the government. Not only did he expect them to
run their departments without coming to him for help,
but he substantially relied on them in drawing up his
legislative programs. Coolidge gave them recommendations less than had Harding. His task, as he saw it, was
to approve, modify, or, on occasion, disapprove their
recommendations. Secretary of State Charles Evans
Hughes retained his primacy in the Cabinet, in terms of
the President's respect and approbation, but Hoover
plainly was not Coolidge's second favorite, although he
generally let the Commerce Secretary have his hand,
even on farm matters in which Wallace became less influential. Treasury Secretary Mellon moved up to second
place in importance, and after Hughes left in 1925 he
became the President's first minister, because their quiet
personalities were so much attuned and they saw eye
to eye on fiscal affairs.

Coolidge had only one emergency to handle before
the opening of Congress in December, and that was the
call for a strike in the anthracite coal fields beginning
September 1. His solution was simple. He told the
mineowners and the miners that he expected them to
come to agreement, for the public would not stand for
a repetition of the coal-short days of the winters of 1919,
1920, and 1922. Then he let Governor Gifford Pinchot,
of Pennsylvania, where the anthracite fields lay, compose the differences between the mine operators and the
workers. Coolidge's only standby weapons were to offer
federal mediation and an investigation of conditions in
the mines, though the hint of sanctioning nonunion

labor to mine coal was also in the air. Pinchot worked successfully and secured agreement by the United Mine Workers and the operators to a 10-percent wage increase and an eight-hour day. Coolidge adroitly claimed credit by suggesting that Pinchot was his agent in the matter, one who deserved great praise, but an agent nonetheless.

Coolidge had four months to prepare for the convening of Congress. That was crisis enough for any President in the fourteen years after World War I, for Congress was then neither a rubber stamp nor a body dedicated to compromise. It was filled with men who were not to be harnessed by any President, as Wilson and Harding had already discovered. Coolidge's tactics were generally to make legislative recommendations, then sit back and let the Republican congressional leaders do their best for him. He seldom pressed an issue or used patronage or spoils to influence a vote. This fitted his unaggressive personality and his concept of the equality of the executive and legislative branches. Coolidge's approach probably worked as well as a more vigorous one would have during the 1920's, since the Democrats were too partisan and the Republicans too unpartisan for coordination by the administration. Coolidge was usually attentive to the wishes of Republican senators, allowing them and even some Democrats easy entrée to the White House and often extending personal courtesies. Although under no pressure, he went out of his way to complete Harding's work in pardoning those, still remaining in federal penitentiaries, who had been convicted of sedition during the Wilson years. If all this was a strange substitute for executive aggressiveness, it undoubtedly softened the antagonism between the White House and Capitol Hill. Coolidge often lost in his struggles with Congress, but he probably lost less frequently than he would have otherwise.

When Calvin Coolidge delivered his first message to Congress on December 6, 1923, it contained no surprises.

He endorsed Harding's foreign policy, and like his predecessor, Coolidge insisted that "our main problems are domestic problems." He, too, declared that lynching should be outlawed, inland waters developed, conservation and highway construction encouraged, farmers further assisted to help themselves, additional steps taken to mediate labor disputes, disabled veterans aided, a new department created to deal with education and the people's character development, a minimum wage for women and prohibition of child labor achieved through a constitutional amendment, and radio and aviation regulated. The big change was one of emphasis. The foremost domestic issues, he declared, were tax reduction and economy in government. Coolidge had spoken. His program was that of a President who sought to satisfy most citizens by picking up the things they wanted and carrying them as long as they did not cost too much. He also urged Americans to do whatever else was necessary to achieve the common good. As he said in his peroration, "We want idealism. We want that vision which lifts men and nations above themselves." Coolidge was plainly telling Congress and the people that government should do only what was essential to promote stability, tranquility, and prosperity, not to guarantee them.

The President, in his budget message given a few days later, detailed his wishes. He recommended a $3,300,000,000 budget. Coolidge envisioned that almost $400,000,000 could be pared from the national debt and that taxes could be reduced by $300,000,000, allowing for abolition of the remaining wartime excise levies and a cut in income taxes. With few exceptions the expenditures of federal agencies would be decreased, and the Post Office Department would become self-sustaining. The net result would be an increase in private funds for spending and investment.

Although the Coolidge budget was controversial, it

was not the central issue of the Sixty-eighth Congress. Politics was to camp on center stage. This was foreshadowed in the fight, early in 1924, by progressive Republicans for fairer committee operations, which delayed the reelection of Frederick Gillett as Speaker of the House of Representatives. A similar struggle ensued in the Senate, where the progressive Republicans successfully replaced Albert Cummins as chairman of the Interstate Commerce Committee with Democrat Ellison Smith. The two battles demonstrated the fragility of the administration's majority in Congress. Insurgency on rules and committee assignments and even the administration's uncertain majority on regular legislation were, however, to be the least of Coolidge's worries with Congress in 1924. The Harding Administration had left a legacy of scandal that would plague Coolidge for months, hamper consideration of his program, and develop poisonous relations between Congress and the executive branch that would have long-term aftereffects.

Before his death, Harding had often been criticized for appointing his political cronies to high office without proper regard for their qualifications. A steady drumroll of fire was aimed at the most prominent of Harding's friends, Attorney General Harry Daugherty, from the day the President announced that he wanted him in the Cabinet. Daugherty often treated the press and even congressmen arrogantly. Although his work was usually adequate, he drew heavy criticism for being laggard in pressing recovery of the overcharges made by wartime government contractors. Rumors of the Attorney General's connection with government graft were widely circulated even before Harding died. Indeed, soon after Coolidge became President, Senator Borah felt so bold as to advise him, "Get rid of Daugherty."

Other things happened, however, before Coolidge entered the White House. Daugherty and Senators David A. Reed and James Wadsworth warned Harding that the director of the Veterans' Bureau, Charles Forbes, was probably involved in corrupt activities. When Harding discovered that Forbes was profiting from the unnecessary sale of medical supplies to private parties, he demanded his resignation early in 1923. That fall Senate investigation showed that millions of dollars' worth of Veterans' Bureau supplies had been sold for private gain and that Forbes had been deeply involved in questionable deals on government land sites and construction contracts. Subsequently, in 1924 Forbes and his chief outside contact, J. W. Thompson, were convicted of conspiracy to defraud the government, and each was sentenced to a ten-thousand-dollar fine and two years in prison.

That was only the beginning. The biggest scandal burst wide open in 1924. The Senate had earlier authorized an investigation of the leasing to private oil interests of the naval oil reserve number three, in Wyoming, known popularly as Teapot Dome. The hearings, which began in October, 1923, under the direction of Democratic Senator Thomas J. Walsh, seemed to be leading nowhere when a contradiction in testimony appeared in January, 1924. Former Interior Secretary Albert Fall told the committee that he had borrowed $100,000 from Washington newspaper publisher Edward B. McLean to buy a ranch. McLean, however, denied that he had given Fall the money. Fall admitted that, but declined to name the source of the loan. Since Fall had arranged for the leasing of the Teapot Dome reserve to Harry F. Sinclair's Mammoth Oil Company, the question arose as to whether Sinclair had been the source of the loan and whether it had been a bribe.

The issue had been joined, and developments followed rapidly. As Senator Thomas Heflin, of Alabama, said, it was like a dog "Whose name was Rover/And when he died he died all over." On January 24 Edward Doheny, whose oil company had leased the Elk Hills

naval oil reserves in California, revealed that he had
lent $100,000 to Fall in 1921, ostensibly as an arrange-
ment between two friends. The next day one of Sinclair's lawyers gave evidence that his chief had lent
$25,000 or $30,000 to Fall in 1922. Rumors sprang up
that the entire Harding Cabinet was implicated in the
oil transactions, and soon the Senate began looking for
evidence of involvement by other officials than Albert
Fall. Coolidge remained calm, denying any recollec-
tion of Cabinet discussions of oil-land leases. He also
made clear that although the evidence required further
explanation and investigation, legal action by the executive branch demanded hard evidence. He was soon to
act, however. Senator Walsh planned to ask the Senate
on January 28, 1924, for a resolution authorizing the
President to stop the flow of oil from the naval reserves,
sue to cancel leases, and employ special counsel to prose-
cute where necessary. Coolidge beat him to the punch
and on January 27 announced that he would engage special counsel to take action in enforcing the law in the
case. To do this work, he named a prominent Republican lawyer, Owen J. Roberts, and a former Democratic
senator, Atlee Pomerene.

Although this took some of the initiative out of the
hands of the Senate investigators, it did not end their
work. Secretary of the Navy Edwin Denby came under
fire for consenting to the transfer of the naval oil reserves
to the Interior Department. On February 11 the Senate
called for Denby's resignation. Coolidge refused to accept
this as an order. Denby may have been naïve, and he
may have been mediocre as an official, but there was no
evidence—and never has been—that he was guilty of
misconduct. Coolidge stated that Denby was under his
jurisdiction, not the Senate's, and added, "I do not pro-
pose to sacrifice any innocent man for my own welfare."
Denby himself, however, decided to resign to lift some
of the pressure from the President.

The senators' next target was, predictably, the rough-and-tumble Attorney General, Harry Daugherty. Although Coolidge was not enamored of Daugherty, he was unwilling to dismiss him on hearsay. He would remove the Attorney General only for cause, despite the mounting pressure from Republicans as well as Democrats. Of course, Coolidge would have been pleased had Daugherty resigned of his own volition, but the Attorney General would be the last man to resign under fire. Meanwhile, it had been made clear that Wilson's Navy Secretary, Josephus Daniels, had fathered the legislation that permitted the private leasing of naval oil reserves and that Edward Doheny was closely linked with the leading Democratic candidate for President in 1924, William Gibbs McAdoo. The involvement of Democrats, however, did not blunt the attack on administration Republicans. On March 1 the Senate voted to investigate Daugherty for failure to probe corruption. Soon evidence was given of questionable transactions by the Attorney General and his friends. It was insufficient to jail him, but the record was disenchanting. When Daugherty refused to open his department's files to Senate investigators, Coolidge asked for his resignation because "I do not see how you can be acting for yourself in your own defense in this matter, and at the same time and on the same question acting as my attorney general."

Even Daugherty's resignation did not end the investigation and the charges. Harding and Coolidge were among those subject to suspicion and scrutiny, although the evidence against Coolidge was so flimsy that it only built sympathy for him. His coolness under attack also contrasted favorably with the antics of some of the senators who allowed their imaginations to run wild in a saturnalia of vituperation. The President bolstered his position by appointing California Chief Justice Curtis D. Wilbur as Secretary of the Navy and Harlan Fiske

Stone, the former dean of the Columbia University Law School, as Attorney General. In promise and performance both were several cuts above the men they replaced. Moreover, Coolidge relied on Special Counsel Roberts and Pomerene to clean up the oil leases, and that they did well. Albert Fall was fined $100,000 and sentenced to a year in prison for receiving a bribe. Harry Sinclair was fined $1,000 and drew three months in jail for refusing to testify and an additional six months for contempt of court. There was insufficient evidence to penalize him further or to convict Daugherty and Doheny. After exhaustive court proceedings the oil leases were canceled. Whether there was criminal intent in the affair was never conclusively proved.

Scandals in the Veterans' Bureau, Department of Interior, and Department of Justice were not all that Coolidge was burdened with. Corruption was revealed in the Office of the Alien Property Custodian, where Jess Smith, Daugherty's closest friend, apparently had illegally arranged transfer of a German company to an American syndicate. Smith committed suicide, and Alien Property Custodian Thomas W. Miller, for his role in the matter, was fined $5,000 and sentenced to eighteen months in prison. During the Teapot Dome affair the Senate also began investigating the Bureau of Internal Revenue and discovered that several corporations had received large tax rebates. This was further complicated by pressure to investigate alleged scandal in the bureau with regard to prohibition enforcement. The probing of the Internal Revenue Bureau quickly degenerated into a fishing expedition, which Coolidge forcefully protested to the Senate. Subsequently, the prohibition investigation was blunted, and it was shown that the tax rebates were legal, even though the bureau's interpretation of the law was most generous. Another issue was Coolidge's encouragement of industrialist Henry Ford to buy the government's properties at Muscle

Shoals in order to develop the area. The Senate put a stop to this as a result of George Norris's charges that such a transaction would make "Teapot Dome look like a pinhead."

Although Coolidge generally handled himself well in these crises, Congress's preoccupation with scandal and the President's jousts with the Senate largely contributed to the blocking of his legislative program. The Internal Revenue Bureau affair built up the opposition to the Coolidge-Mellon tax reduction program, which was defeated as being too favorable to wealthy citizens. Coolidge's and Hughes's unsuccessful struggle with Congress in April against Japanese exclusion demonstrated how far out of tune the legislative and executive branches were. The same could be said of Congress's overriding of the President's veto in May of the Adjusted Compensation Act for World War I veterans. Certainly, the Teapot Dome affair contributed to the defeat of Coolidge's plan to sell Muscle Shoals to Ford.

What it all added up to was that except for confirmation of his several major appointments, the President's 1924 legislative successes were few and generally negative in nature. He maintained the integrity of the executive branch against congressional encroachment, and he blunted the less savory aspects of the Senate investigations of Teapot Dome and the Internal Revenue Bureau. Coolidge also turned aside passage of the McNary-Haugen bill, which was the congressional formulation of the Peek-Johnson agricultural scheme. The bill proposed federal purchase of eight surplus farm products at high prewar prices and their sale abroad for whatever they could command, with the expectation that with domestic supply not exceeding demand, the resulting higher prices at home would exceed the amount lost overseas. Coolidge also successfully vetoed increases in veteran's pensions and the proposed salary raise for postal employees. In effect, though, he had come out of his first round with

Congress as badly as any President in American history. Not one major part of his program had been enacted. The best that can be said is that Coolidge, under most trying circumstances, had kept his head.

By June the country's politicians turned their attention toward the national conventions. When Coolidge assumed office as President in 1923, he did not appear a prime contender for the 1924 Republican nomination. He seemed to lack the aggressiveness and political astuteness needed in a successful presidential candidate. Moreover, Coolidge had no significant power base and was not well known in his party. Yet he skillfully used White House patronage and publicity to develop political strength, and he personally impressed a number of disparate Republican elements, including Chief Justice Taft and Senator Borah, to gain support. Coolidge had handled himself well during the Teapot Dome investigation, and he was further aided by the fact that the nation was beginning to prosper. As important as anything was the growing realization among regular Republicans that they could not repudiate Coolidge lest the voters take that as a sign that the charges of the progressive Republicans and Democrats about government scandals were correct. There was also the increasing awareness that the President's obvious integrity and his old-fashioned ways were probable antidotes to the questionable ways of Harding and his friends.

This did not mean that Coolidge had no opponents for the presidential nomination. There were plenty, including former Governor Frank O. Lowden, of Illinois; Governor Gifford Pinchot, of Pennsylvania; Henry Ford; and Senators Robert M. La Follette, Hiram Johnson, and Charles Curtis. By January, 1924, all of them except Johnson had dropped out of active contention for the nomination. Until spring Senator Johnson gave Coolidge stiff competition. In May, however, the President won the primary election in California, Johnson's home state, which effectively removed the senator as a candidate. Coolidge's men controlled the June convention in Cleveland. The Republican platform was largely a reiteration of the President's December, 1923, message to Congress, and Coolidge was nominated on the first ballot. His only mistake was that he gave insufficient attention to who his running mate should be. He thought of many people, but finally became intent upon Borah. The Idaho senator, however, would have no part of it, and Coolidge found himself in the middle of a convention without a vice-presidential nominee. The delegates took the question out of his hands and nominated Lowden, who declined the honor. Then the congressional leaders and party rebels at the convention united on Charles Dawes. Thus the 1924 Republican ticket was balanced between the solemn Yankee lawyer who was President and an irascible Illinois banker.

The Democratic convention, which met late in June and early in July, presented quite a contrast to the Republican conclave. The Democrats lambasted the Republicans for alleged wickedness and corruption in office. Soon, however, they dissolved into a howling mob, dividing over such issues as the Ku Klux Klan, which the party indirectly deplored, repeal of prohibition, which was not endorsed, the League of Nations, which was endorsed, and oil-tainted Democrats, who were condemned, even though there were not supposed to be any. As for the presidential nomination, prohibition repeal and Catholicism defeated Governor Alfred Smith, of New York, oil dragged under William Gibbs McAdoo, and Alabama's Oscar Underwood's chances were ruined by his criticism of the Klan. The convention was deadlocked as no other party convention before or since. It took 103 ballots before the Democrats agreed on Wall Street lawyer John W. Davis as their nominee. They then turned to William Jennings Bryan's brother, Gov-

ernor Charles Bryan, of Nebraska, to run for Vice-
President.

As the Democrats were concluding their free-for-all
convention in New York, the Conference for Progressive
Political Action was meeting in Cleveland. Here
gathered a coalition of farm and labor elements, reform-
ers, Socialists, and religious liberals to seek an alternative
to the conservatism of the 1920's. They promised positive aid to agriculture, recognition of labor's rights, the
end of monopoly, a housecleaning of government offices,
protection of natural resources, popular sovereignty,
and peace on earth. The Progressives endorsed the presidential candidacy of Senator La Follette and asked Bur-
ton K. Wheeler, the maverick Democratic senator from
Montana, to run for Vice-President.

Coolidge and the Republican National Committee
chairman, William Butler, staked their party's campaign
on economy, prosperity, respectability, and stability.
They declared that government economy would release
more money for private spending and investment, which
in turn would increase and broaden prosperity. Respectability would give people confidence in the government,
and the resultant stability would not only encourage
further economic growth but also spread like a balm over
the strife and discontent still existing in America. Of
course, the government would try to deal, efficiently but
on a small budget, with the social and economic cankers
that private action could not heal.

The Democrats aimed at similar goals in their campaign. They promised to distribute prosperity more
widely, through more federal services and actions, and to
install virtue in government. The Democrats were, however, at a great disadvantage. Coolidge had already
become the procurator of capitalist prosperity, and the
Progressives had outpromised everybody in the area of
expanded government action. As for virtue, how could
Davis, a Wall Street lawyer and former diplomat, com-

pete with the old-fashioned solidity of Coolidge or with the Olympian senator, LaFollette, playing holy prophet?

Coolidge did not formally campaign. He attended to government business and confined himself to occasional nonpartisan speeches. He left the rigors of attack and rebuttal to Charles "Hell'n Maria" Dawes, who could give as good as he could take on the stump. The Republicans generally left Davis to wallow in his obscurity. Their main target was La Follette, who, Dawes asserted, was "leading an army of extreme radicalism . . . a heterogeneous collection of those opposing the existing order of things, the greatest section of which, the Socialists, flies the red flag." This was contrasted to the sturdiness and wisdom of Coolidge who was declared the heir of Washington and Lincoln. The issue was, the Republicans said, "Coolidge or Chaos."

John W. Davis had little to offer. He had not been high in Democratic circles. He was no orator, and like most Democrats, he drove the Teapot Dome issue into the ground. His party was not united, as its convention had demonstrated, and it raised only one-fifth of the amount of money that the Republicans had for campaign purposes. Davis and Bryan also had to bear the incongruity of a ticket composed of a House of Morgan lawyer and a neo-Populist. As Davis later commented, "I went around the country telling the people I was going to be elected, and I knew I hadn't any more chance than a snowball in hell."

The aging La Follette made only twenty speeches, but they were among the oratorical glories of American progressivism. And Wheeler conducted a hard-driving campaign against alleged Republican venality. They were hampered by a lack of funds, but most of all by the facts that little remained of the prewar progressive constituency and that few young voters found progressivism attractive during the 1920's. Most citizens had had enough of promises, largely unkept, of a bright new world through government action. They were easily persuaded that progress would come by allowing people to quest for it in their own ways.

With no crisis developing at home or abroad during the campaign, with employment and farm income rising, and with integrity reigning in the White House, everything seemed to be well handled by the incumbent administration. The result was a smashing electoral triumph for Calvin Coolidge, who polled 15,718,000 votes to 8,385,000 for Davis and 4,831,000 for La Follette. The majority of the voters wanted the prosperity and tranquility that the Republicans promised. As far as most citizens were concerned, internationalism and liberalism had either gone far enough or failed. Neither in his campaign nor in his record had Davis given signs of doing better than Coolidge. La Follette offered a clear alternative, but the progressive program of nationalistic reforms promised to do even less for a troubled world than the Republican and Democratic platforms. Coolidge seemed the only choice for most Americans. Although he did not understand the postwar era, neither did Davis and La Follette, and he was far more reasonable in his misunderstanding of it than were they.

President Coolidge had been shrewd in winning nomination and election in 1924, but he only occasionally in the years to come found the right combination to be successful with Congress. There were several obstacles hindering enactment of his legislative program. Unrest and resentment carried over from his 1924 battles with Congress and from the bitterness of the campaign. This was aggravated by the expulsion of Robert La Follette and three of his Senate followers from the Republican party caucus and their loss of committee seniority in November and December, 1924. The Republican leadership could discipline the progressives; it could not, however, dictate their votes or those of other senators sympathetic to them. Their independence would repeatedly embarrass the administration's efforts on Capitol Hill.

With other senators and representatives Coolidge was amiable. He did not try to influence the election of congressional officers and the composition of committees. Nor did he oppose the raise in pay for congressmen from $7,500 to $10,000. Despite his mollifying tactics, Congress was not amenable to his program in late 1924 and early 1925. Republican party solidarity weakened as economic issues moved members of Congress more than party loyalty. It was clear, too, that what legislation the administration wanted and what bills a majority could be found for were usually two different things. Stalemate was generally the result.

During the lame-duck session of the Sixty-eighth Congress, Senator Oscar Underwood offered, with Coolidge's support, a bill authorizing the leasing of Muscle Shoals. The bill was passed by both houses, with mixed partisan backing. Progressive Republican George W. Norris, however, used a remarkable display of parliamentary tactics to force recommittal of the conference bill that had composed the differences in the House and Senate versions of the measure. More important in the long run was that Norris's struggle turned the tide against disposal of Muscle Shoals by the government. He persisted in battling for federal development of the area until, during the Franklin D. Roosevelt Administration, the property was used as the foundation for the establishment of the Tennessee Valley Authority.

Muscle Shoals was the major legislative issue of the lame-duck session of 1924–1925, and Coolidge let it go at that, for he expected increased support in the new Sixty-ninth Congress. Meanwhile, he had to take up some administrative rearrangements with the Senate. Henry C. Wallace had died in October, 1924, and Coolidge took the recommendation of Farm Bloc leader Arthur Capper for a new Secretary of Agriculture. The nominee was a leader in agricultural education, William M. Jardine, who was easily confirmed by the Senate. Also quickly confirmed was Frank B. Kellogg, the ambassador to

Great Britain, as Hughes's replacement as Secretary of State. The appointment of Harlan F. Stone to take Justice Joseph McKenna's place on the Supreme Court left open the attorney generalship. Also left open was the opportunity for Coolidge's antagonists to embarrass him. The President nominated Charles Beecher Warren for the position. Warren was a lawyer and businessman who had served the government as ambassador to Japan and Mexico. He was vulnerable, however, because he had been a prominent figure in the Sugar Trust, which was under indictment, and because Coolidge had not smoothed the way for Warren's confirmation. Progressive Republicans rose in revolt and got enough Democratic support to block confirmation. Thus, for the first time since 1868 the Senate rejected a Cabinet nomination. Coolidge settled for the appointment of an old friend, John Garibaldi Sargent, of Vermont, and a measure of revenge on the leading progressives in patronage matters.

The President's appointments were adequate, and even outstanding in two cases. Stone, who was Coolidge's only Supreme Court appointee, proved a distinguished jurist, one who was later elevated by Franklin D. Roosevelt to the chief justiceship. Despite a streak of irascibility, Kellogg was highly competent and indeed, for his part in the Pact of Paris, was to win the Nobel Peace Prize and a seat on the Court of International Justice. Jardine strengthened the forces seeking cooperative solutions to farm problems and served as an effective bulwark against McNary-Haugenism. Sargent administered the Department of Justice honestly and conservatively, paying strict attention to his master's admonition that the avoidance of controversy was the golden rule. As with the rest of the Coolidge Cabinet, efficiency and economy were among the characteristic qualities of the three new administrators.

A word should be said at this point about Coolidge and the regulatory commissions. During the Harding and Coolidge administrations, thanks largely to conservative appointments, the nature of the commissions' labors changed from policing business abuses to encouraging business freedom. For example, Coolidge altered the Tariff Commission by luring a low-tariff Republican off the body with a diplomatic appointment and by naming a protectionist Democrat in his place. Reshaping the commissions was a painful chore for the President, who did not like the bargaining and pressures involved. He frequently had to make recess appointments to the commissions because of the difficulties, based as much on patronage as on ideological grounds, of gaining Senate consent to his nominations. But Coolidge was successful in securing regulatory commissions dominated by pro-business elements or, in the case of the Railway Labor Board, with members who sought industrial tranquility by reconciling the interests of management with those of labor leadership. His efforts were augmented by President Hoover's generally conservative appointees and for a time impeded the regulatory work of the commissions and boards during the 1930's when more dynamic action was in demand.

The struggle between President and Congress resumed in December, 1925. In his message to Congress Coolidge pointed up the nation's increasing prosperity and played down the need for government action. He therefore asked for little from the legislators. The keynote was "economy and efficiency" in government, so that taxes and the public debt could be further cut in order to allow for greater private spending as a stimulus to prosperity. His chief legislative goals therefore were to restrain appropriations and to provide tax relief. Coolidge was both astute and lucky in paving the way for focusing congressional attention on these interrelated issues. No major appointments were in the offing, and the minor ones were handled circumspectly. The Harding scandals had lost their force, and there was no Coolidge scandal.

The President kept his other legislative requests to a minimum, while skillfully marshaling public sentiment behind tax relief. A potentially diverting question like prohibition was not one that then commanded much interest in Congress. Coolidge could escape with occasional sanctimonious statements in favor of enforcing the law while he let his chief enforcement officers, Attorney General Sargent and Treasury Secretary Mellon, do what their consciences required, which was little. Fortunately for the President's fiscal goals, the wets in Congress did not attack Coolidge for fear that he would respond with stricter enforcement, and the drys seldom criticized him for fear that he would do less.

Any assault that came was on Congress and in favor of tax relief, as bankers, businessmen, economists, state officials, and tax-reduction clubs demanded legislative action. President Coolidge and Secretary Mellon added to the constant pressure. Consequently, Congress in February, 1926, approved the Revenue Act by overwhelming majorities. Income taxes in all categories were cut, estate taxes were halved, surtaxes on wealth were reduced up to 50 percent, and the gift tax was abolished. The result for the taxpayers was not only a tax reduction but also the exemption of about one-third of them from tax payments. A further dividend was that despite the great tax decrease, plenty of funds remained to pare the national debt because of low congressional appropriations and additional executive economies. Moreover, further money could be pumped into the rising economy because of the some $350,000,000 of national income released for discretionary private spending. There were problems, of course. The government was made more reliant on the tariff for revenue, which was used as an additional argument for keeping duties high. The wealthy benefited more proportionately from the tax slashes than middle-class citizens, and less money was available for financing new and old federal programs. Furthermore, the door was opened for increases in state and local taxes, since it was often reasoned that what the federal government surrendered to taxpayers could now be taken to meet state and local needs.

The Revenue Act of 1926 was followed two years later with legislation lowering income taxes further as well as reducing levies on corporations and granting a substantial number of exemptions on special taxes. Coolidge wanted these, but Congress, on its own initiative and despite the President's opposition, also repealed the 3-percent tax on automobiles. Consequently, the 1928 revenue measure released another $300,000,000 for private spending and increased state and local taxes. There can be no doubt that the fiscal policies of the Harding and Coolidge administrations greatly relieved the federal tax and debt burden. Between 1921 and 1929 the total potential internal-tax yield was cut by one-third; the number of individual income-tax returns declined from 6,662,000 to 4,044,000; the gross federal debt was slashed from $24,000,000,000 to $17,000,000,000; and the annual interest on the debt was reduced from $1,000,000,000 to $678,000,000.

Coolidge's December, 1925, message to Congress contained one minor surprise, one connected to a well-publicized issue. He requested increased appropriations for the government's aeronautical activities. This reflected the administration's sensitivity to the struggles among various cities to become the center of the rapidly expanding aircraft industry and the fierce competition among airplane manufacturers. Coolidge wanted development of airways and of the industry, but on an orderly basis. Thus he not only encouraged cooperation among the contending elements but also sought to spur cooperation through better government financing and coordination of the aircraft industry. A diverting issue resulted from the public charges of the American apostle of air power, Colonel William Mitchell, that the army and navy were negligent and incompetent in developing aviation. Mitchell's brashness led to his conviction of insubordination by a court martial. The situation also led to Coolidge's appointment in September, 1925, of a board, headed by Dwight Morrow, to consider the best ways of developing aviation for the national good. The Morrow group rejected Mitchell's exaggerated contention that foreign air power would soon menace America's security. The board, however, supported further study and development of aviation and recommended the creation of assistant secretaries of war, navy, and commerce for air, with coordinated activities, and the establishment of a bureau of civil aviation. Coolidge, who had been working in this direction since 1923, was able to get from Congress a substantial appropriation for aviation development and approval of most of the Morrow board's recommendations. The President's program of urging stability in the aircraft business and of subsidizing its development was a significant step in the history of aviation in the United States.

Another of Coolidge's domestic concerns, and the most vexing during his second term, was to control the increasingly controversial agricultural situation. Farmers were in serious trouble. Their markets shrank after the war as military needs swiftly contracted and European agricultural productivity recovered. American farmers also found themselves deeply in debt because they had borrowed too much during the war in order to meet the nation's needs and to take full advantage of a rising market. Their usual answer to paying off their debts and making a decent return on their investments was to increase productivity. The result was to keep markets glutted and agricultural prices depressed. The decreasing rates of immigration and births further widened the gap between American agricultural production and consumption during the 1920's, as did the change in middle-class eating habits dictated by the fashionably slim figure of the decade.

Many solutions to low farm-purchasing power were suggested, including better rural credit, businesslike agricultural management, cooperative marketing, crop diversification, mechanization, and soil conservation. Farmers increasingly adopted these, but usually to increase production instead of adjusting production to demand. They reasoned that higher yields, even at lower prices, would adequately increase their income, but all it did was to guarantee a recession for most farmers throughout the 1920's. Unable to find a solution of their own, agriculturalists looked to government for help. Government responded, as we have seen, with higher tariffs, aids to cooperative marketing, better farm information and education, increased rural credit, and improved regulation of wholesalers and processors. But neither the farmers' efforts nor those of the government got to the root of the problem, which was to balance supply and demand. It was clear that there was no mandate for—indeed there was fierce opposition to— federal control of production or expansion of consumption by the undernourished. And the farmers were unable, as individuals and as a group, to limit production in the face of insufficient markets for their products.

By 1923 Agriculture Secretary Wallace and Commerce Secretary Hoover were joined in battle on how to meet the farm situation. Wallace sought establishment of an export corporation that would facilitate marketing overseas. Hoover wanted the further extension of farm credit and development of cooperatives. Neither was willing to recommend tampering with the tariff, nor apparently thought of new programs to distribute farm commodities to underfed Americans. With Wallace's death in October, 1924, Hoover's viewpoint won out as official policy, and with Coolidge's blessing, since he believed that Wallace was advocating class legislation that would not work anyway. The solution, as the President saw it, lay with the farmers themselves. All the government could do was to assist them to become better managers; it could not effectively manage their affairs for them. Nevertheless farmers sought government relief beyond what Coolidge thought wise. This was seen most powerfully in the emergence of the McNary-Haugen bill in Congress. The measure, over the years, took different forms, but what it basically proposed was government purchase of selected surplus farm commodities at an average of prewar prices and then their sale abroad for whatever price they would fetch. The hope was that this would balance supply and demand at home and thereby force domestic farm prices up to a level that would exceed whatever amount was lost in the program's operation. It was not until 1926, however, that the McNary-Haugen bill attracted enough support to become a serious problem for the Coolidge Administration.

It was plain by 1925 that farmers were not sharing in America's growing prosperity. In December Coolidge stated that he would not support anything that would in effect be government price-fixing, in other words, McNary-Haugenism. The administration offered instead a measure to establish a federal farm board with the power to lend up to $250,000,000 to cooperatives in order to remove some surpluses from the market. In the legislative struggle that followed in 1926, neither this bill nor the McNary-Haugen proposal won enough support for passage. Yet the administration secured funds to help cotton-growers manage their surplus and gained enactment of a bill creating a Division of Cooperative Marketing in the Agriculture Department. The President also persuaded Congress to appropriate money for further development of inland waterways. Little as it was, the results of congressional action in 1926 represented the high point of legislative success for Coolidge. This was partly because he had less to request after that year and partly because the 1926 elections resulted in a drop in the Republican majorities in the House and Senate, from sixty to thirty-nine and from sixteen to two respectively. Now insurgent Republicans and Democrats possessed the power often to stymie administration proposals and occasionally to enact their own measures.

The McNary-Haugen forces tried to take advantage of this situation during Coolidge's last two years as President. He tried to deflate the movement by emphasizing what his and Harding's administrations had done for agriculture and by championing further product research, cooperative marketing, and farm education. Yet McNary-Haugenism was not to be stopped by recitations of past favors and promises of others to come. Vice-President Dawes and all the Senate Republican leaders except Borah had gone over to the movement. Also important, the President was not enthusiastic about his own administration's alternative, the federal-farm-board proposal of Secretaries Hoover and Jardine to keep surpluses off the market by extending low-interest credit to cooperatives.

By 1927 sentiment for the McNary-Haugen bill was so high among farmers and businessmen engaged in farm-related enterprises that it passed both houses of Congress by February. Coolidge vetoed it. He condemned it in his veto message for putting "a premium on one-crop farming," penalizing farmers who tried to restrict production to demand, and levying a tax that was therefore unconstitutional. In effect, the measure contemplated "employment of the coercive powers of government to the end that certain special groups of farmers and processors may profit temporarily." That profit, he contended, would be the incentive to expand production and thus worsen, not cure, the root problem. Coolidge pointed out at great length other weaknesses of the bill and inferred that the dumping of surplus commodities abroad would complicate international trade.

Congress was unable to override the President's veto, but McNary-Haugenism was not dead. The House and

Senate approved a revised version of it in 1928. Again Coolidge vetoed the measure, calling it a "preposterous economic and commercial fallacy." And again Congress could not pass the bill over his veto. McNary-Haugenism was now dead, for the coalition behind it began to crumble, with many of its elements either in search of new panaceas, discouraged by the administration's stout opposition, or satisfied with slightly improving farm prices during the Indian summer of Coolidge prosperity.

The President did not have the answer to the serious problems affecting the nation's farmers, but the McNary-Haugen plan was conspicuous economic nonsense. It did not provide for restricting surplus agricultural production and probably would have encouraged further production. Even had the unlikely occurred and production remained stable, it would have raised consumer prices artificially and offset the modest gains in purchasing power that the urban lower classes had made during the 1920's. The world prices of surplus commodities would have been further depressed as a result of dumping farm produce overseas. Foreign governments would undoubtedly have reared still higher walls against American exports and probably have indulged in reverse dumping where possible. In short, the unstable international trade situation would have become even more unstable, with only short-range advantage for a small group of Americans and long-range disadvantages for all. Deservedly unsuccessful as McNary-Haugenism was, the movement did, of course, force the administration to do more for farmers than it would probably otherwise have done. It is possible, however, that McNary-Haugenism also diverted the energy, thought, and imagination that might have led to the formulation of sounder measures for agricultural relief.

Among other issues during the Coolidge years was the establishment of the Federal Radio Commission to halt the scramble for broadcasting rights and to provide for an orderly assignment of radio wavelengths. The catastrophic floods on the Mississippi, Missouri, and Ohio rivers in the spring of 1927 and later that year in New England led not only to prompt federal relief efforts but also to the formulation of a flood-control program along the Mississippi. Although President and Congress wrangled over the size of the program and the amount of government participation, compromise legislation emerged in 1928, thus marking the first substantial federal attempt to control the threat of floods. Because of Coolidge's frugality, the program was not as effectively wide-ranging as it could have been, but neither did it authorize as many questionable benefits to private interests as Congress wanted. Coolidge supported the improvement of waterways as arteries of transportation, with appropriations increasing from $47,000,000 in 1923 to $70,000,000 in 1928. The number of miles of federally assisted road construction grew from 169,000 in 1923 to 190,000 in 1929. Although the President was cool to Secretary Hoover's plan for large-scale federal development of hydroelectric power, he eventually backed construction of the huge Boulder Dam on the Colorado River to regulate the river's flow, provide for increased electric power, and help distribute waters equitably among seven western states. During the Coolidge Administration the area of national forests did not shrink, as some conservationists feared would happen, but increased slightly from 182,100,000 to 184,565,000 acres. Thanks to the dynamic leadership of the National Park Service, national parks, monuments, and historical areas expanded substantially, from seventy-one to ninety-six and from 8,790,000 to 10,538,000 acres.

Coolidge's administration, like Harding's, did bring changes to the United States. It was not an overwhelming record, but neither was it insignificant. And it was made better by Coolidge's ability, at which he surpassed Harding, in securing able and economical performance from public servants and in making maximum use of the Bureau of the Budget. He also deserves credit for extending the civil-service and foreign-service merit systems, raising the level of competence among federal judges, and releasing the remaining wartime political prisoners.

Nevertheless there were serious flaws in the administration's policies and practices. Coolidge's lack of aggressiveness, his limited insight into the country's needs, and the similar paucity of insight and the combativeness of Congress account for much of the administration's failure. Labor reform was not seriously considered, nor were railway consolidation and expansion of welfare services. The government's response to black America's entreaties for more equal rights was feeble, consisting only of a few additional appointments to office, moderate increases in appropriations for Negro educational institutions, some improvement in civil-service job opportunities, and occasional rhetorical gestures. This did little to help blacks, and the result, born of disappointment, was to loosen the traditional ties of Negroes to the Republican party. Except for Indians, who were the subject of some reform interest in the government, even less was done for other racial minorities in the United States.

Yet what Coolidge did or accepted or presided over was popular with most Americans. Prosperity was the keynote, and during the Coolidge Presidency prosperity seemed to depend upon tranquility and low taxes. Thus these were the two policies that the President emphasized. Tranquility appeared to spur business enterprise, as did the release of potential federal revenues to private investment. The majority of Republicans and Democrats approved in general Coolidge's policy of encouraging business. Indeed, during the 1920's, even the American Federation of Labor opposed a strong antitrust policy. Certainly, there was insufficient support for federal action in other economic sectors. While the farmers struggled for government aid, they were seldom willing to assist labor in a similar fight, and labor was not eager to lend a hand to farmers. Furthermore, for labor, agriculture, and others to secure privileges equivalent to those gained by business would have required positive legislation. Clearly, however, positive legislation usually ran against the wishes of a majority of Americans and contrary to the traditionalist viewpoint of the country's jurists. Approval from the administration, Congress, courts, and the people was reserved largely for the federal action and inaction that encouraged business expansion and in turn seemed to provide more jobs, additional purchasing power, and a greater variety of goods and services. Most Americans, remembering what economic conditions had been but a few years earlier, could agree with Coolidge when he told Congress on December 4, 1928,

No Congress of the United States ever assembled. on surveying the state of the Union, has met with a more pleasing prospect than that which appears at the present time. In the domestic field there is tranquility and contentment, harmonious relations between management and the wage earner. freedom from industrial strife, and the highest record of years of prosperity. In the foreign field there is peace, the good will which comes from mutual understanding, and the knowledge that the problems which a short time ago appeared so ominous are yielding to the touch of manifest friendship. . . . The country can regard the present with satisfaction and anticipate the future with optimism.

If Calvin Coolidge was by and large pleased. so was the nation. If Coolidge by and large lacked the foresight to see what the future would bring, it must be said that so did the nation.

[5]
Prosperity, Release, and Reaction

HOWEVER transitory, there was a great deal to President Coolidge's "pleasing prospect." In a time of relative tranquility the United States was more prosperous than ever before. The average industrial workweek declined from 47.4 hours in 1920 to 44.2 hours in 1929. There was a 13-percent increase in the real wages of industrial workers between 1922 and 1929, and many factory employees enjoyed new fringe benefits. The average unemployment rate was 3.7 percent between 1923 and 1929, compared with 6.1 percent between 1911 and 1917, which was a fairly prosperous period itself. Work stoppages from labor-management disputes dropped markedly, from 3,411 in 1920 to 637 in 1930. Consumer prices remained fairly stable during most of the decade. Most of this resulted from the jump in gross national product from $73,300,000,000 in 1920 to $104,400,000,000 in 1929, in terms of 1929 prices. Equally significant was the 50-percent leap in the quantity of manufacturing production between 1922 and 1929.

There were many reasons for the expanded production of the 1920's. One was the rising efficiency of American industry. Production was increasingly harnessed to mechanization and more effective power modes, and the assembly-line method, pioneered by Henry Ford in 1915, was applied in growing numbers of factories. The industrial efficiency movement, associated with the names of Frank Gilbreth and Frederick W. Taylor, moved into high gear to cut down on wasted time and motion by workers. It led to better plant layout and use of manpower, with the result that the index of man-hour productivity rose from 44.6 in 1920 to 72.5 in 1929. Increasingly professional plant managers, men trained to do their jobs, took the places of the owners' relatives and heirs. Business consolidation probably contributed to efficiency by eliminating marginal producers. And one cannot overlook the role of new inventions that boosted production as well as expanded the variety of commodities for sale.

Transportation was another important component of increased production and distribution. Although the nation's railway system remained stable in size and in types of equipment, the average tractive effort mounted by about 25 percent and freight tonnage rose by 10 percent between 1919 and 1929. Inland-water traffic also increased substantially. The bulk-freight tonnage jumped from 91,762,000 in 1919 to 138,574,000 in 1929 on the Great Lakes and doubled on the New York State canals. More impressive were the leap in the number of truck registrations from 898,000 in 1919 to 3,550,000 in 1929 and the increase in bus registrations from 17,800 in 1925, the first year of reliable statistics, to 34,000 in 1929. Surfaced roads under state control grew from 350,000 to 662,000 miles between 1919 and 1929. By the end of the 1920's it was clear that although rail and water traffic still dominated commercial transportation, they had lost their monopoly. Buses and trucks could compete in prices and often speed with trains and go places that railways could not reach; trucks had an even greater advantage over the cheaper water transport in speed and in where they could travel. Aviation was the other main transportation development. A novelty at the beginning of the decade, by 1929 there were thirty-eight domestic operators carrying 162,000 paying passengers and flying seventy thousand ton-miles of express and freight.

The heightened efforts to create a buyer psychology also helped to produce the prosperity of the 1920's.

Salesmanship rose to new levels as a career. It was widely proclaimed as one of the easiest ways to make money in a decade when the earning of money seemed the highest goal. Articles on salesmanship appeared in newspapers and magazines with great frequency, and salesmanship courses entered the academic curriculum. The emphasis was not so much on serving the customer as on convincing him of the advantages of the wares that one had to sell. Thus the proprietor and the clerk became salesmen, and old-line salesmen became super-salesmen.

Salesmanship was reinforced by advertising, which, already a big business, became a bigger business during the 1920's. An increasing proportion of newspaper and magazine space was devoted to advertising copy as the modest, even staid advertisements of the prewar era burgeoned into large, eye-catching testimonials to the efficacy of this, the low cost of that, or the status-raising properties of this and that. The old colorful advertising curtains still remained in vaudeville houses, but filmed advertisements flooded the screens of the rapidly growing number of motion-picture theaters. Commercials quickly became an integral part of radio programming. Increasing numbers of roadside billboards extolled the virtues of the various products to be found just down the pike or around the bend. Sloganeering rose to previously unreached heights as a way to capture the public's attention and favor. "They Satisfy" was all one had to say about one brand of cigarettes, and for those who were not thus satisfied, the advice was "Reach for a Lucky instead of a Sweet." "Halitosis" and "B.O." became household terms along with the names of the products that could prevent such social offenses. Ballyhoo seemed to receive the imprimatur of many churches, which adopted techniques of salesmanship and advertising in their proselyting. Bruce Barton expressed this convergence of church and mammon when he wrote in his best-selling book, *The Man Nobody Knows,* that Jesus "would have been a national advertiser today."

If the methods were increasingly available to produce, transport, and sell commodities, the goods themselves were becoming more attractive to buyers. A choice of colors was available in many products. Variety was the watchword, whether applied to automobiles, vegetables, or clothes. Moreover, new products were turned out in increasing abundance. A greater variety of fabrics was found on the market as rayon became a commonly used material and as celanese came into production. Many items were geared to the vastly increasing use of electricity in the home, such as radios, electric irons, vacuum cleaners, and even by the late 1920's refrigerators, washing machines, and electric razors. There were plenty of other new products including cellophane, cigarette lighters, Pyrex cooking utensils, various Bakelite goods, and lacquers, which testified to the fast-paced technological advances in industry.

The single most important product during the 1920's was also relatively new, the motor vehicle. It was important just in itself, as between 1919 and 1929 the factory sales of passenger cars jumped from 1,652,000 to 4,455,000 and those of trucks and buses from 225,000 to 882,000. In addition, the manufacture of motor vehicles created or greatly advanced other industries, as can be seen in the corresponding increase in the production of tires, batteries, window glass, upholstery, and various accessories. The rise of motor-vehicle manufacturing also contributed to the expansion of the petroleum industry, for the use of gasoline shot up from less than three billion gallons in 1919 to fifteen billion in 1929. Add to all this the development of tourism, roadside advertising and merchandising, garages, automobile dealerships, and various other enterprises catering to motor traffic, and it is plain that within a decade the automotive industry and related businesses had become the most important and attractive element in the American economy.

Another essential ingredient of the phenomenal economic spurt of the 1920's was the growth of the super corporation. Increasingly American business was conducted by large organizations. It was the giant corporation that mainly exploited the earth and the forests, both at home and abroad, for the raw materials necessary for manufacturing; it was the supercorporation that did the manufacturing, distributed the products to consumers, and even financed the operations. More and more, consumers were to use as parts of their everyday vocabulary the names of Standard Oil, A & P, Westinghouse, General Motors, United States Steel, Bell Telephone, Eastman Kodak, Bank of America, and similar firms.

By 1929 the largest two hundred corporations possessed about 20 percent of the nation's wealth and almost 40 percent of business wealth. This was attributable in part to expansion of corporate business with its total assets rising from $262,000,000,000 to $336,000,000,000 between 1926 and 1929 alone. The share of total corporate net income for the wealthiest 5 percent of corporations grew from 76.73 to 84.34 percent between 1919 and 1929. Their rise was also due to an increased number of recorded mergers, which in manufacturing and mining mounted from 438 in 1919 to 1,245 in 1929. Contrary to widespread belief, however, the number of corporations, and of business concerns, did not decrease during the 1920's. The total of American business concerns jumped from 1,711,000 in 1919 to 2,213,000 in 1929. What was happening was a grand expansion of private enterprise in response to a rising market and easier financing. More and more Americans were entering business to take their chances. What was also happening was that the supercorporations were profiting the most, gaining a larger share of the market and therefore the wealth.

It is not surprising that the greatest benefits went to the biggest businesses. They had the resources to expand operations vastly and to make them efficient and to produce and market new commodities. With mass methods of exploitation, purchasing, production, advertising, and distribution, the giant corporations could hold down their costs. With their research departments, they could put out new products and improve old ones. Most of the increase in American patents issued for inventions was accounted for by corporations, as between 1921 and 1929 the number of patents that they had received almost doubled. Large corporations could also staff their operations with specialists in various phases of business instead of relying on family skills or jacks-of-all-trades. At least as important, supercorporations could, by themselves or in conjunction with others, move toward controlling their sectors of the economy.

There were two basic ways to accomplish this dominance. One method was to control the whole industrial process, including the extraction of raw materials, the fabrication or refinement of products, and their distribution to wholesalers and even retailers. This pattern of vertical integration was well established before the war in the petroleum industry and was increasingly seized upon by other large corporations during the 1920's. Another method commonly employed, and by no means at variance with the one described above, was to join with supposedly competing firms to regulate an entire industrial segment. This could be carried out in several ways. Illustrative of one pattern, United States Steel was so dominant in its sector of the economy that it could usually force other steel firms to adhere to common price, labor, and marketing practices. Another method was the use of interlocking directorates whereby a group of industrial executives would turn up sitting on each other's boards of directors, thereby forming a superdirectorate for a number of related industries. There was also the holding company, which by 1929 became the prime method of economic concentration, with ninety-four of the largest ninety-seven industrial corporations being such organizations. Under this method one gigantic corporation would possess the controlling interest in two or more operating corporations. Holding companies sometimes grew to bewildering proportions, as with Samuel Insull's electric-power empire, which included 111 companies organized in twenty-four layers of operation between Insull and the companies actually distributing power. Often a holding company could gain control through shrewd business maneuvering of properties of tremendous value. One of the best examples of this was the railway complex directed by O. P. and M. J. Van Sweringen. Using $500,000 of their own money and another $500,000 from some associates, the Van Sweringen brothers were able to obtain control of ten railroads holding more than 29,000 miles of track.

The trade association was another major technique of arranging business matters to the satisfaction of industrial leaders. This method was encouraged by the Department of Commerce under Herbert Hoover's guidance. It was seen as an effective way to minimize cutthroat competition in industries that were not dominated by holding companies, huge leading corporations, or interlocking directorates. The objective of the trade association was to organize firms engaging in a common industrial activity so that they would exchange information that would allow them to keep their prices in line, standardize tools, measurements, and product sizes and shapes, and to take advantage of the latest technological, managerial, and distributive techniques. Some two thousand of these associations already existed by 1920, and hundreds more came into existence by 1929. Although they were criticized as being in violation of antitrust laws, the Republican attorneys general of the 1920's rarely acted against trade associations, and when they did, the Supreme Court held that associational activities were legal so long as they were not aimed at increasing prices.

The last essential ingredient of the prosperity of the 1920's was easy financing. As the largest corporations grew, they had more money in their pockets to invest, and increasingly they financed their own operations and sometimes those of other firms. Yet the growing financial independence of supercorporations did not hinder the expansion of traditional lenders. Bank assets jumped from $48,000,000,000 to $72,000,000,000 between 1919 and 1929. Proportionately more dramatic was the rise during the same period in the assets of savings-and-loan associations from $2,000,000,000 to $12,000,000,000, and the assets of America's life-insurance companies shot up from $7,000,000,000 to $17,000,000,000. Obviously, plenty of money was available for lending, at reasonable rates, and it was borrowed at a previously unheard-of volume, especially by small businesses. Moreover, corporations, to finance their activities, not only took from their expanding assets but borrowed substantially as well. The amount of corporate stock grew from $76,000,000,000 to $186,000,000,000, and the amount of corporate debt increased from $58,000,000,000 to $88,000,000,000 between 1922 and 1929. The mass consumer was also well financed, expanding his buying capacity well beyond his mounting income. Between 1919 and 1929 the amount of consumer nonfarm credit grew from $32,000,000,000 to $60,000,000,000, thanks to the liberality of loans from banks, savings-and-loan companies, insurance concerns, loan companies, and merchants. "Just a little bit down and a small monthly payment" increasingly became the American way of buying and therefore of financing one's dreams and the country's prosperity.

Few of the ingredients of the prosperity of the 1920's were new, for most of them had been developed before 1920. What was new was the frequency of their use and the recognition of them as forming the bases of a new, even revolutionary economic system. All together they signaled the domination of the economy by giant corporations that were producing for the mass consumer. Thereby a greater variety of standardized goods could be produced more cheaply. Ideally, the advantages of the mass-production-consumption system were tremendous. The large corporations could more efficiently and profitably coordinate their operations and maintain mass employment at wages and salaries sufficient to provide the mass consumer with the wherewithal to buy their goods and services. Market and employment stability would make the mass consumer a better credit risk so that his purchasing power could be supplemented with larger loans and more installment buying than ever before. The resultant prosperity would theoretically beget more prosperity as industry and creditors could expand, thereby providing additional jobs, higher income, and further credit.

It was all so logical and seemed to be working. No wonder that by 1929 most Americans believed that prosperity would be permanent. That they were wrong, however, should not obscure the fact that the basic components of the economy of the 1920's would survive. Giant corporations would continue to dominate, and the customer, for whom they produced, would still be the mass consumer. The supercorporations would still seek more efficient methods of production and distribution, and all, producers and consumers alike, would continue to believe in the efficacy of salesmanship, advertising, technological improvement, and organizational expertise.

The results of the prosperity of the 1920's were indeed impressive, even those that were short-lived. As already noted, the United States made more progress than ever before in purchasing power, employment levels, employee benefits, and product availability and variety. On top of that, industry was operating more efficiently and indeed had taken the place in society that it was to hold for the next two generations. But there was more to it than strictly economic and technological results. Prosperity also contributed immensely to social, cultural, and intellectual changes.

To a considerable extent the postwar decade was a time of emancipation, of release. World War I had already loosened home and community patterns of restraint. The beckoning opportunities of the new prosperity added to geographical, social, and economic mobility. The movement from farm to city continued apace, as between 1920 and 1930 the rural population rose only from 51,553,000 to 53,820,000, whereas urban population grew from 54,158,000 to 68,955,000. The period's prosperity, along with the great reduction of newcomers from abroad, permitted further acceptance and assimilation of immigrants and especially their children. Increased job possibilities and purchasing power as well as additional orientation to American society allowed them to partake further of the opportunities to gain more adequate housing and clothing and occasional luxuries. Tension lessened between native-born and immigrant Americans and among the various categories of immigrants. Increased numbers of their children completed high school, and some went to college, with a concomitant later improvement in their economic and social status. Some of the immigrants' children were motivated to leave their neighborhoods; some intermarried with other ethnic groups and with the children of native Americans. Politically the vast blocs of ethnic-group voters gained more attention from

government and even ran their own candidates for public office. It would not be long before an Anton Cermak
was mayor of Chicago and a Fiorello LaGuardia mayor
of New York. Assimilation was to be a long story, and
what happened during the 1920's was only a chapter in
the middle of the book, but it was a heartening chapter.

The story for America's black people was far less
encouraging. The movement of Negroes from the South
to the North continued as an estimated 783,000 migrated
from the area of the old Confederacy. In other sections
of the country black people found slightly better economic and educational opportunities and living conditions. They could vote, and a few could run for political
office and even be elected, as Oscar DePriest's election to
Congress from Chicago in 1928 showed. Economic
advances were modest, but the percentage of unskilled
Negroes decreased by 1930. As Donald Young commented in 1928, "Industrial changes and the checking
of the entrance of unskilled immigrant labor gave the
colored people of both sexes an opportunity to demon-
strate their fitness for industrial occupations previously
considered by a majority of the population to be beyond
their ability." Educational achievement continued to
rise between 1920 and 1930 as the percentage of young
blacks between ages five and twenty attending school grew
from 53.5 to 60.3. Life expectancy among blacks mounted
from 45.3 to 48.1 years, although the increase was greater
among whites during the decade. New York City's Harlem became a cultural Mecca for Negroes, for there in
the 1920's numerous black painters, musicians, and
writers developed their arts. Especially important among
them were the poets Countee Cullen, Langston Hughes,
Alain Locke, and Claude McKay, who advanced the
struggle for a literature that responded to the black
condition in America.

Yet the performance of the 1920's for Negroes nowhere
matched the potential. The burdens of discrimination

and segregation had not been relieved. Government had not acted to outlaw lynching and restore voting rights in the South, much less to desegregate public facilities. In short, black Americans shared only incidentally in the prosperity of the decade, as no attempt was made to give them or smaller racial minorities a fair share.

Although the opportunities and advances of the 1920's were largely confined to whites, there were liberating features that in some way affected almost all Americans. The new or relatively new commodities of the decade contributed substantially to that. Radio burst onto the scene in 1920 with the establishment of KDKA in Pittsburgh. By 1922, 30 radio stations were operating, and by 1929, 606 were on the air. During those years the number of families with radio receivers grew from 60,000 to 10,250,000. Radio was conceived as an emancipating force and to some extent served as such. Even the most house-bound person could enjoy a great array of listening experiences that were otherwise unavailable at home or in the community. These ranged from symphonic music conducted by Walter Damrosch to the jazz of the Coon-Sanders "Nighthawks," from police calls to news and sports broadcasts, from university lectures to soap operas, from sermons to political speeches, from farm-market reports to labor news and business advice. If radio did not greatly edify most of its listeners, it did broaden their range of experience, even though most of the experience was entertainment. It raised material aspirations, not only through the ubiquitous commercial but by revealing what pleasures awaited people who lived like the characters in comedies, musical shows, and even soap operas. It further liberated many listeners from the starchiness of earlier American society and incidentally provided better music, news, education, and market information for those who would seek them out.

Radio's role in freeing the public from the bounds of family and neighborhood and from the cares of the day was matched by the great expansion of the motion-picture industry. Movies had been established as a medium of entertainment before the 1920's, but the decade saw the development of the cinema as an art form as well. The amount of cash laid out by Americans for admission to motion-picture theaters rose from $301,000,000 in 1921 to $720,000,000 in 1929, and the average weekly attendance mounted from forty million persons to eighty million. If radio brought sounds from afar, the movies brought visual experience. Educational and religious films were widely distributed, usually to school and church audiences. More people, of course, saw commercially made films that emphasized adventure, romance, and comedy. The cinematic reproductions of great literature and drama were often crude and certainly limited, until the end of the 1920's, by the lack of sound. Yet the emancipating force of motion pictures was substantial, as they covered more and more ambitious themes and played to larger audiences. The results, as with radio, expanded experience and aspirations, for audiences found it difficult to avoid identifying with the modes of behavior portrayed on the screen. Every watcher of the movie romances found a little of the vamp or the sheik in herself or himself or tried to emulate the dash if not the daring of Douglas Fairbanks. In a sense, radio told the masses what to do, and movies showed them how to do it, with the result that patterns of courtship and social interchange were altered. And those alterations were generally on the side of release from the conventional patterns and aimed at a greater celebration of the enjoyment of life.

Another emancipating commodity was the automobile, of which there were some 23,121,000 registered by 1929. The motor car opened up the city and the countryside as no earlier form of transportation had. With it the driver could escape the bonds of family and community, for he could travel far beyond the vision of prying eyes to do what he wanted, and lovers could be transported beyond inquisitive eyes and ears. It made more accessible the varied pleasures and opportunities of the city and of the entire country, as the United States was quickly spanned by highways. The automobile, along with the bus and the truck, greatly expanded the suburban frontier for living purposes and rural areas for commercial enterprises. The automobile's possibilities were also quickly seized upon by criminals, who now had a swifter method of carrying out their operations over a broader area. In brief, because of its speed and privacy, the motor vehicle made possible a vastly wider range of activities, whether legal, questionable, or illegal.

With money, means, and models, increasing numbers of Americans took advantage of the opportunities to enjoy themselves. The church and the family declined in importance as many people took their cues on how to conduct themselves from other sources. This development was endorsed by some of the best and the most popular authors of the day. Most writers of the 1920's not only urged freer patterns of behavior and thought but lambasted American society. Older literary figures, such as Theodore Dreiser, Upton Sinclair, and Lincoln Steffens, excoriated what they saw as America's limiting factors. Authors who rose to fame after the war used different forms and targets to express their feeling of alienation.

Sinclair Lewis scathed the restricted life of the small town in *Main Street* (1920), the middle-class businessman and middle-sized city in *Babbitt* (1922), the medical profession in *Arrowsmith* (1925), the clergy in *Elmer Gantry* (1927), and the big-business man in *Dodsworth* (1929). F. Scott Fitzgerald became the prophet of rebellious youth who had grown up to discover "all Gods dead, all wars fought, all faiths in man shaken." In *This Side of Paradise* (1920), *The Beautiful and the Damned* (1922), and *The Great Gatsby* (1925) Fitzgerald portrayed the "lost generation" that was seeking, often by burning the candle at both ends, to make up for what they took as the meaninglessness of life. Ernest Hemingway depicted the same generation in more vigorous if less engaging language in *The Sun Also Rises* (1926) and *A Farewell to Arms* (1929). Henry L. Mencken was probably the most frequently read social critic. Often printed, reprinted, and quoted in magazines and newspapers, he wrote six volumes of essays entitled aptly enough *Prejudices* (1919–1927). Mencken was the bullyboy among those who found America banal and rudderless. According to Mencken, the South was the "Sahara of the Bozart." It was advisable to be watchful of clergymen, particularly when young girls and boys were about. Americans were, Mencken further declared, "the most timorous, sniveling, poltroonish, ignominious mob of serfs and goose-steppers ever gathered under one flag in Christendom since the end of the Middle Ages." Other prominent postwar authors, including Malcolm Cowley, E. E. Cummings, John Dos Passos, William Faulkner, Edna St. Vincent Millay, and Edmund Wilson, expressed disillusionment and contempt with both traditional and contemporary society. Although their work constituted a remarkable flowering of style, it did not offer a constructive program for a new America.

The new literary lights were not shunned by the public or cut out of their share of prosperity. As Malcolm Cowley commented, "The public was as grandly hospitable to young writers as it was to young movie actors and financiers just out of Yale." Cowley added a telling comment about his generation when he wrote that "in those days we were splendidly ignorant of the American literary past." Moreover, though they would not say it, Faulkner, Hemingway, and Wilson shared the success orientation reflected in Fitzgerald's remark to Wilson that "I want to be one of the greatest writers who ever lived, don't you?" What these authors also wanted was adventure and freedom, and they sought them in the way they lived and wrote. In doing so they were just as much a part of the 1920's as were George Babbitt and Jay Gatsby. They too wanted all the fruits of prosperity; what they did not like was the technology and business that accompanied the rising economy. The new breed of the 1920's might have done well to develop the compassion for the human condition demonstrated by one of the surviving worthies of an earlier literary period, Willa Cather, as seen in her novels *The Professor's House* (1923) and *Death Comes to the Archbishop* (1927).

Nevertheless the literary repudiators of American society had great impact. Their leaders gave the nation's letters a great boost, with greater emphasis on the individual, sharper characterization, and more vigorous and sophisticated writing. They lent additional authority to the quest for individual self-determination and enjoyment. Although their works did not sell in the volume that the westerns of Zane Grey and the detective stories of S. S. Van Dine did, they had a broader readership than mere book sales would indicate. Their writings were widely circulated by those who did buy them and by libraries. Their story ideas and themes were often copied by lesser writers and used by motion pictures, and their short stories and essays frequently appeared in popular magazines. Even if theirs was chiefly a middle-class audience, that was the group that led in seeking emancipation from traditional restraints and set living models for the lower class.

There were other figures in the new literary elite of the 1920's who had considerable influence. James Branch Cabell repudiated American society in his singular retreat to the fictional medieval province of Poictesme. Employing an elaborate writing style, he opened up discussion of previously taboo subjects while puncturing man's pretentiousness in, among other works, *Jurgen*

(1919) and *The High Place* (1923). The playwright
Eugene O'Neill was the greatest innovator in theme and
form among the American writers of the 1920's. In *The
Emperor Jones* (1920), *The Hairy Ape* (1922), *Desire
under the Elms* (1924), *The Great God Brown* (1926),
and *Strange Interlude* (1928) O'Neill pioneered the
stream-of-consciousness mode in the nation's drama and
disseminated the ideas of Sigmund Freud. His was not
a repudiation of society, but a concern with the wells
of violence and irrationality in men that could easily
push through the thin crust of civilization. As such, it
was a more universal theme than those treated by the
other writers of the time and one that he dealt with
powerfully. O'Neill recognized that all men are sinners
and suffer from guilt, which other leading young American authors during the 1920's seldom accepted for
themselves or their friends. In the instances when they
did, they justified it by the circumstances of the time and
made distinctions among sinners without approaching
the skill of Dante. O'Neill's catalog of sins and his
concern for man were both more profound and timeless
than those of his contemporaries.

It is plain that the writer in America was breaking
through as never before to deal with themes that appealed to him, whether they were anticlericalism, dis-
sipation, psychological alienation, marital infidelity,
homosexuality, or philistinism, and he was finding an
audience. Much the same trend could be observed in
nonfiction writings, where intellectual and scientific
discussions of topics increasingly sheared themselves of
the earlier moralism. The fact was that intellectuals
were building on an already established tradition of
probing the problems and fetters of society. By the
1920's they had more freedom to do so in America than
ever before, which accounted for not only a wider range
of writing styles and topics but also a higher level of
complaint. Governments did little to censor their work,

and private groups were less able to exercise control over these inquiring spirits or over the minds of their readers. Social restraints had considerably eroded, and if it did not make the United States an intellectual paradise, it did encourage a substantial increase in the freedom of thought and expression.

Other intellectual and cultural areas blossomed. Science, social science, and cultural scholarship as a whole prospered during the postwar decade. Psychology, Freudian and otherwise, became well established as a research field, as business, government, and the public became interested in its findings. Philanthropists increasingly gave money to researchers in the expectation that shortcuts would be found to solving the problems of the time. The 1920's was the decade of the foundation of the American Council of Learned Societies and the Social Science Research Council. Colleges and universities encouraged the expansion of academic and scientific probing, and government agencies and businesses increasingly engaged researchers to advance their work. Just as psychology in America had been stimulated by development in prewar Europe, so the shattering discoveries during the 1920's of European scientists such as Niels Bohr, Albert Einstein, and Max Planck furthered the growth of science in the United States. The rising quality of the nation's scientists was mirrored in the award of three Nobel prizes, in physics to Robert Milliken in 1923 and Arthur Compton in 1927 and in medicine to Karl Landsteiner in 1930. The quantity also spurted ahead as, for example, the number of persons classified as chemists grew from 28,000 in 1920 to 45,000 by 1930.

This was, of course, related to changes in education. The number of American colleges and universities rose from 1,041 to 1,409 between 1920 and 1930, the faculty grew from 49,000 to 82,000, and the enrollment increased from 598,000 to 1,101,000, far in excess of the country's population growth. More dramatic was the number of degrees conferred, which during the decade rocketed from 48,622 to 122,484 bachelor's degrees, 4,279 to 14,969 master's degrees, and 615 to 2,299 doctorates. A larger pool of advanced-degree holders was thus able to serve the personnel requirements of education, government, and business. The financing of colleges and universities was equally startling in its advance, from a total income of $199,922,000 in 1920 to $554,511,000 in 1930.

The growth of the elementary- and secondary-school system was only slightly less impressive. Enrollment increased from 23,278,000 students in 1920 to 28,329,000 in 1930, and the average length of the school year expanded from 161.9 to 172.7 days. A larger proportion of students was able to complete school, as 667,000 young people were graduated from high school in 1930, compared with 311,000 in 1920. The change in curricular patterns that had emerged by 1915 was accelerated. In addition to courses in business, industrial arts, home economics, agriculture, music, and art in the public high schools, physical education, geography, sociology, economics, world history, and simplified courses such as general science and general mathematics took their place in the curriculum. The American secondary school was becoming broader ranging and less academic in its offerings. It was also coming increasingly under the influence of at least two of the ideas of the philosopher John Dewey: to be more practical in school offerings and to propel students through the curriculum, although that often meant lowering standards of learning. Nevertheless it did result in the production of a greater number of graduates. On balance, it is difficult to avoid the conclusion that despite the dilution of standards, large numbers of students were learning more in the nation's grade and high schools than ever before. One other important change was beginning, and that was connected to the coming of the automotive age. With easy transportation available via school buses, the old country school began to disappear, replaced by the consolidated school. The result substantially upgraded education for rural children, because the larger school could recruit better teachers and offer a broader course of study in modern facilities.

The development of art and music in America took a back seat to literature, scholarship, and education. Nevertheless there was increased interest in art. During the 1920's sixty new museums opened, more people sought to buy paintings and sculpture, and the number of art students grew considerably. Modernism and experimentalism predominated among painters, as was seen in the work of such artists as John Marin, Georgia O'Keeffe, and Max Weber, although established prewar painters like George Bellows attracted more attention. American sculptors tended to remain conventional. One exception was Gutzon Borglum, who undertook works in fairly traditional form but of monumental scope in his likenesses of Confederate leaders on Stone Mountain, Georgia, and in the 1930's the faces of Washington, Jefferson, Lincoln, and Theodore Roosevelt on Mount Rushmore, South Dakota. Naum Gabo was another exception and one of the few American sculptors and painters who won an international reputation, which was based on his pioneering work in the use of manufactured materials to depict the beauty of the clean lines of the material stuff of modern technology. Nevertheless serious American art and sculpture were still essentially in their adolescence, learning from European artists and offering little in return. The most popular native painters were commercial artists who worked in uninspired takeoffs on nineteenth-century models. Clearly, to most Americans of the 1920's, a painter was still someone who would apply a brush to the outside of one's house.

Serious music offered more promise in both originality and popular acceptance. Radio, phonographs, and the growing number of music students offered economic support for professional musicians. America's three best-known schools of music were founded during the 1920's: the Eastman School in Rochester, the Juilliard School in New York, and the Curtis School in Philadelphia. They were to draw the best of faculty and students and to provide a stimulus for producing a superior type of musician. The leading American orchestras drew and kept world-renowned conductors. Leopold Stokowski continued his long tenure with the Philadelphia Orchestra, and Serge Koussevitsky and Arturo Toscanini became the directors of the Boston Symphony and the New York Philharmonic during the decade. American composers began to receive national and even international attention. George Gershwin bridged the gap between popular and symphonic music, becoming an established figure in both. He was particularly outstanding in blending jazz and symphonic forms in his compositions "An American in Paris," "Rhapsody in Blue," and Concerto in F. Aaron Copland used asymmetric rhythms to great effect in his Piano Concerto. Howard Hanson's music was more influenced by European styles but was marked by robustness and experimentalism, as demonstrated in his symphonic poems "North and West" and "Pan and the Priest." His music was less popular than Gershwin's and Copland's but no less influential on composers to come, partly because of his position as head of the Eastman School.

The improvement in the area of health care is also noteworthy. The life expectancy of Americans continued to rise, but at no time during the twentieth century as between 1920 and 1930, when it increased from 54.1 to 59.7 years. This was attributable to a number of things, especially the effectiveness of the reforms in medical training set in motion before World War I and the greater application of advances in medical science. The death rate for diphtheria, whooping cough, measles, influenza and pneumonia, gastritis, duodenitis, enteritis, and colitis was more than halved during the 1920's. Substantial inroads were also made on infant and maternal mortality rates and the death rate from tuberculosis and typhoid and paratyphoid fever. Nursing care was remarkably expanded as the number of nurses per 100,000 Americans jumped from 98 to 174. The proportionate number of hospital beds available to patients remained stable. It was more commonly accepted, however, that one should go to the hospital when ill, as seen in the growth of the average daily hospital census between 1923 and 1930 from 553,000 to 763,000.

Earlier trends in the nation's occupational structure continued during the 1920's. Manual workers remained the largest group, growing from 16,974,000 to 19,272,000, but white-collar and professional workers became the second largest group, increasing from 10,529,000 to 14,320,000. Farmers and farm workers declined in numbers from 11,390,000 to 10,321,000, therefore settling into third place. The proportion of women working rose slightly, growing during the decade from 8,637,000 to 10,752,000 while the female population increased from 51,810,000 to 60,638,000. Although that did not match earlier promises of economic liberation for women, it revealed some expansion of economic opportunities. Reinforcing this was the considerable increase of women employed in professional, technical, managerial, clerical, and sales work from 3,353,000 to 4,756,000.

There was a remarkable and adverse change in the state of organized labor during the 1920's. Union membership had jumped from 2,722,000 in 1916 to 5,034,000 in 1920, thanks to favorable wartime and postwar recruiting circumstances. The figure had melted to 3,629,000 by 1923 and remained in that vicinity until 1931. It is clear that the depression of 1921-1922 and the labor-management

strife of the same period scared off many union
members. Those who lost their jobs often severed their
affiliation, and some of those who remained employed accepted management's alternative to unions, the "American plan," under which nonunion members would
supposedly receive the same benefits that union members
did. Industry often employed two other tactics during
the decade with considerable success in keeping organized labor out of the shops. One made it aggressively
clear that union members were unwelcome in the factories. The other gave wages and benefits to workers
beyond what the unions were likely to obtain, on the
condition that employees remain unorganized or at
best organized only in company-sponsored unions. Thus
workers' purchasing power often increased, many factories improved employee facilities such as cafeterias,
washrooms, locker rooms, social programs, cleaner shops,
and the like, and some industries went so far as to establish retirement and incentive programs.

Two other factors accounted for the small role played
by trade unions during the 1920's. One was that the
government was probusiness and, in judicial decisions,
was even antilabor. Of course, government did encourage
the improvement of working conditions and the mediation of labor-management disputes. In a showdown,
however, it was obvious that government during the
1920's would not favor labor. The other factor was that
union leadership grew flabby. The American Federation
of Labor under Samuel Gompers, and after his death in
1924 under William Green, thought largely in terms of
preserving the core of the labor movement, the skilled
worker. The A.F.L. made little effort to recruit the
unorganized and especially the unskilled worker. Moreover, what organized labor asked for or obtained was
seldom imaginative or matched what most unionized
and nonunionized shops could reasonably afford to grant.
With few exceptions, labor leaders were content to keep

their fiefs intact and to get some share of the national prosperity. Consequently, during the 1920's labor unions marked time intellectually and in influence while the rest of the industrial economy marched forward.

Another social trend worthy of observation is the much-discussed struggle between the city and the countryside. There was conflict, but the heat and nature of it are frequently exaggerated. For census purposes by 1920 a majority of Americans was classified as urban for the first time in the country's history. That majority grew steadily throughout the decade, so that by 1930 about 57 percent of the people lived in urban areas. This did not mean, however, that they lived in large cities. Of the 68,955,000 persons classified as urban, only 36,325,000 lived in places with 100,000 or more inhabitants. Even if one added the 12,917,000 Americans who lived in communities with between 25,000 and 100,000 inhabitants, the total fell well short of a majority of the nation's population. Moreover, many of the people living in cities of any size came from the countryside or small towns and frequently did not fully identify with the city or were not sympathetic to it. In addition, many city dwellers were influenced by the still considerable national celebration of the virtues of country and small-town life. Although they did not see themselves as part of the so-called urban menace, large numbers of them accepted the idea that the city was sinful and corrupt. The point is that the number of genuinely urban-minded Americans was a decided minority and would remain so well beyond the 1920's.

There is, of course, another side of the issue that softened some of the antagonisms between city and countryside. While many farmers and small-town inhabitants fulminated about how the city was destroying the fabric of American life, they were gradually succumbing to urban ideas and forms of living. Those of their children —and there were many—who lived in the city often served as channels of communication that tempered their attitudes. Automobiles and buses released the people of the countryside from bondage to the farm and village, so that they, too, could get more accustomed to and take advantage of the opportunities and pleasures offered by the city. They were also affected by advertising, salesmanship, radio, and the movies. Consequently, rural Americans aspired to a share in the nation's prosperity and the goods it could buy, and they increasingly accepted many of the urban values that accompanied it.

This does not mean that the alteration of the countryside's values took place so swiftly or that so few city dwellers had solid urban attitudes that there was no struggle. The urban-rural conflict, however, was not quite as intense as it is often pictured, and the results of it in the 1920's were not the repression of the city by the countryside, but the retarded advance of urban interests. Of course, rural sentiments influenced many Americans to endorse the old ideals of self-reliance, social control of personal behavior, hard labor, and simple living. But more pervasive media were teaching the concepts of interdependence, personal freedom, leisure, and prosperous living, and the countryside was learning these lessons more rapidly than it was shucking away its traditional rhetoric. Larger state budgets were adopted for vastly expanded highways, improved schools, new social services, and other requirements of the burgeoning industrial, urban society; and they were being financed to a considerable extent out of land, motor, and gasoline taxes, which the farm and small town felt keenly. State expenditures mounted from $388,000,000 in 1913 to $1,397,000,000 in 1922 to $2,047,000,000 in 1927. State debt and state aid to local governments rose concomitantly. The balance sheets of state governments showed that countryside traditions were losing the fiscal battle to urban needs. Parenthetically, it should be observed that the greater increase in state and local government functions and expenditures indicated that there was a new deal in their activities well before the 1930's.

The influence of farmers and small-town residents did not lose ground quite as quickly in social and moral matters. Although prohibition had been fastened upon the United States before the 1920's, it was kept on the law books largely because of the countryside's wishes. Implementation was, however, another matter. Enforcement was already flagging by 1925 and would limp along until prohibition was repealed in 1933. Clearly, those forced to abandon alcoholic beverages because of the law largely were the urban immigrant and laboring masses, who were often the objects of rural scorn and fear. They could not make their own beer and liquor as easily as their imbibing country fellows, nor could they afford as easily as the upper and middle economic classes the bootleggers' services and visits to speakeasies and roadhouses. Prohibition may have benefited their health, as diseases associated with alcoholism decreased in incidence, but it certainly ruffled their feelings as the class discriminated against. As we have seen, the campaign to cut drastically the flow of immigration was successful, and it largely reflected the influence and attitudes of rural and small-town America. Shut off the tap of immigration, it was reasoned, and traditional national values would be able to recuperate. Vice could supposedly be reduced, corruption eliminated, and industriousness and self-reliance reemerge. Accompanying this was a continuing effort to crack down on radicalism. The most notorious example of repression was the prosecution on flimsy legal grounds of two aliens who were philosophical anarchists for the killing of a paymaster in Massachusetts. After seven stormy years of trial and appeal the two men, Nicola Sacco and Bartolomeo Vanzetti, were executed. The upshot of the affair, however, was that xenophobes were put on the defensive.

The Ku Klux Klan was largely a postwar reaction of the countryside's worst elements. Although Negroes were the Klan's chief target, others included Mexican-Americans, immigrants, Jews, and Catholics. The hooded order's hundreds of thousands of members spread terror through most of the South and much of the Midwest. The Klan's work was not unknown elsewhere in America, even in the cities. Lynchings, whippings, and other assaults on the human objects of their contempt happened often enough to make fear an everyday companion of many minority-group members. All racial, ethnic, and religious minorities, even those safe from bodily harm, felt oppressed by the very existence of the Klan and by the barrage of calumny upon them and their ways of life. Minorities suffered in the marketplace as economic opportunities were somewhat restricted because of the virulent prejudice of the nightshirt knights and their sympathizers. Although the size and effectiveness of the Ku Klux Klan tapered off rapidly after 1925, its violence, intimidation, and propaganda left wounds that took a long time to heal.

The countryside's struggle against the city was taken up in other ways, such as legislation against prize fights, racetracks, gambling, and Sunday entertainment and commercial activity. Yet even here rural beliefs were receding. Increasingly, movies were shown on Sunday, prize fights and racetracks prospered in many states, and gambling went on almost everywhere in one form or another. Ballroom dancing, also an object of rural disfavor, became more frequent, energetic, and intimate.

Worst of all from the standpoint of farm and small-town moralists was what was happening to women, at least to urban middle-class women. Two old taboos, drinking with men and smoking in public, were vanishing. Hemlines rose, clothing became more colorful and flamboyant, hairstyles more dramatic, and swimming suits revealed more flesh. Lipstick, rouge, and eyeshadow became common implements in making up the ladies' appearance. Women were less passive partners in dancing and more active in social conversation. And this was all at the time when American women received the right to vote and run for public office and as their job opportunities expanded somewhat. Of course, this did not mean that women were "emancipated," as it was often declared. The man was still the head of the family, and the wife and daughters followed his decrees to a large extent. Economic opportunity and remuneration were far from equal between the sexes. Nor did women follow up all their opportunities, as was indicated by the handful who sought public office and by the disintegration of the unity of organized women's movements during the decade. If women had come a long way by the end of the 1920's, they also had a long way to go toward equality and were to experience setbacks before the women's liberation movements of a later time.

In short, the United States by 1929 was a greatly different nation from what it had been even ten years before. It had emerged as an urban, industrial, consumer-oriented society. Prosperity and pleasure were the goals of most Americans, and a greater range of opportunities and experiences was available and acceptable. It was by no means a polished country, for its culture and science were second-rate, except perhaps in literature. Business attitudes and an accompanying philistinism dominated society. America was more open and varied in its styles of living, but it was not a libertine nation, for there was an innocence about even those who tried to be emancipated and sophisticated. What the United States was trying to do was adjust to the vast postwar technological, economic, demographic, and political changes. Its adjustment was at best successful only for the 1920's, for the country was too quick in formulating its answers, too many of which turned out to be invalid. And the changes themselves were more far-reaching than anyone, in America or abroad, perceived. The United States, moreover, was still captive to many past ideas, some of which were obsolete while others were not successfully converted into workable implements for the new era. In retrospect, the general problems of Western society during the Industrial Revolution were set in bold relief by the specific problems of the 1920's and, as shall be seen, of the 1930's. Americans, existing on the advanced frontier of the Industrial Revolution, were not adequately equipped to recognize the implications of the increasingly swift developments of their society and time. Their adaptability, great as it was, was insufficient. They dropped old ideas too slowly and did not devise enough valid new concepts or apply them skillfully enough.

[6]
Hoover's New Day

"I DO NOT choose to run for President in nineteen twenty-eight," Calvin Coolidge told reporters on August 2, 1927. It took several months for most Republican leaders to take the popular President at his word, but by winter, a large number of contenders was vying for Coolidge's place. Secretary of Commerce Herbert Hoover was very early the front runner, and with good reason. During his years of public service he had made his name a household word and had developed a broad network of supporters among politicians and businessmen. Hoover was the leading example of a man who had been both an economic and a political Horatio Alger character, an orphaned lad who had made himself into a multimillionaire and a world statesman. More than anyone else except Coolidge, he symbolized prosperity, and he could legitimately claim to be a humanitarian because of his extraordinary relief achievements. Hoover capitalized on all this with a whirlwind series of primary election contests and a huge publicity campaign. His opponents had neither the political strength nor the reputation to withstand him.

When the Republican national convention met in Kansas City, Missouri, in June, 1928, the fifty-three-year-old Hoover gained the presidential nomination on the first ballot. Senator Charles Curtis, of Kansas, his far-distant nearest competitor, accepted the second place on the ticket. The Republicans positioned themselves firmly on the accomplishments of the Coolidge administration; the party platform promised more of the same, particularly government efficiency, debt cutting and tax reduction, maintenance of a high tariff, "pacific settlement of international disputes," and additional support for highway construction and development of inland waterways. Favorable mention was made of prohibition, conservation, antilynching legislation, furthering Indian rights, and restricting the use of court injunctions in labor disputes. Endorsement of the McNary-Haugen farm proposals was pointedly missing, but the Republicans reiterated their support of cooperatives, orderly agricultural marketing, establishment of a farm board, and other methods of helping farmers to help themselves. In short, it was a moderate, business-oriented document. No one doubted that most Americans would find its contents acceptable.

The Democrats had done little to ready themselves for a presidential campaign. There had been virtually no Democratic national organization between 1924 and 1928, and their national committee chairman, Clement L. Shaver, had been an obscure and amateurish political figure. The Democrats had not developed any new national political leaders or compelling new issues. Most of the Democrats either fought battles long since lost or repeated the prosperity creed in accents that lacked originality and appeal if not conviction.

The campaigns for nomination of William Gibbs McAdoo and Senator Thomas Walsh, of Montana, aborted well before convention time. It was clear that only one Democrat, Governor Alfred E. Smith, of New York, could attract enough support to be nominated. Smith was fifty-four years old and had risen from the poverty of the "Sidewalks of New York" to make a career for himself as a politician. During his years in the state legislature he established himself as a champion of the interests of workingmen and consumers and as a faithful servant of Tammany Hall, the New York City political machine. Smith was elected governor in 1918, serving in that position for eight of the following ten years and winning a reputation as an administrator who could achieve ground-breaking reforms and still cut costs. Well before 1928 it was plain that Alfred Smith had accomplished more as a public servant than any other Democrat and had established an effective national political organization.

The delegates at the Democratic convention in Houston, Texas, nominated Smith for President on the first ballot. The selection of a northern, Catholic, urban politician was balanced by the nomination for Vice-President of Senator Joseph T. Robinson, of Arkansas, a southern, Protestant, farmer-oriented politician. In one important respect, however, the ticket's balance was a contradiction. As one observer wrote, "The Democratic donkey [left Houston] with a wet head and wagging a dry tail." That soon became clear when Smith asserted that despite his party's pledge to enforce the Eighteenth Amendment, he would work to change the prohibition laws. Yet if the Democratic plank on liquor did not square with the views of its presidential nominee, the rest of the platform did.

Not only had the Democratic convention become as dull as the quadrennial Republican gathering, but their platforms were almost indistinguishable from one another, that of the Democrats being only slightly less conservative. The Democrats made no mention of the League of Nations, and there was substantial acceptance of Republican issues, which the Democrats promised to manage better. These included debt and tax reduction, essential maintenance of the high tariff, orderly farm marketing, a federal farm board, encouragement of cooperatives, outlawry of war, and better transportation facilities. There were also a hint of something like McNary-Haugenism for farmers, a strenuous statement against labor injunctions, recognition that some unemployment existed, a suggestion of a bit more federal regulation here and there. But basically the Democrats, too, had become worshipers at the altar of a permanent, all-controlling prosperity that employed business as its high priests and agriculture and labor as acolytes. The Democrats reinforced their commitment to business by choosing a General Motors executive and a former Republican, John J. Raskob, as their national committee chairman. Four other millionaires, James Gerard and Herbert H. Lehman, of New York City, Texas businessman Jesse Jones, and Senator Peter Gerry, of Rhode Island, took leading roles in setting the party's strategy and raising money. New York banks even lent the party $1,600,000, and for the first time in recent years the Democrats came close to the Republicans in attracting campaign funds.

There was little political alternative to the prosperity parties available in 1928. The third-party activity, so abundant in 1924, had dwindled to almost nothing. The Communists, labeled the Workers party, ran a national ticket for the first time, headed by William Z. Foster. Socialists nominated Norman Thomas, a former Presbyterian minister, who thus began his career as their perennial presidential candidate. An intellectual rather than an agitator, Thomas was to serve more as America's political conscience than as its prod. These and lesser third parties found little support in the United States during the high tide of prosperity. Thomas received only 267,000 votes and Foster 49,000. No other minor-party candidate attracted even half as much as Foster.

Alfred Smith's campaign was based on an amalgam of issues designed to appeal to both economic liberals and conservatives. He indicated that labor and agriculture could expect more from him than from Hoover but that business could be confident that he would not shatter the vessel of prosperity. He was sympathetic to the objectives of McNary-Haugenism, even if he did not endorse the plan as such. He endorsed collective bargaining for labor as well as the protective tariff. Although his campaign promises were rarely detailed, Smith strove to give the impression that he was a dynamic, constructive politician who would further business prosperity while attending to the needs of farmers and workingmen.

Herbert Hoover expected that the nation would prefer to entrust the expansion of prosperity to those who had managed it to that point. Therefore, he stood squarely on the Republican party's record and platform. Not as vigorous and interesting a campaigner as Smith, Hoover had been intimately involved in dealing with economic questions, which were uppermost among the voters' interests. His mettle had been tested in a variety of fields, and he had been found more than satisfactory. Because of that, he enlisted confidence when he said, "We in America today are nearer to the final triumph over poverty than ever before in the history of any land. . . . We have not yet reached the goal but given a chance to go forward with the policies of the last eight years, and we shall soon with the help of God be in sight of the day when poverty will be banished from this nation."

Smith brought some of the McNary-Haugenites over to his side and won Senator George Norris's support because of his endorsement of government development of water power. He also gained the favor of many independents for his dynamic approach to the issues. Certainly the New York governor won back many Democrats who had strayed from the party in 1920 and 1924. Yet where Smith lost ground was on the basis of what he seemed to represent. Many voters, especially outside the East, could not stomach his Lower East Side accent and the flaunting of his urban background. To these people he was not just a city man, but from New York City, which represented to them the greatest threat to traditional American values. Moreover, Smith was not just a machine politician but a member of Tammany Hall, reputedly the most corrupt of all political organizations. To many Americans he also personified rising and menacing alien elements. He championed immigrants and their children; he was a Catholic and opposed prohibition legislation. Therefore, large numbers of voters could only consider Smith as a man who would open the doors again to the saloon and fresh hordes of immigrants as well as put the government in the hands of the Pope. This widespread interpretation swung to Hoover the votes of many independents and Democrats, particularly in the South, who might otherwise have voted for Smith.

It was therefore Smith himself who was the biggest issue in 1928 and caused the major division of ballots, making inroads on the Republican urban vote as a large percentage of voters of immigrant background and of Catholic affiliation rallied around him. Even greater, though, were the losses he suffered outside the cities as armies of people voted for Hoover against the alleged apostle of liquor, corruption, the city, and Rome. Although Hoover did nothing to encourage this reaction, the result was a sweeping victory for him: He polled 21,392,000 votes to 15,016,000 for the New York governor. There is no doubt that Smith would have lost despite the personal and social issues held against him, but there is also no doubt that those issues added considerably to Hoover's margin of victory. Yet the Republican gains in the South were temporary, while Smith's advances forged another step, already seen in the combined Progressive and Democratic urban election returns in 1924, in the decline of Republican strength in the cities. That trend would accelerate during the 1930's.

Herbert Clark Hoover's background was rare for a President. Born in the farming village of West Branch, Iowa, in 1874, he was orphaned at an early age. He put himself through the engineering program of Stanford University, and working as a mining engineer all over the world, he became a wealthy man before World

War I. Then came his years of public service as chairman of the American Relief Committee in London and of the Belgian Relief Commission and as head of the United States Food Administration during the war. After the armistice he was the guiding force behind economic relief to Europe and Russia and became Secretary of Commerce in 1921.

The quantity of Hoover's work was matched by its quality. He earned a reputation as a hardworking, innovative, productive, and thoughtful public servant. No one labored more diligently than he to come to grips with the various changes in the pace and nature of life in the postwar era. Hoover was cognizant of the interrelatedness of economic, technological, and social trends, and he strove to harmonize them in order to improve the quality of life, primarily at home but also abroad. He believed that only by working together for positive goals could people achieve the maximum of their potential. Harmony, industriousness, and inventiveness in all areas of human endeavor were needed, and he thought he could engineer a social and economic structure that would bring these qualities to the fore. Certainly no other Democratic or Republican leader had a better grasp of the problems of the 1920's or of the interdependence of people and their activities. Hoover believed that by intelligent application of knowledge and technology society could substantially eliminate the waste of human and natural resources. Production must be for the good of all. No area of the economy could be permitted to lag, for not only would it suffer in itself but it would retard progress in other areas. Agriculture must be brought up to the mark. High levels of employment must be maintained, with improved working conditions and a rate of pay necessary to sustain a mass-production-consumption economy. Attention must be given to bettering social services and to heightening the dignity of life. Above all, technology must be employed to the fullest to accomplish these objectives. This demanded orderly development of machinery, power, transportation, management, and personnel. Efforts must also be made to achieve smooth and peaceful relations among nations, for anything less jeopardized the expansion of prosperity.

Between his election and inauguration, Hoover busied himself with staffing his administration and formulating his policies. He also made an unprecedented tour of Latin America to increase goodwill and to inform himself of the tension points between North and South America. In choosing his Cabinet, the President-elect retained Treasury Secretary Andrew Mellon and Labor Secretary James J. Davis from the Coolidge Administration. The new men would be Henry L. Stimson as Secretary of State, William D. Mitchell as Attorney General, James W. Good and after his early death Patrick J. Hurley as Secretary of War, Charles Francis Adams as Secretary of the Navy, Walter F. Brown as Postmaster General, Arthur M. Hyde as Secretary of Agriculture, Ray Lyman Wilbur as Secretary of the Interior, and Robert P. Lamont as Secretary of Commerce. Except for Stimson, who had been Taft's Secretary of War and governor general of the Philippines under Coolidge, none of these men reached more than adequacy during Hoover's Presidency. The only other outstanding figure in the Cabinet, Ogden L. Mills, would not come along until he succeeded Mellon in the treasury post in 1932. The main problem was that Hoover's Cabinet members were men largely attuned to the 1920's, and they were caught unprepared by the economic problems of depression. Moreover, the new President gave few of them any room to pursue their own conceptions of excellence. Where Coolidge had largely presided over his Cabinet, Hoover too often commanded his, and he was little better equipped to deal with a monumental depression than they were.

Hoover intended to have a Presidency of accomplishment, "The New Day," as he called it in a moment of political inspiration. In his inaugural address on March 4, 1929, he pledged his administration to "give leadership to the realization" of a variety of ideals. He went on to catalog them: "preservation of self-government," the perfection of economic and social justice, "the denial of domination by any group or class," "equality of opportunity," "the stimulation of initiative and individuality," governmental integrity, the fitness of officials for office, "the direction of economic progress toward prosperity and the further lessening of poverty," "freedom of public opinion," "the sustaining of education and of the advancement of knowledge," "the growth of religious spirit and the tolerance of all faiths," "the strengthening of the home," and "the advancement of peace." As one rustic observer commented, the new President "got a lot of hay down."

And this Hoover meant to do. He approached Congress repeatedly with fresh approaches to achieve or maintain these ideals, and he often used the powers of the Presidency to stimulate executive and private action. No one could accuse Hoover of lack of dedication. He fully intended to make up for what he considered the general governmental inaction since 1914 in seeking "reform and progress." The time had come, he believed, for easing the "strains of growth and giving impulse to progress." With the arrival of depression, Hoover was to be frustrated in realizing that hope. Nevertheless he attempted to set in motion a vast array of changes, some of which were achieved during his Presidency.

In the Watres Act of 1930 Hoover was able to gain authorization from Congress to revamp the relationship between the government and aviation carriers. Consequently, better mail, express, and passenger service was provided. The administration also acted to clean up some of the waste in the subsidization of merchant ships and to encourage the building of new, more efficient vessels. The President envisioned a vast new program of housing for government agencies, all over the country, and particularly for beautifying the nation's capital. Out of this came hundreds of new federal structures, including Washington's huge federal triangle area and the monumental Supreme Court Building. In four years the national government spent or earmarked about $700,000,000, which was almost three times as much for such public works as had been spent during the previous three decades. Similarly, Hoover's concern for the improvement of transportation was reflected in the growth of federal support for state highway construction from $105,000,000 to $260,000,000.

The conservation and development of natural resources was also a field in which Hoover struck hard by his own lights. Soon after taking office, the President forbade the further leasing and disposal of federally owned oil lands except where ordered by Congress. The administration also moved to reduce waste in the exploitation of other oil and gas properties by promoting state and private efforts at conservation. Hoover appointed a commission, headed by former Interior Secretary James R. Garfield, which made recommendations to conserve grazing lands, water storage, and mineral resources. Congress was not in the mood to follow these recommendations, however, and the problem passed to the next administration. National forests were nevertheless increased in size by over two million acres, and national parks and monuments by almost five million acres. Moreover, Hoover pressed the development of cooperative federal-state projects to build large dams that would serve to control floods, store water for irrigation, generate electric power, and in appropriate cases, improve navigation. This led to completion of Boulder Dam, the beginnings of the Grand Coulee Dam, and the construction of a series of large dams in California's Central

Valley. It also resulted in continuous battles between the administration and Congress as to whether private enterprise or government should distribute the electricity and held up development of the damming of the Tennessee River. Whatever the arguments over private versus public power distribution, the big dams did serve their primary goals of water storage, flood control, and the production of electricity. They also set a pattern of dam building that would a generation later explode into sharp controversy over whether the big dams destroy too much scenic beauty and the balance of nature as compared with small dams. Some critics would even question whether dams were really necessary in a nation that was overproducing farm commodities and had plenty of sites for economic development elsewhere.

Herbert Hoover had long been interested in raising the quality of houses Americans lived in and in facilitating the buying of them by more people. As Secretary of Commerce he had established the Division of Building and Housing and created a private organization called Better Homes in America. During his Presidency he called a White House conference to encourage state and private housing efforts and to promote the reduction of blighted areas and slums. Hoover wanted not only more but better housing, for he believed that a home was basic to social health. For all his interest, however, all that he accomplished during the depression was to slow down the rate of decline in home building.

Hoover used White House conferences and presidential committees to a greater extent than any previous chief executive in order to publicize problems and solutions and to enlist state, local, and private energies in meeting national problems. His best-known conference was probably that on the health and protection of children, another long-standing concern of his. Preparations began in July, 1929, and Hoover raised $500,000 from private sources to meet conference costs. By the time the conference met in November, 1930, research committees had long been at work to identify the problems relating to children. The conference and its research committees turned child life inside out and published a multivolume report dealing with children's physical, mental, economic, and social problems and the ways of treating them through community and private action. A "Children's Charter," which set out nineteen standards for child care and protection, was widely distributed. As never before expert information and advice were available to the public. Action was stimulated in the states and localities and by private parties, although Congress failed to approve the President's requests for funds to help develop rural agencies for children's health. In addition, Hoover appointed the Research Committee on Social Trends to inventory the social state of the Union as a basis for formulating policies on old-age security, unemployment insurance, housing, and child care. This massive report and accompanying monographs appeared in 1933 and helped focus the country's attention on the need to cope with undesirable social trends. The information was available too late, however, for a one-term President to do anything about it.

The administration made strenuous efforts to improve the quality of criminal justice and to upgrade the personnel involved in it. Hoover's three appointments to the Supreme Court were above average, with Charles Evans Hughes named as Chief Justice in 1930 and Owen J. Roberts and Benjamin N. Cardozo as associate justices in 1930 and 1932 respectively. One of the President's major legislative victories was the reform of the federal prison system in order to relieve overcrowding and to apply some of the most advanced penal concepts of the time, especially systems of rehabilitation and segregation of convicts by the nature of their offenses.

Agricultural and tariff questions plagued Hoover as

they had Harding and Coolidge. At Hoover's urging, Congress created the Federal Farm Board in 1929 in an attempt to relieve the farm problem. The new agency was allocated $500,000,000 to facilitate cooperative marketing, to encourage the retirement of marginal crop lands, and to raise farm receipts by reducing surplus production. All this was to be done by lending money to farm cooperatives, which were expected to take the necessary steps to achieve the stated goals. Hoover also labored to revise the tariff, with the objectives of raising duties on agricultural imports and slightly reducing some industrial tariffs. The President also wanted more power to adjust duties upward or downward depending upon the differences in foreign and domestic costs of production. What he got from Congress in the Smoot-Hawley Act of 1930 was a higher level of protection than he wished, as the average level of the tariff rose from 13.83 percent under the Fordney-McCumber Act of 1922 to 16 percent and the proportion of duty-free imports declined somewhat. Thus the United States joined almost thirty other countries that had already increased obstacles to trade with the intent of protecting home markets as hard times came. Hoover's only consolation was that Congress, after a bitter and protracted struggle, granted the President additional power to adjust tariff levels. This provision led to executive changes—most of them decreases—in duties on some seventy-five commodities. That, of course, was a negligible number in the vast universe of trade. The American tariff therefore generally remained high, and it encouraged other nations to rear further obstacles to foreign commerce at a time when international trade was more vital than ever to the world's economic health.

Hoover was much concerned with gaining greater government efficiency. To this end he increased the number of civil servants under the merit system and enlisted a number of citizen volunteers to tackle a variety of tasks. The President also endeavored to reorganize the federal government to make economies in administration and reduce competing and overlapping agencies. It made little sense, as he observed, that federal educational services were scattered among five agencies and water conservation among fourteen. He succeeded in placing the various prohibition units under the Justice Department and gathering together veterans' operations under the administrator of veterans' affairs. But Hoover wanted authority for a more far-reaching reorganization of federal agencies. He therefore asked Congress for power to reorganize the agencies by executive orders that would become effective unless disapproved by joint legislative resolution within sixty days after issuance. The legislators in 1932 would only agree, however, that executive orders regarding reorganization would be valid only with express congressional approval. Soon afterward President Hoover sent up twenty executive orders consolidating fifty-eight agencies into nine, all of which were denied approval by the House of Representatives. Government reorganization had no more success under Franklin D. Roosevelt. Substantial changes had to wait upon the work of a commission on reorganization established during the Truman Administration and headed by Herbert Hoover. The former President was nothing if not tenacious.

Hoover also tried to visit reorganization upon the nation's long-ailing railways. Working with the Interstate Commerce Commission and the major railroads, in 1930 he proposed a plan to consolidate the major lines of the North, East, and West into four or five rail systems. Congress failed to approve this, too, largely because of the opposition of otherwise conflicting forces—labor, the smaller railway companies, and the advocates of government control. The President tried again in 1932, even enlisting his erstwhile opponent, Alfred Smith, in the venture, which called for far-reaching railroad reorganization and improvement. With Hoover's defeat for re-election, however, nothing was done. Not until 1970 was any great plan to save the railways implemented, after it was too late to maintain adequate passenger service. Hoover suffered another disappointment in Congress's response to his proposal for the establishment of the Federal Power Commission. The F.P.C. was created in 1930, but Congress refused to give it the power requested to regulate interstate electric-power rates and the financing and accounting of the corporations that distributed power across state lines. Again the opposition came mainly from opposites: those who wanted government control of electric power, particularly Senator George Norris, and those who opposed regulation. As in so many other things, Hoover was caught in the middle.

President Hoover also set out to promote more healthful and cooperative relations between the United States and other countries. The changes included the negotiation of treaties of arbitration with twenty-five countries and of conciliation with seventeen and the expansion of cooperation with the League of Nations in areas such as radio, narcotics, transportation, copyrights, slavery, and health. He was even able to appoint an ambassador-at-large, Hugh Gibson, with special responsibility for League affairs. Like Harding and Coolidge, Hoover sought American membership in the world court, and, like them, he failed.

Hoover, too, pursued the chimera of disarmament. During the spring of 1929 he proposed that another naval disarmament conference be convened, in order to extend earlier limitations to all classes of warships. After a great deal of preparation, which included a meeting in the United States between President Hoover and British Prime Minister Ramsay MacDonald, the conference met in London early in 1930. Out of it came essential equality between England and the United States in cruisers, destroyers, and submarines. Japan received parity with the two larger powers in submarines and a seven-to-ten ratio in cruisers and destroyers. Tonnage was restricted in those classes as well as further limited in capital ships. France and Italy only partially accepted the pact, as they could not reach agreement with the other three nations on cruiser ratios. The Senate quickly ratified the treaty, which was effective until the end of 1936. Later attempts, in 1935–1936, to extend the London agreement and the earlier Washington treaty came to little, as world tensions increased, spurred chiefly by German and Japanese militarism. For all practical purposes naval disarmament died with the expiration of the treaty of London.

Hoover also took a hand at trying to reduce land armaments, for which the League of Nations had been preparing for almost a decade. A League-sponsored conference to that end met in Geneva early in 1932, and Hoover, despite considerable opposition at home, sent a delegation headed by Ambassador Gibson. After four months of dawdling by the conference, the President tried to force action. He proposed through Gibson that "all land armies over and above the police component" be cut by one-third and that "aggressive" arms, such as tanks, bombing planes, chemical weapons, and large mobile artillery, be abolished. He further urged reductions of between one-third and one-quarter in the number and tonnage of naval vessels. Although the conference's Army Technical Committee accepted nearly all of the American plan, the conference itself, largely because of British and French opposition, did not. Hoover had made a bold attempt to force action through the League, one that his successor, Franklin D. Roosevelt, tried to follow up outside League channels. Neither succeeded because of the failure of the powers to agree upon the nature and extent of land disarmament.

Hoover was greatly interested in putting relations with Latin America on a better basis, because tensions in that nearby area affected the United States quite directly and because it was an obviously fertile field for expansion of North American trade. In April, 1929, the President asserted that "it ought not to be the policy of the United States to intervene by force to secure or maintain contracts between our citizens and foreign states or their citizens." To show that that was not just a verbal gesture to Latin America, he eventually ordered the withdrawal of marines from Haiti and Nicaragua. Hoover made it plain that his administration was not concerned with the domestic affairs of the Latin American republics and that military interventions would be countenanced only when American lives were at stake. He also acted energetically to improve transportation between the United States and Latin America and discouraged unwise business ventures and investments in order to stabilize relations. In his Latin American policy Hoover built upon the efforts of Harding and Coolidge, thereby broadening the basis for the Franklin Roosevelt Administration's Good Neighbor Policy.

Despite Hoover's concern for reducing tensions in the Americas, one aspect of his 1929 conference with Ramsay MacDonald must be noted. The President proposed to the Prime Minister that Great Britain should not maintain fortified bases in the western hemisphere, which Hoover defined generously as running from just east of New Zealand to slightly west of the coasts of Africa and Iceland. He also suggested that Bermuda, British Honduras, and Trinidad be sold to the United States, with the sale price being deducted from the British debt. The Admiralty rejected the idea relating to fortifications, and MacDonald did not respond to the proposed sale of British territories in the Americas. Hoover ingenuously observed later, "I had a hunch he did not take the payment of the debt very seriously." The abandonment of British fortifications might have obviated possible future tensions, if there had been any, between the

United Kingdom and the western-hemispheric republics, but it is improbable that such action would have significantly improved England's financial position. As for the sale of territory, the American need to use Trinidad and Bermuda for defense purposes was not pressing in 1929, and the cession of British Honduras would not have contributed greatly, as Hoover asserted, to "cure certain frictions between Mexico and Guatemala." It appears unlikely that Hoover wanted the possession to trade to Mexico to keep either Mexico or Guatemala from some rash action. Certainly, for one of the architects of the Good Neighbor Policy to engineer the acquisition of British Honduras would not have been taken as neighborly by Latin Americans.

The thorniest foreign problem of the Hoover Administration resulted from Japanese aggression in China beginning September 18, 1931. On the basis of an incident fabricated by Japan and blamed on China, Japanese forces occupied key points along and near the Southern Manchurian Railway. Soon they started to seize other parts of the huge province, and Chinese troops were unable to resist effectively because of the civil war that was going on in other parts of the country. The Japanese action was plainly in violation of the covenant of the League of Nations, the Nine-Power Treaty of 1922, and the Kellogg-Briand Pact, all of which Japan had adhered to. When China appealed to the League for help, President Hoover directed Secretary of State Stimson to cooperate with the League and authorized an American representative to sit in on the deliberations of the League Council. Independently, the United States Government protested the incursion to Japan on September 24. Six days later, the League Council reprimanded the Japanese and urged China and Japan to do nothing that would aggravate the situation. The Council also took note of Japan's promise to return its troops to their prior positions when safety permitted.

Japanese troops, however, continued to fan out over Manchuria. Secretary Stimson suggested that the situation called for a stronger response from the United States. He asked the President to consider the application of either further diplomatic pressure and international public opinion against Japan or "some form of collective economic sanctions against Japan." Hoover agreed to the former policy but would not approve the latter. The boycotting of Japanese goods or the embargoing of goods to Japan would demoralize that nation's economy, with ensuing great hardship, he believed, and would lead to hatreds that would seriously affect relations or even lead to a long and costly war. Moreover, he thought that economic sanctions would probably not force a Japanese withdrawal even if other nations joined the United States in applying them. The President nevertheless sounded out the British on the question and was advised that they would not get involved in economic sanctions against Japan. It soon became clear that this was also true of the French and Italians.

Hoover stated his position to the Cabinet. Branding the invasion of Manchuria "immoral" and "outrageous," he called for the use of "moral pressures" against Japan in cooperation "with the rest of the world" and the League. It was not America's role to settle by force a conflict between two other nations. Moreover, he declared, it should be observed that China was not maintaining order in her territory, Manchuria, in which Japan had a legitimate interest, and that Japan felt threatened by "Bolshevist Russia to the north and a possible Bolshevist China on [its] flank." Certainly there was no direct peril to the United States that called for abandoning principle or risking war with Japan. No, Hoover thought, moral pressure was the only medium available.

The League Council meanwhile was meeting and on October 24 demanded the withdrawal of Japanese forces by November 16. Two weeks later Secretary Stimson seconded the call for the withdrawal of troops. The Japanese did not recognize these demands, and the League Council again met to consider the problem in mid-November. Former Vice-President Charles Dawes, who was now serving as ambassador to Great Britain, met with representatives of China and Japan in Paris to try to work out an agreement, but without success. The League Council established a commission headed by the Earl of Lytton to investigate the Manchurian situation. The United States supported this effort and appointed General Frank McCoy as its representative on the Lytton Commission. In December the liberal government of Japan, which had been striving unsuccessfully to control the army's moves in Manchuria, fell and was replaced by a ministry that was under strong military influence. Therefore, by the end of 1931 the situation looked cloudier than ever.

Out of this came the American action variously called the Hoover or the Stimson Doctrine. In early December the President proposed to the Cabinet that the United States recommend to the League that its members refuse recognition of any area occupied by Japan in violation of its international agreements and withdraw their diplomats from Japan. Stimson drew up an identical note to be sent to both China and Japan and asked England and France to send similar notes. The secretary's note was dispatched on January 7, 1932, and in it Stimson declared that the United States "can not admit of the legality" of any arrangement that would impair the sovereignty of China and violate the open-door policy or the Kellogg-Briand Pact. The British and the French declined to take this position.

The refusal of England and France to endorse the nonrecognition doctrine seemed to encourage the Japanese militarists, for in late January their forces seized Shanghai in an effort to break the Chinese boycott of Japanese goods. Great Britain, which could not ignore this direct threat to their interests in Shanghai, joined the United States in sending armed forces to the city for the protection of their citizens there. American naval strength in the Pacific was also reinforced. Hoover's suggestion of a joint appeal from the heads of state of the major Western powers to the Emperor of Japan was not accepted, but America, Britain, and the League promoted negotiations between China and Japan that by May led to the withdrawal of the Japanese forces from Shanghai beyond the strength normally kept in the city's International Settlement.

Meanwhile, in February, 1932, Secretary Stimson again urged the imposition of economic sanctions, but Hoover declined to approve the idea because of Congress's almost sure refusal to approve it and the possibility that sanctions might lead to war. The President agreed with Stimson, however, that the time had come again to try to enlist international support of the nonrecognition doctrine. This was done publicly on February 23, despite the discouragement of the British cabinet. To Hoover's surprise, the Assembly of the League of Nations, on March 11, adhered to the nonrecognition position, with English and French concurrence. Probably this reaction was strongly influenced by Japan's action in reconstituting Manchuria into the puppet state of Manchukuo. Except for contributing to the suspension of Japanese aggression in Shanghai, however, these actions had no effect.

The next step was to wait for the results of the investigation of the Lytton Commission. Its report, issued in October, 1932, condemned Japan's aggression in Manchuria and recommended the withdrawal of both Chinese and Japanese troops from Manchuria and their replacement by a special police force. The commission also called upon China and Japan to negotiate a series of treaties recognizing Chinese sovereignty in Manchuria, protecting Japanese interests there and pledging amity between the two nations. Japan refused to accept the terms of the report, and after the League endorsed it in 1933 and asked its members not to recognize Manchukuo's existence, Japan withdrew from the League of Nations.

It is difficult to evaluate America's position in the Manchurian crisis. There are those who contend that America's trade was so important to Japan that the application of sanctions would have brought about a withdrawal from Manchuria. Others say that although unilateral sanctions would probably not have been effective, other major powers would soon have joined the United States in an economic boycott of Japan, which would have been successful because Japan was already in a poor economic condition with the onset of depression. Yet depression affected the major Western powers, too, and it is clear that they were reluctant to lose their trade with Japan. It is also possible that Japan would have gone to war with the United States over economic sanctions, a war that America was ill-prepared to conduct and one that had no significant support at home or abroad. Certainly, one cannot say that the Hoover Administration was insensitive to events in the Far East or that it failed to try to bring the Manchurian crisis to a conclusion acceptable to both China and Japan. Because of widespread hostility to the League in the United States, it took courage for the administration to cooperate with that organization. Moreover, Hoover and Stimson were responsible for formulating the non-recognition policy. That, along with other efforts of America, Britain, and the League, contributed largely to halting Japanese aggression in Shanghai if not in Manchuria. In retrospect, it is too easy to conclude that the United States, at great risk and with only fragmentary domestic and almost no foreign support, could have done more. Clearly the blame for not turning back Japanese aggression in Manchuria rests with the League

of Nations for failing to use the powers given in its covenant, whether of promoting the withdrawal of legations
from Japan, imposing economic sanctions, or even using
force. The result was the rape of China and the eventual
disintegration of the League as a consequence of its
demonstrated ineffectiveness. The responsibility for
neither of these can be fairly placed upon the Hoover
Administration. In the most important world crisis since
World War I, the United States had played a major
peacemaking role, one well in advance of those of either
the League or other major powers.

The "New Day" of which Hoover spoke turned out to
be quite different from the one that he and the American
people anticipated. Instead of expanding prosperity, the
administration was soon faced with rapid economic decline. Peace was maintained for the United States, although the Manchurian episode augured the great
hostilities of the future. Herbert Hoover and his administration endeavored to bring about the New Day, even
after the onset of depression, but with little success. Most
of the administration's energies had to be turned to
coping with the monumental economic problem that it
had not foreseen and that it was ill-prepared to treat.
It is bitterly paradoxical that at a time when a President
unusually well prepared to deal with prosperity came
on the scene, the script was drastically changed, and he
found himself cast as the lead in the drama of depression.

7

The Great American Trauma

OBSERVERS often write about the Great Depression as though it were mainly caused by the collapse of the stock market in the United States in 1929. The stock-market crash did play an important role, but its larger significance was as a trigger and as a dramatic symptom of deeper and more complicated national and international causes of the depression.

The world's economic instability had been clear throughout the postwar years and had proceeded largely from the dislocations stemming from World War I. What appeared to be established certainties in 1914 had been swept away by the war and the political settlements following it. Old continental empires and their political systems had been destroyed. England, France, and Italy had been badly shaken up, as had dozens of smaller countries. Only Japan and the United States left the war stronger than they had entered it. New nations emerged from the ruins of old empires in Europe and the Near East, as did radically new forms of government, most notably Communism in Russia and Fascism in Italy. In various countries and colonies the mass of the people demanded, sometimes successfully, more of a voice in their governments and a bigger share of the wealth.

These rapid and far-reaching changes were to have serious economic consequences, for national economic requirements were altered, often drastically, in response to changes in a country's size, resources, and new economic expectations. Moreover, not only did new markets and sources of supply frequently have to be found, but new managers and management systems had to be adjusted to. As we have seen earlier, a greater emphasis was placed on national self-sufficiency, and additional barriers to international trade rose. There was also a shift in the roles of various nations in the world's trade. England and France never recovered their prewar positions, Germany fluctuated immensely, and Russia was considerably an unknown quantity. Japan and the United States continued their phenomenal rise among the world's importers and exporters during the 1920's. Remote countries and colonies were increasingly looked to for imports of raw materials and as markets for exports and investments. The upshot of all this was a fierce international struggle for economic advantage, with rationalization of the world and even national economies too infrequently contemplated.

The situation was complicated by the huge structure of intergovernmental debts and reparations left over from the war. There seemed few ways to pay off such obligations and no way to forgive them without jeopardizing the economies of either debtors or creditors or both. The trend in most countries to raise tariffs and in many to impose import quotas, prohibitions, quality controls, commodity categories, surtaxes, excise, and even export imposts made trade even more difficult, robbed producers and workers of some of their potential profit, and contributed to increased tensions among peoples and states. The emphasis on national self-sufficiency and the often unwise lending of money further aggravated the situation by encouraging the proliferation of unstable enterprises and the production of surplus and sometimes shoddy goods. The national economies could not satisfactorily adjust to postwar developments by trying to protect their home markets while seeking markets abroad for their surpluses; and they were always unwilling to take their chances in a less restrictive world market. Consequently, many countries were in economic trouble throughout the 1920's. Between 1927 and 1929 Australia, Bolivia, Brazil, Bulgaria, Germany, and Italy were among those that showed serious economic difficulties, and Great Britain suffered during most of the 1920's from a high level of unemployment.

All of this contributed to American economic instability. The United States could not expand its foreign markets as rapidly as its production, and exports mounted only 38 percent between 1922 and 1929, compared to a manufacturing increase of 50 percent. Moreover, American capitalists too often made the mistake of investing in questionable enterprises abroad. The United States, of course, partly had itself to blame for its international trade problems. It had not done enough to facilitate imports or to stabilize economic relations with other major industrial countries. The fact that most of the nation's import and export increases came from trade in Africa and Latin America reflected the effectiveness of European and American export controls against each other. Then, too, through its vast private investments abroad, the United States helped to stimulate and subsidize overproduction and unwise economic developments elsewhere in the world. America had become a readily accessible filling station full of dollars to fuel the world's economy, and all comers, the fair and the foolish, took advantage of the proprietor's easy terms. When the world economic crash came, America lost much of its private investment abroad and, for all practical purposes, all of its public loans. The country could not lose so much of its capital without grave economic consequences, any more than it could allow its productivity to exceed its domestic and foreign markets.

This is not to say that the United States would have avoided a serious economic crisis if the world economy had been stable. Although the chaotic international situation contributed to the coming of depression in

America and added considerably to its severity, the domestic economy had manufactured a large number of its own problems. Obviously there had been insufficient economic planning and regulation in both the public and the private sectors. Wartime controls had been withdrawn almost immediately after the war's end by the Wilson Administration, and an economic free-for-all had been allowed to occur with ensuing inflation and then depression. The Harding and Coolidge governments had diminished regulation of business and thrown off whatever feeble controls over investments abroad that Wilson had exercised. Only one out of every three of the nation's banks was under the jurisdiction of the Federal Reserve Board, and state-banking regulatory bodies presented a spectacle of conflicting energies and rules. Moreover, the F.R.B.'s powers were limited largely to restricting short-term loans, and in view of the board's wishy-washiness, it is questionable whether it would have braked America's headlong dash to economic calamity even if it had been given more power. The result was widespread instability among banks, with an increase in the number of them suspending their operations from 168 in 1920 to 659 in 1929. Indeed, between 1926 and 1928 about 8 percent of the nation's banks went out of business. Private planning and regulation were equally insufficient. Although the number of industrial and commercial associations and farm cooperatives increased, with government encouragement, they did not work effectively toward balancing production and consumption. Furthermore, no one was doing much to help lagging industries get on their feet. Even had government and private enterprise devoted more of their energies and resources to economic stabilization, it would have been difficult to carry out because of the still primitive state of economic knowledge and the inadequate distribution of the theory and information that existed.

Depending upon whom one read, the problem seemed

to be that the United States was either producing too
much or consuming too little. Actually it was a good
deal of both. In agriculture, for example, production
spurted upward while domestic and foreign consumption
lagged behind. There were, of course, millions of Americans who were undernourished, and the system found
no way to distribute a satisfactory amount of the products of the fields and orchards to these people. Yet many
consumers of farm commodities had legitimately cut
their requirements. The great reduction in the number
of fodder-consuming animals, made redundant by the
increased use of machinery, and the rise of the healthy
and fashionable slim figure are examples of this. As
world agriculture recovered from the effects of war, so
the foreign demand for American farm products declined. Negotiated reductions in trade barriers and providing the undernourished with means to improve their
diets could have expanded the American farmer's markets. Nevertheless the fact remains that most farmers
produced far beyond what their existing markets called
for and therefore earned and bought less than what
maintenance of a national mass-production-consumption
economy required.

The exaltation of business during the 1920's also contributed to the coming of depression. Opportunities
seemed unlimited. As F. Scott Fitzgerald wrote in retrospect, "Even when you were broke you didn't worry
about money, because it was in such profusion around
you." The economy was moving ahead by the middle
of the decade, and the few remaining problems could
ostensibly be solved by salesmanship and advertising.
Everyone was optimistic, and that included the great
majority of economists. The businessman was king. He
had brought America so far down the road to prosperity
by 1929 that he must know what he was doing, and anyway Herbert Hoover was in the White House. In short,
most Americans had been so well sold on the idea of a

permanent pervasive prosperity that they could not properly evaluate economic trends. The few who sounded alarums were seen as Cassandras.

In looking back upon the 1920's, however, it is apparent that overproduction and underconsumption had become rife in America by 1929. As we have seen, manufacturing productivity was up by 50 percent over 1922, but neither domestic buying power nor exports were keeping up. Certain sectors of the economy were ailing and therefore unable to do their part in stimulating mass consumption. Cash farm receipts increased only from $8,500,000,000 to $11,300,000,000 between 1922 and 1929. The building trades had been one of the boom industries of the mid-1920's, rising from new construction worth $7,600,000,000 in 1922 to a high point of almost $12,100,000,000 in 1926. That fell away, however, to $10,800,000,000 by 1929. Coal was another lagging industry, chiefly because of the application of new power sources. The value of bituminous, lignite, and anthracite products declined from $1,549,000,000 to $1,339,000,000 between 1922 and 1929. The woolen-cloth industry was badly hit by the appearance of new materials and limped throughout the decade. There was also a paucity of reliable lending facilities for small-business men and farmers, partly because of the instability of banking during the 1920's and partly because lending opportunities seemed so much better in other directions. This contributed to the fairly high annual average business-failure rate of 104 firms per 10,000 between 1921 and 1929, compared with 90 out of 10,000 between 1901 and 1909.

Of course, economic dislocation and technological unemployment played a role, albeit small. As new industries and processes took the markets away from old ones, some firms declined or failed, and the economies of certain geographical areas shriveled, with attendant unemployment. Moreover, some industries, in order to survive, moved to other areas to take advantage of lower taxes, wage rates, and overhead. The application of laborsaving devices also took its toll in what is called technological unemployment. The only solution was for the unemployed to move to where jobs were to be had or for the stricken localities to develop new job opportunities, neither of which was an easy matter. Yet these were unavoidable developments in a time of national economic and technological growth. In terms of 1923–1929 unemployment, the problem did not loom large, as the percentage of jobless registered at 3.2 in both 1923 and 1929, with a low of 1.9 in 1926 and a high of 5.5 in 1924. This is a record that compares highly favorably with any other seven-year peacetime period in American history. Therefore, it cannot be concluded that economic dislocation and technological unemployment, however painful to those immediately affected, were major factors in the coming of the Great Depression.

Maldistribution of income during the 1920's was a far greater problem. While real wages were up an average of 13 percent for workers, industrial returns increased by 72 percent, and although the distribution of national income to employees rose from 53.2 between 1910 and 1919 to 60.5 percent between 1920 and 1929, still not enough of the country's buying power was in the hands of the mass consumer, the customer for whom the economy was primarily producing. If he could not buy the products of the factory and the farm, then the system had to either limit its operations or collapse. It was in no mood to cut back in either prices or production, partly because business did not generally see the danger and partly because too many businessmen were afraid that to cut back would be taken as a sign of weakness by creditors. Moreover, the signs of danger were obscured by the great expansion of consumer credit, which until 1929 enabled the mass consumer to keep up sufficiently with production. It was becoming clear, however, that the mass consumer, without a substantially larger part of national income going his way, would be reluctant or unable to handle much more credit and therefore could not absorb much more production. The doubling of business inventories in 1929 was a sign of this.

Similar to this problem was the overinflation of the stock market. In a decade with so much business and industrial development it is obvious that a great deal of capital had to be raised. Issues of new stocks and bonds, therefore, proliferated, and plenty of money and credit was available to buy the new issues. Yet investors were not attracted mainly by stock dividends, since the yield from common stocks, for example, declined fairly steadily from 6.49 percent in 1921 to 3.98 in 1928. The lure was the market value of stocks, which began its phenomenal upward spiral in 1924. Prices rose almost steadily, from an average value of $9.05 that year to $12.59 in 1926, $19.95 in 1928, and $26.02 in 1929. With selective buying the increase could be greater still. One spectacular rise in market price was in a stock that paid no dividends, the common stock of the Radio Corporation of America, which was quoted at $85 a share early in 1928 and at $505 a share by September, 1929.

There were several problems with this highly speculative stock market. One was that stock prices had gone well beyond actual business values, which presaged a readjustment of prices sooner or later, one that would be all the more severe the longer it was postponed. Another was that many of the stock purchases were made on 50-percent credit, which meant that in a market decline investors would have difficulty raising the money necessary to cover their borrowings. A third problem was that the number of stock-owners had considerably expanded, to more than a million and a half active customers, thereby rendering vulnerable to stock-market reverses a greater number of people with a wider range of economic interests. Those who extended credit to investors were also vulnerable if their debtors could not repay them, and these creditors included not only brokers, bankers, and the like but also large corporations such as Standard Oil of New Jersey.

Despite these problems, confidence in the market remained high until September, 1929. Then stock-market prices began fluctuating as some investors tried to consolidate their positions, which was enough of a sign that the confidence of big investors had declined, and the market began to edge downward in a series of short breaks. Business analyst Roger Babson declared as early as September 5 that "sooner or later a crash is coming, and it may be terrific," a prediction that further heightened fears. More and more stockholders became concerned with hedging their investments, for it was becoming clear that America's frantic pace of industrial and business development was flagging. The indexes of industrial production had been slowly dropping since June. The high priests of the bull market assured people that both the economy and the stock market were sound and would continue to advance, but still the market fluctuated, going more often down than up. By the end of the third week in October many investors had lost heavily, and a few had been ruined because they could not cover their margin requirements. Then came October 24, Black Thursday, and a great rush to sell stocks for whatever they would bring. That day 12,894,650 shares of stock were traded, at discouragingly low prices.

Organized attempts were made to bolster the stock market, by purchases and words of optimism, but they were only temporarily successful. No sooner had one rally been effected than another slump came. The many investors who remained in the market only deepened their losses. The downward trend of prices prevailed and carried much of the economy with it. Stock values contracted by $30,000,000,000 within a month. Over a period of two and a half months brokers' loans dropped from $8,000,000,000 to $3,500,000,000. Within three months personal bank accounts in 141 cities were drawn upon for $35,000,000,000, or more than one-third of their total.

The market collapse triggered the depression. The drastic reduction of stock prices substantially cut the personal wealth of those who owned stocks. Those who bought stocks on credit were often wiped out, and their creditors greatly disadvantaged, because they could not pay off their debts when called upon to do so. Because creditors and investors made up an essential stratum of American business, the entire economy was bound to be adversely affected. They controlled many of the funds necessary to carry on the day-to-day operations of business. With their capital greatly depleted they were in no position to carry on their lending functions to the degree they had earlier. Creditors and investors were also understandably less venturesome in using whatever remained of their capital. Indeed there was a rush to withdraw funds not only from the stock market but often from banks and businesses. Capital was far safer, it seemed to many people, in one's own hands than in anyone else's. Americans had, and quickly, lost confidence in their economy. Inevitably, business activity slackened as credit contracted. Credit was not to be expanded without a revival of confidence, and after October, 1929, there was little about which to be confident.

The American economy spiraled almost continuously and calamitously downward. The Federal Reserve Board's index of manufacturing productivity sank from fifty-eight in 1929 to forty-eight in 1930, thirty-nine in 1931, and thirty in 1932. Agricultural, forestry, and fishery income plunged from $8,300,000,000 in 1929 to $6,200,000,000 in 1930, $4,900,000,000 in 1931, and $3,300,000,000 in 1932. The number of banks operating declined from 25,568 in 1929 to 14,771 in 1933. Steady and precipitous drops were seen in almost every other major aspect of the nation's economy.

The personal toll was tremendous. Unemployment grew from about 1,550,000 in 1929 to 4,340,000 in 1930, 8,020,000 in 1931, 12,060,000 in 1932, and a peak of 12,830,000 early in 1933, by which time one out of every four Americans in the labor force was jobless. Because of the depression's long duration, millions of people lost their savings and possessions. Between 1929 and 1933, for example, one out of every eight farmers was forced to give up his property. There was a hierarchy of despair that lasted not just until 1933 but until prosperity returned with the coming of World War II. There were those unfortunates who were out of work and unable to get work. Then there were those who could get work only occasionally and usually at low wages. Of those who remained employed, some did so only by shifting from one position to another. Most people who kept their jobs did so with a considerable cut in pay and with the nagging fear that they would soon be discharged. Most entrepreneurs suffered similar problems, either losing their businesses, having to swing from one enterprise to another, or keeping shop only with a relatively small profit.

The paralysis of depression afflicted almost everyone. Living standards dropped along with income. Families often doubled up to cut down on housing overhead, and children were sometimes parceled out to relatives who were economically a bit better off. One of the common activities of the 1930's was hiding from the landlord because money was unavailable for rent. Such situations led to considerable psychological stress, with people getting on one another's nerves and "Papa" being blamed for not being a good provider. Not surprisingly, separations of married couples increased, and divorces rose, apparently when people could begin affording

them, during the last half of the 1930's. Young people
were among the worst hit by the depression. They often
found that when jobs were open, the advertisements
carried the discouraging notice "Experience required."
When they did get jobs, it was frequently not in the
lines of work for which they had been trained, and it
was normally at low pay and with few opportunities for
advancement. For them living was far from easy, and
marriage was often deferred, despite the popular advice
that "two can live as cheaply as one." Most of the unemployed young constituted an extra burden on their
family's slender resources, and others roamed the cities
and the country in search of jobs or whatever the morrow might unexpectedly bring.

The depression was, in short, the most traumatic experience that the American people had suffered since
the Civil War. Materially, they were affected as though
a war had been fought from coast to coast. Psychologi-
cally, they felt pressed as never before to explain what
had happened to them. Spiritually, the dreams of prosperity and of unlimited opportunities had been severely
challenged. Most Americans had to hustle, not just to
keep in place but to keep from falling further behind.
For over three years they saw their business civilization
crumble, and they were unable to do anything about it.
The result was the creation of a generation of disillusionment, one suspicious of individual worth and responsibility. When that generation commenced picking
up the pieces, it would strive above all to gain security.
This does not mean that this generation did not want
to reachieve the prosperity of the 1920's, but that seemed
beyond reach for the time being. Bare sustenance was
the immediate goal, and after that some guarantee of
job and property security. Slowly and uncritically, the
people turned to government to provide those commodities. The result was a considerable, though not radical,
alteration of the relations between the people and gov-

ernment. This new relationship would pose its own
problems, although those would not be monumental by
the end of the 1930's. There was no acceptable alternative, however, for few Americans were willing to return to the economic patterns of the nineteenth century
or to create a new society. The institutions of the 1920's
had to be revamped.

The Coolidge Administration and Congress did virtually nothing to keep the boom of the 1920's within
bounds. They usually gave business a free rein and
largely left the Federal Reserve Board to its own devices
regarding banking and credit. The board was limited
in its powers. To deal with excessive credit and a run-
away stock market, it could sell government securities to
absorb some of the money available for speculative investment, but it was limited in the amount of securities
it could sell. The F.R.B. could raise the rediscount rate,
the interest level at which member banks borrowed
funds from reserve banks, and thereby limit further
lending. It could also issue discouraging statements.

What did the board do? In the spring of 1927 the key
federal-reserve bank, that of New York, lowered the rediscount rate from 4 to 3.5 percent in response to pleas
from England, France, and Germany for action that
would discourage the escape of their moneys to the
United States. Government securities were also purchased from member banks in order to release more
funds to fuel the economy. The idea was that these
actions would raise prices, making America a less favorable place to buy from and ostensibly lowering the
return that foreign investors might receive. This was not
entirely a goodwill gesture, as it was certainly to the
liking of those Americans who wanted more speculative
capital, including banks, which were largely represented
by the directors and governors of the Federal Reserve
System.

This is not to say that the stock market or credit

generally was out of control as early as 1927, though such operations were growing excessive. There were, by 1928, internal pressures in the Federal Reserve System to do something to keep credit within bounds. Therefore, during the year, the system sold $389,000,000 worth of government securities, some 60 percent of its holdings, in an effort to divert funds from speculation. Moreover, the rediscount rate of the New York Federal Reserve Bank was raised to 5 percent, an action that did little if anything to restrain the upward trend of the stock market. In February, 1929, the bank proposed increasing the rediscount rate further from 5 to 6 percent, but that was overruled by the Federal Reserve Board as being meaningless, which it probably was in view of the interest rate of up to 12 percent that brokers' loans were commanding. Small sales of government securities were made early in 1929. More effective was the mild warning of the board in February that it might act to restrict the use of federal-reserve credit by banks to finance speculation. This statement caused a small break in the market, but it was counteracted by the expectations of greater economic opportunities with the coming of Herbert Hoover's inauguration in March. Retiring President Coolidge did not help the situation with his observation that the economy was "absolutely sound" and that shares were "cheap at current prices."

Whatever action was taken by the Federal Reserve Board was timorous and not even up to the limit of its small powers. The rediscount rate remained at 5 percent until August, when it was advanced to 6, with little effect. The F.R.B., however, was not to divest itself of its remaining government securities. Furthermore, it did not ask Congress for additional power, especially the obvious one—that of regulating margin requirements so that credit extended to stock-market investors would be substantially reduced to below 50 percent. Why the board did no more is clear. It did not want to accept the criticism that was sure to follow if it deflated the bubble of speculation and prosperity, however adroitly. Then, too, the management of the Federal Reserve System contained a large proportion of "mediocrities"—as Herbert Hoover later called them—and, by law, a great number of directors and governors with banking and credit ties. Obviously, such men had a conflict of interest, and many of them feared that they would be financially injured or ruined in a downward turn of the stock market.

Yet neither the Federal Reserve Board nor the new President could be unconcerned with credit and stock-market trends. On March 6, 1929, Hoover encouraged the board to act and persuaded Treasury Secretary Mellon, on March 15, to tell investors to be cautious and to buy bonds in order to hold down speculation. On March 16 the F.R.B. chairman, Roy A. Young, asked banks to restrict the extension of credit for speculative purposes. Toward the end of the month the board met daily, even on Saturday, without issuing any statements. The secretive meetings so unnerved the stock market that it broke seriously, and a record number of shares changed hands. Stock prices declined, and interest rates on brokers' loans went up to a discouraging 20 percent. Then Charles E. Mitchell, the board chairman of New York's huge National City Bank and a director of the New York Federal Reserve Bank, came to the bull market's rescue. He announced that the National City Bank would lend money to avert the collapse of the speculative market and that it would even borrow from the Federal Reserve Bank to do so.

The Federal Reserve Board had met its match in Mitchell, as the stock market rallied and financial pundits severely criticized the board for trying to interfere. This counterattack was successful, for the gentle efforts of President Hoover and the board in April and May to deflate speculation had virtually no effect. By June whatever doubts people entertained in March had disappeared. The last chance for skillful deflation of the stock market had been lost. Indeed the government, except for the F.R.B.'s small increase in the rediscount rate in August, stayed on the sidelines.

When the stock-market crash arrived in October, Hoover was quick to recognize the potential consequences and to try to shore up what remained of the market. Confidence was the key. The President declared that "the fundamental business of the country . . . is on a sound and prosperous basis," a view heartily seconded by industrialists, financiers, and businessmen. Others acted, too. In order to encourage stock purchases in the collapsed market, stock exchanges slashed the margin requirement to 25 percent, and the Federal Reserve System lowered the rediscount rate from 6 to 4.5 percent and bought back government securities from member banks. The Ford Motor Company and other firms cut their prices to stimulate retail buying. The $500,000,000 revolving fund of the Federal Farm Board was authorized to be lent to support agricultural prices and to encourage farmers to limit their production. President Hoover, in November, called a series of meetings with the leaders of agriculture, business, industry, and labor to devise a program to sustain employment and wages until the crisis was past. This had the effect of cushioning prices, wages, and employment for several months. It was a considerable success, except that the emergency was to last several years.

When Congress convened in December, Hoover asked it for banking reform and increased public works, among other measures, so that government could further help meet the economic crisis. He continued his campaign of public confidence, indicating from time to time that the worst was about to pass. Whatever the reason, the stock market responded favorably during the first quarter of 1930. Then in April it leveled off and by June

broke again, despite the passage of the Hawley-Smoot
Tariff to protect the home market for American producers. Employment and wage levels had been substantially held until April, but employers could not hold
out forever, with their income dropping. During the
spring of 1930 employment sagged badly, and wage reductions were announced in some industries. By then
the hope was that the bottom would soon be reached
and that in the meantime private charities, local relief,
and federal public works and farm aid would take care
of the most needy persons.

In September Hoover halted immigration to the
United States in order to reduce competition for whatever jobs were available and to keep newly arrived aliens
from becoming public charges. In October, more than a
year late to the thinking of many people, he told the
officials of the New York Stock Exchange that they must
reform their rules and enforce them or consider federal
regulation inevitable. The same month the President
announced that the government would sponsor the coordination of relief for the needy. He appointed Colonel
Arthur Woods to head federal relief work and to encourage and coordinate the activities of national, state,
and private relief agencies. The administration made
it plain, however, that there would be no direct federal
relief for the unemployed. State and private efforts
should suffice, augmented by the federal public-works
programs. If it became necessary for the national government to go further, then federal assistance would
be funneled through state organizations.

The outlines of President Hoover's program to combat the depression had been drawn. It would stimulate
confidence by occasional optimistic statements and encourage cooperative action by economic organizations.
This would be supplemented by some economic reform.
The country's relief resources would be mobilized to
meet the most pressing needs of the growing number of

the jobless. The credit of the national government would be kept secure with a balanced budget in order not to upset the economy further and to maintain confidence in the government's fiscal integrity. Credit would be extended to agricultural cooperatives so that they could act to ease the plight of farmers. The administration would attempt to ameliorate an additional problem, widespread drought, by negotiating the reduction of railway freight rates for farm commodities and by giving seed loans.

In February, 1931, Hoover urged the establishment of federal employment offices across the nation to facilitate the placement of people in jobs. This resulted in the hiring of over three million persons, but given the short-term nature of many jobs, it did little more than dent unemployment. During the first quarter of 1931 some signs of economic recovery appeared. Unemployment leveled off, wages and stock prices increased, and industrial production and construction began to climb. It was a modest upturn, but it gave hope that the worst was over. If that had marked the end of the depression, the crisis would have been no worse than the postwar depression of 1920–1922. It was not the end, however, basically for two reasons. One, the footing of the upturn was precarious in view of the serious dislocation of the domestic economy since October, 1929. Two, the full impact of the decline of the world economy, not prosperity, was just around the corner.

The economy of the United States was not the only one to suffer during 1929–1931. Other industrial nations had in varying degrees received economic shocks, many as a result of the American depression. Although their governments had usually been better prepared to manage their economies, they had about exhausted their supply of remedies. The liquidation of inflated values had not yet run its course, but it had seriously weakened the structure of private finance and business throughout the world. Intergovernmental and private debts sat heavily on various countries, which with monetary deflation were in a worse position than ever to handle them. The financial position of many governments was further weakened as a consequence of their efforts to meet the ever-growing demands for relief of the needy. Equally important, by imposing a variety of new trade and financial controls during the economic crisis, governments made international commerce even more difficult. By 1931 too many countries therefore were too deeply in debt and lacked the resources to earn more money. Many creditors responded to the deteriorating world economic situation by withdrawing many of their investments and sharply restricting new loans. Others who had liquid capital frequently sent it to what they considered safer countries, which additionally weakened less safe national economies. Even sound businesses, banks, and governments were adversely affected by the situation. The result was that many debtors began paying creditors only in part or in debased currency, and, indeed, some were forced to default altogether.

The worldwide economic collapse and financial panic had several effects upon the United States by the spring of 1931. In the scramble for liquid assets, foreign owners cashed in their American stocks and bonds, thereby reversing the slight upward trend in the prices of securities. Overseas creditors also pressed for payment of money owed them by Americans. The sagging of the world debt structure made it difficult if not impossible for Americans to collect on their investments abroad. Furthermore, the decline in foreign purchasing power dealt a serious blow to American exports. The result was further cutbacks in production, employment, and prices in the United States. The overall situation caused many Americans to withdraw more of their deposits and investments at home, thereby restricting domestic credit all the more. There was, of course, a similar constriction of American credit and buying abroad, which additionally injured world finance and trade. The lifeblood of commerce and finance, both at home and abroad, was growing ever more anemic. If the United States had had any chance to turn the trend of depression early in 1931, world developments killed it.

The response of the American Government was to fortify its credit so that it could pay off demands upon it and also keep the nation on the gold standard to prevent the debasement of money. This was achieved by restricting expenditures somewhat and increasing taxes. To maintain circulation of currency, the Federal Reserve System, the Federal Land Banks, and the Federal Farm Board were employed to expand the amount of credit available. In a bold action President Hoover in 1931 proposed a one-year moratorium on the payment of all intergovernmental debts and reparations in order to relieve the strain on debtor economies and to prevent future defaults of payments. In July this was accepted by all of the governments involved and resulted in a small upturn in business confidence and activity. The administration also encouraged European governments to work together to solve the situation, with American cooperation. The result, coming out of the London Economic Conference of July, 1931, was action to support the economy of Germany, the most threatened of the major economic powers. This included acceptance of Hoover's proposal that banks not press Germany for payment of short-term notes. Continued interest and cooperation by the administration at least contributed to the stabilization of the world economy during the summer of 1931.

Yet the war against depression at home had to continue. Direct and indirect employment on public-works projects rose to 760,000 by August, 1931. The federal government extended further loans to drought- and depression-stricken farmers and spurred state, local, and private relief agencies to greater efforts to take care of the needy unemployed. Deportations of jobless aliens became common. The administration also pressed Congress for establishment of federal home-loan banks, government reform of banks and stock markets, reorganization of railways, regulation of utility finances and rates, and government reorganization. Most of this was frustrated, however, as Hoover lost control of the Senate and the House of Representatives as a result of widespread Republican defeats in the 1930 elections.

President Hoover resisted what he considered more radical ideas to deal with the depression. Among these was the proposal of many business leaders to allow industry-wide agreements so that corporations could assure themselves of a specified part of the market that would thereby ostensibly permit them to maintain prices and wages. Hoover rejected this plan for industrial self-government, not only because it was probably unconstitutional and unacceptable to the people but because he apparently believed that it posed economic problems greater than those already confronting America. Congress, especially after the Democrats and maverick Republicans gained control in 1931, pressed for direct federal relief to the needy and for a huge public-works program. The President would not approve direct relief because he thought it destructive of the liberties and responsibilities of the people and the states. Moreover, he was determined to hold down appropriations for relief and public works, for fear that they would lead to a rapid expansion of the national debt that might jeopardize the federal government's ability to pay off its obligations and in turn result in a complete collapse of the economy. The legislators were unable to surmount Hoover's opposition.

Congress did, however, in 1931 enact over the President's veto a bill authorizing veterans to borrow up to one-half of the face value of their adjusted-compensation certificates. Veterans immediately began agitating for payment of the full value of the so-called bonus, and legislation to that end was introduced in Congress. Veterans from all over the country, organized as the Bonus Expeditionary Force, marched on Washington in May and June, 1932. By the middle of June some fifteen thousand of them and their families were camped out in the capital. They met with congressmen and other officials to exert pressure for full payment of the bonus. The House of Representatives passed the full-payment bill, but it was defeated in the Senate. Most of the B.E.F., largely because they were unemployed and had no place else to go, remained in Washington, hoping for reconsideration of the bonus bill. Despite their general orderliness, the government began moving them out of abandoned buildings. In the process tensions developed, and two veterans were killed. Rumors then swept official circles about the veterans taking a stiff stand and even rioting, and the army was ordered to move the B.E.F. completely out of the capital. The veterans' shanties on the Anacostia Flats were destroyed, and the men and their families were cleared out of Washington. The government had panicked and put itself in the disgraceful position of using bayonets to drive unarmed and generally peaceful citizens from the capital, an episode that would be remembered by many voters during the next election. Passage of the full-payment bonus bill, at a probable cost of over $2,000,000,000, would have jeopardized Hoover's attempts to balance the budget. It certainly was special-interest legislation, and Congress would have been as irresponsible in yielding to veterans' pressure as the administration was in straining at the B.E.F. gnat. Were such a sum to have been expended, it would have been far better applied, economically and morally, to the relief of the jobless and needy in general. It is clear in retrospect that such an appropriation would not have seriously damaged the government's credit, although by itself it would not have greatly stimulated the economy.

Hoover and Congress, however, compromised on a couple of innovative relief measures in 1932. At the President's request Congress established the Reconstruction Finance Corporation in January and authorized the new agency to lend up to $2,000,000,000—later $3,500,000,000—to businesses whose maintenance was deemed essential to the national economy. The R.F.C.'s lending operations saved many key banks, railways, and insurance companies from failure, thereby considerably supporting employment, payments to depositors and beneficiaries, and a needed flow of business credit. Nevertheless the nature of the agency's work generated criticism of the Hoover Administration as being willing to assist big business only. The Emergency Relief and Construction Act of July was another compromise measure. That legislation authorized the R.F.C. to lend up to $300,000,000 to the states for relief purposes and appropriated $322,000,000 for public works. Although with these two laws the federal government had moved positively to meet the economic emergency, it was a clear case of providing too little, too late.

Congress was able to secure Hoover's agreement to one reform, the Anti-Injunction Act of March, 1932, which was sponsored by Senator George Norris and Representative Fiorello LaGuardia. The statute dealt with two issues that greatly irritated workingmen. It considerably restricted the issuance of court injunctions against labor strikes. The Norris-LaGuardia act also outlawed the "yellow-dog" contract, which was a device to force employees to pledge not to join unions. As a result of the new legislation, unions were to play a greater role in sustaining the pay and improving the working conditions of employed labor. The President's grudging acceptance of it, however, did nothing to help him politically.

Hoover in turn received some action from Congress on his requests. He successfully urged the $300,000,000 in loans to the states for relief and the strengthening of the Federal Land-Bank System. He also saw the establishment of the home-loan banks in 1932 to reinforce mortgage institutions and through them to preserve home ownership. In the Glass-Steagall Act he secured an increase in the number of banks eligible for membership in the Federal Reserve System, liberalization of federal-reserve lending policies, and expansion of the amount of currency in circulation. Congress also approved his request to distribute surplus stocks of wheat and cotton for relief purposes. The legislators did not, however, agree to his proposals for banking reform, public power regulation, railway consolidation, revision of war debts, and rigorous reduction of government expenditures, or hear his faint appeal for regulation of the stock market.

It is obvious that Herbert Hoover was not a do-nothing President. He recognized the gravity of the economic crisis from the beginning and acted to do something about it. Indeed he did far more than any previous chief executive had when confronted by the specter of depression. Self-help was encouraged and coordinated in all strata of the economy. Private economic and charitable reserves were mustered for the fight, as were the resources of state and local governments. Federal lending facilities, public-works projects, and regulation were extended. Words of confidence and encouragement were spent (but profligately, for by 1932 most Americans no longer believed what Hoover was telling them). The President leaned over backward by 1931 to foster international economic cooperation, yet he resisted plunging the federal government deeply into debt by taking on great relief obligations, because he believed that "we cannot squander ourselves into prosperity."

Hoover's prime goals were to get the nation's economic

institutions operating effectively and to gather together the scattered remnants of confidence into a durable new material with which to rebuild the superstructure of prosperity. Relief and reform would serve as implements, when necessary, to achieve those objectives. The problem was that the President's approach was not working. What he and his administration did either was insufficient to combat the deep and long-extended economic crisis or came too late, and Congress was of little help. It is plain in retrospect that Hoover was too cautious, that much larger appropriations for relief and public works would not have bankrupted the United States, that if anything the basic economy was sounder than he thought. Yet it is equally clear that however hard he worked for stability and recovery, the depression, once started, would be severe. The price had to be paid for a generation of national and international economic errors, and the great majority of American leaders was too conservative and too divided to make effective changes, at least until 1933. Whether under the circumstances anyone else could or would have done a better job from 1929 to 1933 than Hoover can be only a matter of conjecture.

8

The Coming of Franklin Roosevelt

DESPITE the claim of President Hoover's apologists that "the battle against the depression had been won" by the summer of 1932, evidence of that victory was hard to find. Breadlines, soup kitchens, and hastily built collections of makeshift housing, sarcastically called Hoovervilles, were commonplace in the cities. Private construction had almost come to a halt, as cities were scarred with unfinished houses, factories, and office buildings. Vacant stores and idle factories were found everywhere. Hundreds of thousands of farmers and homeowners had lost their property by foreclosure and forced sale. One-fifth of the working force was jobless. Although the economic crisis reached a plateau by summer and there was a business upturn during the election campaign, the plateau was barely above sea level, and the upturn was merely a lift up a sand dune by the sea of despair.

What is remarkable was the calm that reigned over the land. Except for a few clashes resulting from occacasional picketing, boycotts, and demonstrations, there was little violence. Certainly there was no sign of revolution. The Bonus Expeditionary Force had been dispersed without trouble, and the strikes of the Farm Holiday Association were not widespread. Agitation by Communists and other radicals was puny and elicited little response. Third-party movements were not enlisting a great amount of backing. It was obvious that the vote totals of the Socialist and Communist parties would rise, but not significantly. Other third-party movements made claims for support that were clearly exaggerated.

It was plain that the American people were standing by the traditional political parties.

Of the major-party national conventions of 1932, the Republicans met first, in Chicago, during the middle of June. No serious attempt was made to defeat Herbert Hoover for renomination, for most Republican politicians clung to him as drowning men to a life preserver. He was nominated on the first ballot almost unanimously. Some show of opposition was made to Vice-President Charles Curtis, but he, too, secured renomination. The Republican platform was an endorsement of the administration's policies. The document pledged the party to continue encouraging the states, cities, and private agencies to meet relief needs, to keep the nation's money and credit sound, to operate the federal government economically and efficiently, to explore the possibilities of world economic cooperation, to help farmers meet their problems cooperatively, to maintain a properly protective tariff, and to promote international harmony and arms reduction. The only plank the delegates showed much concern for was that dealing with prohibition. Here dissidents forced a compromise on administration forces, so that the party's position was altered from adherence to national prohibition to acceptance of a constitutional amendment that would allow the individual states self-determination on the liquor question. It is paradoxical that in the midst of a grave depression the Republican delegates should find this the most engrossing issue confronting them.

The preparations of the Democrats for the 1932 elections were quite different. Since all indicators showed that they had an excellent chance to win the Presidency, there was a heated struggle for the Democratic nomination. The two front-runners were Alfred E. Smith and Franklin D. Roosevelt. Smith, the 1928 nominee, was somewhat interested in having another chance for election, but above all he was determined to prevent the more liberal Roosevelt from being nominated for President. In this Smith was supported by the party's eastern conservatives, who had retained control of the Democratic National Committee. Franklin Roosevelt was a cousin of President Theodore Roosevelt and had served in the New York State Legislature and as a vigorous assistant secretary of the navy under Woodrow Wilson. The Democrats had nominated him for Vice-President in 1920, and despite his subsequent affliction with infantile paralysis, Roosevelt had played a prominent role in state and national politics during the 1920's. Smith had picked him to be his successor as governor of New York in 1928. As governor, Roosevelt ran his own ship, offending Smith by not asking him to be the pilot. The new governor proved a capable administrator and a skillful manipulator of the legislature. He also developed an effective political machine managed by James Farley and Louis McHenry Howe, who soon began to lay the foundations for a presidential campaign. Roosevelt stood for reelection as governor in 1930, emphasizing economic issues under the catch phrase of "bread not booze," and he won a smashing victory, carrying not only New York City but also upstate New York. Now he was clearly a front-runner for the 1932 Democratic presidential nomination, which looked increasingly desirable as the depression deepened.

The Smith group tried to find an appealing conservative Democrat who could defeat Roosevelt out-and-out. They were unsuccessful in their quest. Therefore, Smith himself carried the main burden of opposition and used favorite-son candidates to try to keep Roosevelt from getting the necessary two-thirds of the national convention delegate votes for nomination. Roosevelt helped himself by revamping New York's relief system and by preaching that more vigorous action had to be taken in America to meet the problems of depression. The governor's forces also deftly reached out all over the country to gather support for his nomination. By the time the Democratic convention met in Chicago on June 27, Roosevelt commanded the backing of a majority of delegates. His vote strength, however, fell well short of the necessary two-thirds, as the other delegate pledges were scattered among Smith, House Speaker John Nance Garner, of Texas, and various favorite sons.

Roosevelt's supporters were able largely to dictate the Democratic platform. That document was mercifully brief and to the point. Blame for the depression was fastened on the Republicans. The platform called for "a drastic change in economic governmental policies." These included "reduction of governmental expenditures," government reorganization aimed at greater efficiency, a balanced budget, sound currency, stock-market and banking reforms, an international monetary conference, "a competitive tariff for revenue," expansion of public works and of credit to the states for relief purposes, spreading work around by reducing the workweek, better financing of farm mortgages, "effective control of crop surpluses," support of farm prices above the cost of production, strengthening of antitrust laws, development of natural resources, and the promotion of international peace and harmony. Plainly, this was a moderate platform, much of which Herbert Hoover himself might have accepted. As with the Republicans, the only ripple of excitement over issues at the convention concerned prohibition. The Roosevelt plank called for a national referendum on the question, but the governor was not rigid and allowed adoption of a plank advocating outright repeal of the Eighteenth Amendment.

The voting for the Democratic presidential nominee began early the morning of July 1. Roosevelt led Smith 666¼ to 201¾ on the first ballot, with Garner and seven others dividing the rest of the votes. On the next two ballots Roosevelt moved ahead slightly, Smith lost a bit, and Garner's total rose. James Farley's goal was to get Garner's some 100 votes for Roosevelt, and the House Speaker was a ripe target, for he wanted neither a dead-locked convention nor Smith's nomination. If Garner would run for Vice-President, his Texas supporters were ready to back Roosevelt for President. Garner's answer was a reluctant Yes, and on the fourth ballot Roosevelt won the presidential nomination, though not unani-mously, because Smith refused to release his delegates to a man whom he considered his Cain. Garner was duly named for Vice-President.

Roosevelt then did the unprecedented by going to Chicago by airplane to make his acceptance address. His airplane flight was a dramatic indication that he was abreast of the times; his immediate acceptance of the nomination demonstrated his belief that no time should be wasted in observing formalities for tradition's sake. In the address Roosevelt vigorously attacked the Repub-licans and affirmed the Democratic platform. He vowed to lead a "crusade to restore America to its own people" and to achieve the nation's hope to restore its old stan-dard of living. And he added, dramatically, "I pledge you, I pledge myself, to a new deal for the American people." Not only had Roosevelt begun the campaign, and with a flourish, but he had given an era a resounding name.

The Republican and Democratic election campaigns were fought intensively, both being well financed and or-ganized. The seeming guarantee of victory heartened the Democrats; the Republicans were spurred by the grow-ing realization that whatever the election results, the country would never again be the same. Hoover and his supporters warned the electorate against scrapping the Republican government's carefully laid policies and con-tended that the alternative would be a slapdash and squandering Democratic version of what the Hoover Ad-ministration was doing. Carefully, dolefully, and at length, the President outlined what had been done by his adminis-tration and how he believed this would soon rescue the nation from the miasma of depression without impairing America's heritage or jeopardizing its economic and political institutions. Yet the majority of Americans did not want more of the same, especially when it was wrapped up with President Hoover's dour personality. His gloomy countenance and flat tones seemed to indicate a lack of confidence in what he was saying. Even had he been more dynamic in his expression and ideas, the suffering of the mass of the people made him as popular in America as Katisha had been in Titipu.

Roosevelt made a great contrast. His movements were dynamic, and there was verve in his voice. He was handsome and articulate and showed great confidence in what he was saying, even if it was occasionally contradictory. He was sparkling with ideas and hope. He may have been, as Walter Lippmann wrote, "a pleasant man who, without any important qualifications for the office, would very much like to be president." Roosevelt's very pleasantness and ambition worked to his advantage, however, as did the vigorous support he received from both civic-minded and office-hungry Democrats all over the country. Moreover, although the Republicans had a well-organized and well-oiled campaign machine, James Farley, as the new Democratic national chairman, outdid them in spurring and coordinating his party's efforts. Nevertheless Roosevelt was the center of attention, and he held it magnificently. Despite the fact that he had been crippled by poliomyelitis, he engaged in a strenuous campaign, traveling widely over the nation and frequently taking to radio, where he used his resonant voice to good effect.

Roosevelt attacked Hoover from the right for waste in government spending and from the left for not doing more to alleviate the people's suffering. Of course, he went beyond the attack, promising aid for farmers, strict regulation and even some government operation of public power, and federal policing of the irresponsible use of private economic power. He also pledged greater government concern for unemployment relief and social welfare. Roosevelt could not say how that could be reconciled with his promise to avoid deficit financing nor did he clarify how he was going to maintain tariff protection and yet lower import duties. Moreover, much of what he did say was highly generalized, even platitudinous, so that not even the Seven Sages of ancient Greece could have predicted what a Roosevelt Administration would actually do. Yet these campaign deficiencies were of no great importance to the voters. Roosevelt had impressed most of them as a dynamic man of the times who was interested in doing something about their problems. Hoover, on the other hand, seemed to represent not only the source of their problems but an administration that could do nothing about them.

Roosevelt and the Democrats scored an overwhelming victory in the November elections. Receiving a great deal of independent and Republican support, Roosevelt polled 22,822,000 votes to 15,762,000 for Hoover. Socialist Norman Thomas and Communist William Z. Foster registered 885,000 and 103,000 votes respectively. The Democrats added 90 representatives for a total of 310 in the House and gained undisputed control of the Senate, picking up twelve seats. It was the largest turnover of seats in Congress in several generations. It was noteworthy, of course, in view of the depth of the economic crisis and the administration's unpopularity, that Hoover drew as many votes as he did. That fact added credence to the observation that the United States was not ready to alter its political institutions in 1932.

After the election came one of the most discouraging periods in America's history. For almost four months, between the November election and Roosevelt's inauguration in March, 1933, the ship of state drifted almost entirely at the mercy of the currents of depression. Because of the country's vote of no confidence, the outgoing

Hoover Administration felt unable to take any significant action to cope with the growing distress. And Roosevelt, not yet having been vested with authority, was in no position to act. Moreover, the President and the President-elect could not agree on any joint program. Hoover was unwilling to implement any of Roosevelt's ideas, not that he was asked to, and Roosevelt was unwilling to support the programs that Hoover urged. For example, the two men could not agree on further postponement of the payment of intergovernmental debts, which Hoover wanted and which Roosevelt feared was a political trap. It was not, but Roosevelt was not greatly impressed with the problem anyway. The lame-duck Congress did nothing to help, producing not one piece of legislation that would meet the emergency.

During the winter of 1932–1933, unemployment mounted, and all other economic indicators dipped. Distress was abroad in the land. Demonstrations, riots, and acts of theft and violence became more common. Scattered farmyard and courthouse-step rebellions led by the Farm Holiday Association effected an informal moratorium on farm foreclosures in much of the Midwest. State and local officials urged creditors not to press collections, and many judges advised lawyers, for safety's sake, not to handle foreclosure cases. Legislatures were besieged by men and women demanding assistance. Merchants were offering "sacrifice prices" as never before or since in order to lure the few dollars that were available into their almost empty tills. It was a tragic and dangerous interlude, and both Republicans and Democrats share the blame for it. Action had to be taken soon. It was increasingly evident that a complete collapse of the economy was close and that the corollary of it could be revolution.

Action was near at hand. Despite Roosevelt's airy cheerfulness he was hard at work sifting possible policies for the new administration. During his campaign for nomination and election he had assembled a brilliant group of intellectuals to advise him. This group, popularly called the Brain Trust, consisted of three college professors—Adolf Berle, Jr., and Rexford G. Tugwell, of Columbia, and Raymond Moley, of Barnard—who served as speech writers and to give Roosevelt a broad education in economics. Although the Brain Trust was dissolved after the election, Roosevelt still drew heavily upon its leader, Moley, for advice. He also reached out in many other directions for assistance. Additional advisers included not only his Dutchess County neighbor, banker Henry Morgenthau, Jr., and members of his New York administration, Frances Perkins and Harry Hopkins, but economists, farm experts, businessmen, lawyers, and politicians by the dozen. The variety of advice that he received greatly reinforced Roosevelt's tendency toward experimentalism and interest in social reform, central direction of the economy, large-scale direct relief, inflationary devices, and economy in government. Yet little of the advice led Roosevelt to draft specific proposals for legislative and executive action until after he took office, partly because of the broad range of problems confronting the incoming administration. Flexibility was his guiding principle.

The President-elect was also busy constructing the membership of his administration, and this was no easy task. The Democrats had been out of office for twelve years. Most of the able men of the Wilson Administration were too old for active service or had not kept abreast of the times, and few Democrats of exceptional merit had emerged in the meantime. Roosevelt needed remarkable subordinates in order to deal with the extraordinary economic crisis and to fit in with his ways of doing things. He was faced with a paucity of able candidates for office, however, even at the same time he was confronted with mobs of job-hungry political supporters. For Secretary of State he chose Cordell Hull, of Tennessee, an expert on tariff matters whose long experience in Congress and service as Democratic National Committee chairman might keep party regulars and veteran Democratic congressmen happy. A close personal friend, industrialist William Woodin, was named to head the treasury, partly to satisfy campaign contributors and partly because he was a conservative but not a rigid one. Roosevelt's choice for Attorney General, Senator Thomas J. Walsh, died before the inauguration, and a middle-of-the-road Connecticut politician, Homer S. Cummings, got the job. Utah Governor George H. Dern was to serve as Secretary of War, because of his able campaign support and because the President-elect liked him personally. Senator Claude Swanson, of Virginia, became Secretary of the Navy, largely because he would do exactly what Roosevelt wanted in his favorite department. A Wilsonian progressive acceptable to business, Daniel C. Roper, of South Carolina, was selected Secretary of Commerce. Not surprisingly, the new President made Democratic National Committee Chairman James A. Farley Postmaster General.

Those seven appointments reflected some of the problems Roosevelt had in finding men of the first rank and also his concern for political balance, for they obviously represented what most Democratic leaders considered safe even though their service gave the administration flexibility more than genius. The other three ministerial appointments were remarkable, though. New York Industrial Commissioner Frances Perkins became the first woman, and an able one, to serve in the Cabinet, as Secretary of Labor. Two progressive Republicans who had effectively backed Roosevelt's presidential campaign rounded out the Cabinet: Henry A. Wallace as Secretary of Agriculture and Harold L. Ickes as Secretary of the Interior. These two men may have been Roosevelt's ablest early Cabinet members; certainly they became among the most controversial.

Obviously, Roosevelt himself was by far the most important person in the new administration. The suave squire of Hyde Park, just passing his fifty-first birthday, wore his aristocratic lineage effortlessly and commanded respect for it. Yet he was the supreme pragmatist, committed only to personal success and the survival of basic American ideas and ideals. He was the man in the middle who could sway with the ferocious tides of his time. Touched with megalomania, he could make it clear who was boss. A man who had conquered a crippling disease, he would try anything within reason, and he felt he could conquer anything at all. Sensitive to the people's needs and will, and above all charmingly articulate, he was a master at dealing with his subordinates and communicating with the people.

The first essential problem to be met ripened just before Roosevelt took office. The nation's banks were being struck as never before by depositors demanding withdrawal of their funds. In February Maryland and Michigan closed their banks in order to save them from ruin. By inauguration day, March 4, the banks had been closed in a majority of states. The nation's economic circulatory system was failing, for without banking operations business would collapse. States hastily readied scrip to be used in lieu of money, and barter arrangements were made in some areas. President Hoover and President-elect Roosevelt could not reach agreement on joint action to meet the banking emergency. The outgoing and incoming treasury officials, however, were busy persuading the states to declare bank holidays to forestall further runs on deposits.

Meanwhile, Franklin D. Roosevelt took the oath of office and delivered his inaugural address. He declared that "the only thing we have to fear is fear itself—nameless, unreasoning, unjustified terror which paralyzes needed efforts to convert retreat into advance." What was required was "action, and action now." People must be put to work, resources better used, purchasing power increased, farms and homes protected, relief provided, and government costs cut, the new President said. Domestic affairs would have to receive priority, and then efforts could be made to improve the world's economy. He pledged to ask Congress for "broad executive power to wage a war against the emergency, as great as the power that would be given to me if we were in fact invaded by a foreign foe." The address was electrifying. Roosevelt had conveyed to the nation that where his predecessor had waged a war of attrition against depression, he would go on the offensive. In a few minutes he had restored a measure of hope to the American people.

Then he acted. He instructed Secretary Woodin to draw up emergency banking legislation within five days. The next day, March 5, Roosevelt called a special session of Congress for March 9, and using the 1917 Trading with the Enemy Act, he stopped gold transactions and shut down the country's banks. These were drastic actions, taken on dubious legal authority, but they pointed up the seriousness of the crisis, gave the banks a respite, and halted the drain on gold. People had to make do with whatever currency and change were in circulation, with scrip, I.O.U.'s, and credit. They suffered, but willingly, for a change for the better seemed on the way.

When Congress met, Roosevelt asked for control over gold transactions, the issuance of new federal-reserve notes, and authority to keep banks closed until they could be certified as sound. Sight unseen, the House approved the bill, and later on March 9 the Senate passed it overwhelmingly. It was a moderate measure, one mirroring the work of both Ogden Mills and William Woodin, the old and new treasury secretaries. It was an action, however, that bolstered the monetary and banking systems and restored people's confidence in them. On March 10 Roosevelt requested the slashing of

$400,000,000 from veterans' payments and $100,000,000 from government salaries; this economy bill became law two days later. On the thirteenth the President demanded an end to the prohibition of beer sales, partly out of respect for his party's platform pledge and partly out of the hope that the legal flow of beer would contribute to increased economic activity. (In February Congress had passed the Twenty-first Amendment, but this was not to be ratified by the states until December.) The House and Senate responded quickly by approving the production and sale of 3.2 beer and wine. By April Americans once again had the right to drown their sorrows and celebrate their joys in watered-down wine and beer. Breweries, saloons, and pretzel factories sprouted up over the nation, and they were not lacking for business.

All this was just the beginning. In the special session of Congress, popularly called the Hundred Days, proposals whipped in and out in a fever of executive and legislative accomplishment matched previously only in time of war. The Agricultural Adjustment Act was enacted in May. Despite considerable controversy over its provisions, Roosevelt got basically what he wanted: subsidies to farmers aimed at restoring their prewar purchasing power. In return the agriculturalists were to agree to restrict their production. Millers, packers, canners, and other processors of farm products were to be taxed to help pay the cost. The measure represented a compromise of what various farm groups wanted, and although it satisfied none of them completely, it was acceptable. Congress and the more radical agricultural advocates got into the act by forcing Roosevelt to accept an amendment authorizing him to work for inflation by juggling the monetary system. Even before the farm bill was passed, Roosevelt responded to this pressure by banning the export of gold. What that meant was that the United States was off the gold standard, and the dollar could seek its natural level in trading. The result was to raise prices and spur economic activity a bit, therefore making it somewhat easier for debtors to pay their creditors. Although going off the gold standard was not "the end of Western civilization," as Director of the Budget Lewis Douglas declared, neither was it the economic panacea that "funny-money" advocates claimed it would be, for the increase in prices and business was limited. In other attempts to help agriculture Congress approved the Emergency Farm Mortgage Act in May and the Farm Credit Act in June in order to make it easier for farmers to refinance their mortgages and to negotiate reduction of their debt burdens.

With some thirteen million people out of work, unemployment relief also came high on the administration's list of priorities. In March Roosevelt asked Congress to create an army from among the youthful jobless to work on the conservation of natural resources. At the behest of Frances Perkins, Harry Hopkins, and several senators, the President also requested massive grants to the states for relief and expanded appropriations for public works. This led to authorization of the Civilian Conservation Corps as well as the granting of $500,000,000 to the states for relief and of $3,300,000,000 for public works. In May that was followed by passage of the Federal Emergency Relief Act which established a national system of relief.

The Civilian Conservation Corps was the most popular of the New Deal relief programs. Headed by Robert Fechner, a colorless but able labor leader, the corps was a superb example of cooperation. Army reserve officers were employed to run the camps; the National Forest Service, the National Park Service, and the state agencies drew up conservation projects; and the Labor Department recruited men for C.C.C. service. By the middle of June thirteen hundred camps had been established, with 300,000 young men from relief families enrolled by August. These men and the more than 2,000,000 who followed them in the "C's" were given clothing, food, shelter, and a small stipend. Additional payments were sent to their families. Not only did the C.C.C. men work on forest, soil, and water conservation projects, but they were offered opportunities for further education and to learn a trade. Their bodies became toughened, their minds disciplined, and their morale heightened. In short, the C.C.C. contributed substantially to the conservation of natural resources and the relief of the youthful unemployed and their families as well as injecting federal funds into the national economy.

Of greater impact during the 1930's, however, was the work of the relief agencies managed by veteran social worker Harry Hopkins. Appointed head of the Federal Emergency Relief Administration on May 20, Hopkins rolled up his sleeves immediately to get assistance to the needy. A man dedicated to his work, he was described as having "the purity of St. Francis of Assisi combined with the sharp shrewdness of a race track tout." Hopkins's immediate task was to funnel $500,000,000 into state and local relief agencies on a matching-grant basis and to coordinate their activities. He approved any feasible project that would get men and women to work and allocated money and surplus goods for direct relief. During the critical winter of 1933–1934 he also operated the Civil Works Administration. This agency was a completely federal operation, striving side by side with F.E.R.A. to pick up the slack in state and local relief functions. C.W.A.'s goal was to provide work-relief for the unemployed on some 400,000 construction, social-welfare, educational, and cultural projects. It put more than four million people to work and put almost a billion dollars of purchasing power into the economy. If what Hopkins had done in launching F.E.R.A. was remarkable, the establishment and operation of C.W.A. was monumental. Hopkins had proved himself a worthy field marshal in the war against need, a struggle in which the emphasis was shifted from the unproductive, degrading dole to payment for work received. His work projects served not only relief recipients but also the public through the labor performed by the needy in the national interest.

The spring of 1933 also saw the enactment of the Truth in Securities Act, which authorized the Federal Trade Commission to prevent misrepresentation in the issuance of new stocks and bonds; the abrogation of the gold clause from all contracts in an attempt, which was far from successful, to increase prices and relieve debtors; the Home Owners' Loan Act to refinance mortgages, which gave considerable assistance to both homeowners and mortgage holders; and the Glass-Steagall Banking Act, which separated commercial and investment banking and, despite the President's reluctance, established the Federal Deposit Insurance Corporation to guarantee depositors' bank accounts, a popular and successful measure. Furthermore, Senator George Norris finally found a presidential champion in Roosevelt for government development of the Tennessee River Valley. The result of their alliance was the Tennessee Valley Authority Act of May, 1933. That measure provided for the construction of dams along the river to generate and distribute inexpensive electric power and control floods. The Tennessee Valley Authority was also permitted to manufacture cheap fertilizer, engage in conservation projects, and develop area social and recreational experiments in cooperation with state and local authorities. It was the most revolutionary and controversial single action of the New Deal, obviously aimed at regional economic and social planning by the federal government and meant to set a pattern for similar developments elsewhere in the future.

President Roosevelt had acted to meet the threats of economic paralysis in banking and agriculture and to provide unemployment relief. What he was slow to develop was a program to revive industry. His aides and allies formulated a variety of programs for industrial recovery, but none met with his approval. On April 6 he was prodded to act by the Senate's adoption of Hugo Black's bill to require a thirty-hour workweek in factories producing for interstate commerce and thus spread employment around. This, Roosevelt thought, was too harsh a remedy for business to swallow. Therefore, White House advisers accelerated their quest for a plan of industrial recovery that would meet with the approval of both labor and business. Finally, during the middle of May the President was able to present a recovery proposal to Congress. It called for the authorization of the various sectors of business to regulate their industries exempt from antitrust legislation. What this meant was that trade groups could act cooperatively to set rules of fair competition and in effect to fix prices. It also provided for federal licensing of businesses, legalization of collective bargaining between labor and management, and the establishment of maximum hours of work and minimum wages.

The House of Representatives rubber-stamped the measure. Debate in the Senate was sharp and protracted, however, with some of the opposition coming from senators who feared monopolistic price-fixing and some from those who thought labor was being given too much power. Yet a majority was mustered for the bill, and on June 16 the National Industrial Recovery Act became law. Its objectives were to stop cutthroat competition, discourage industrial overproduction, inflate prices, give labor a fair deal on negotiations, wages, and hours, and provide industry and labor the opportunity to accomplish all this cooperatively. The administration believed that achievement of these goals would allow business to make a reasonable profit again, thereby motivating it to expand operations and provide additional employ-

ment and investment opportunities. The negotiated reduction of work hours would also tend to permit more
employment, which along with the maintenance and
even increase of wages would generate further mass
purchasing power. The economic spiral could thus be
turned upward.

Two agencies were established to administer the act's
provisions: the National Recovery Administration,
headed by General Hugh Johnson, and the Public
Works Administration, directed by Interior Secretary
Harold Ickes. Although sorely disappointed by not being
given charge of both agencies, Johnson jumped into his
task with evangelistic fervor. Bulling and bullying his
way, he started the various industries drawing up regulatory codes. Coordinating their activities was all but
impossible, but Johnson eased his job by launching a
national campaign aimed at getting the public to pressure employers to agree to N.R.A. minimum-wage and
maximum-hour standards. The idea was that buyers
would boycott firms that did not cooperate, that did not
display the official sticker bearing a blue eagle and the
legend "We Do Our Part." The response was tremendous among both citizens and employers. Moreover, with
this demonstration of national solidarity, the troubles
Johnson had encountered in procuring effective codes
melted swiftly.

If General Johnson's promises of what his agency
could accomplish—for example, six million new jobs by
September—were exaggerated, the National Recovery
Administration had significant impact on the economy.
It is true that some small businesses that could not abide
by N.R.A. standards were hurt, that there was a trend
toward business concentration, and that Johnson, with
his high-handed methods and extreme statements, often
embarrassed the government. Jobs were nevertheless
created for some two million workers, threats to the inflationary spiral were deflected, business ethics improved,

and cutthroat competition restrained. Moreover, N.R.A. strengthened organized labor, made the concept of minimum wages and maximum hours a continuing national objective, and considerably reduced sweatshops and child labor. N.R.A. operations did not bring recovery, or indeed come anywhere close to it, but Johnson's agency helped substantially to reverse the downward economic trend.

Harold Ickes's management of the Public Works Administration was quite different. Unlike Johnson, Ickes was cautious and thorough. He was not going to waste federal money on hastily conceived projects or funnel it down the ratholes of municipal corruption. He would see that the taxpayer got a dollar's worth of construction for a dollar's investment and that workingmen would be hired primarily for their skill, not their need, and be paid accordingly. Consequently, P.W.A. did relatively little to take up the slack in employment, provide relief to the needy, or even, until 1934, give the economy a boost. The slow pace of P.W.A. was attributable not just to Ickes. It took time to get worthwhile projects proposed by federal, state, and local agencies and even more time to get decent construction plans drawn up and to secure appropriate building sites. Moreover, President Roosevelt agreed with Ickes that scandal must be avoided and that P.W.A.'s operations should have a long-term value.

Nevertheless the results were impressive. P.W.A. put several hundred thousand persons to work at prevailing wages. Billions of dollars eventually flowed into the economy, through payrolls and the purchase of land, equipment, supplies, and materials. P.W.A.'s activities helped change the face of the nation as never before. Its work led to the construction or improvement of 12,702 school buildings, 628 municipal and county office structures, and 50,000 miles of roads and highways. Among other P.W.A. projects were the building of dams, bridges, sewage systems, state and federal buildings, naval vessels, airports, and hospitals and the pioneering of federal slum clearance and inexpensive housing.

Another development during the early New Deal worthy of mention concerns the restructuring of the Reconstruction Finance Corporation. Roosevelt entrusted this agency to Jesse Jones, a Texas banker whose goal was not so much to save what was in economic jeopardy as to spur business development. Instead of lending federal funds to banks, F.R.C. bought their preferred stock in order to expand their credit operations. Under Jones the agency also branched out into selective financing of mortgages, farm commodities, electrification, and foreign trade. R.F.C. and its subsidiaries consequently became America's largest single investor and bank. As such, they not only placed supports under the nation's economy but also propped up its courage for new ventures, which contributed to the slow upward climb toward recovery.

The administration placed great emphasis on the stabilization of agriculture. Many New Dealers believed that the overall economy could not be revived if the farm sector lagged behind. Farm purchasing power also had to be supported for human reasons, for too many people were dependent upon agriculture for their living. It was with these things in mind, as well as in response to farmer political pressure, that the Agricultural Adjustment Act and farm-credit measures had been enacted. As head of the Farm Credit Administration, Roosevelt's friend and neighbor, Henry Morgenthau, Jr., did a splendid job. F.C.A. plunged into the battle to save the farms, refinancing within a year and a half 20 percent of the country's farm mortgages on easier terms and helping farmers renegotiate their debts on more liberal terms. For his agency's great success, Morgenthau would be named Secretary of the Treasury upon the death of William Woodin in 1934.

Yet saving farms was not enough. They had to be made into viable enterprises. This was the job of Secretary of Agriculture Henry A. Wallace. He knew agriculture as no farmer did. The son of former Agriculture Secretary Henry C. Wallace, he had succeeded his father as one of the nation's foremost farm editors, and, in addition, he was a first-rate geneticist and farm economist. Yet because of Congress's tardiness in passing the Agricultural Adjustment Act, Wallace was at a disadvantage in 1933 in carrying out the government's program to restrict production and distribute subsidies. Moreover, the program could not be launched overnight because of the difficulties of organizing it and enlisting the farmers' cooperation. Something had to be done, however, for crops had been sown and were already sprouting. During the summer Wallace and his aides tried to combat the glutted commodity market by persuading farmers to uproot their cotton and slaughter their hogs. It was an emergency action designed to give a badly needed measure of support to agricultural prices. Despite the reason, the nation's reaction was unfavorable, as public opinion mourned the "little pigs" and many Americans thought that surpluses should be grown for distribution to the needy.

A more orderly program to reduce surpluses and subsidize farmers was on the way, but it would take more time than was available to avert trouble and foolishness. Farm prices had mounted between March and July, 1933, but then they began to dip, and cries were raised for compulsory restrictions on production and for price-fixing to guarantee farmers income above their cost of production. This Roosevelt and Wallace on the whole avoided, for they were determined to go ahead with the program of subsidizing farmers who volunteered to curb production. As wheat and livestock prices dropped and the costs of what farmers bought climbed, the Farm Holiday Association scheduled a farm strike for the

Midwest to begin October 21. The federal government looked to the states to deal with the farm strikes, but they had little with which to work except persuasion. Pressure increased rapidly for price-fixing and inflationary devices. Governor Floyd Olson, of Minnesota, demanded federal relief for farmers; otherwise, he warned, "the sound of marching feet . . . will not be strange." The farm strike came about with attendant bombings, burnings, pitched battles between farmers and police, and sabotage of the produce of nonstrikers. Then the federal government began to act. Henry Wallace and Hugh Johnson went on extensive speaking tours to persuade farmers that the future was propitious. The New Deal's farm-loan program was accelerated, the corn-hog production-control programs were put into effect, and the Farm Credit Administration's operations were intensified, all of which tended to deflate the farm strike.

In Washington Roosevelt and his aides initiated government buying of gold above the world price in the belief that it would raise prices. That panacea did not work, though it possibly slowed down a deflationary farm trend, and the policy was dropped early in 1934. It was replaced by the Gold Reserve Act of January, 1934, which allowed Roosevelt to set the price of gold at $35 an ounce and cut the gold content of the dollar to 59.06 percent of its 1932 value. This was an inflationary measure that inflated very little except the ire of those conservatives who worshiped at gold's altar. In December, 1933, the President committed the government to another inflationary money-juggling scheme, the massive purchase of silver at more than 50 percent above the market price. This was followed by the Silver Purchase Act of 1934, unwanted by the White House, which forced the treasury to buy silver until the world price reached $1.29 per ounce or until silver amounted to one-quarter of the nation's monetary reserve. Silver certificates were issued to finance this and to expand the amount of currency in circulation. Consequently, almost $1,500,000,000 was spent to support the minuscule silver industry that had lobbied ferociously for the measure. While this legislation pandered to both the silver interests and the agricultural inflationists, it cost the government more than did farm subsidies, and it failed to achieve inflation. It was a boondoggle of the highest order, one for which Congress and the "funny-money" men had to take full responsibility. Nevertheless these various government actions, though especially the pouring in of funds from the new federal farm program by December, 1933, cooled farm tempers.

The New Deal's economic policies had been almost completely nationalistic. The experiments with gold and silver had been undertaken without concern for the world's economy, and indeed the Silver Purchase Act was to visit disaster on the currencies of China, Mexico, and Peru. Roosevelt's one venture in the area of international economic cooperation was to encourage the holding of the International Economic Conference in London in June and July, 1933. After the American delegation got to London, the President reneged on his promise to Secretary of State Hull that he would ask Congress for reciprocal tariff legislation, which gave Hull nothing with which to bargain. Then as some agreement on stabilizing world currencies drew near at the conference, Roosevelt decided that would jeopardize his efforts to inflate prices at home. He issued a message in July that rejected his earlier commitment to world currency stabilization, observing that the "old fetishes of so-called international bankers" were healthily "being replaced by efforts to plan national currencies." Only after nations began living within their means, he declared, could international currency stabilization be profitably discussed. President Roosevelt was probably correct in opposing currency stabilization at a low price level. Nevertheless, he missed an opportunity, the last

during the 1930's, to provide some leadership for cooperative world action to deal with economic affairs. He
could at least have championed tariff reciprocity, which
he would adopt a year later anyway. As it was, he contributed substantially to the outbreak of national economic warfare that would increasingly mark relations
among states during the coming years, and he lost considerable goodwill.

The United States did take one positive action in 1933
to try to improve its foreign relations and trade. This
was the recognition of the Union of Soviet Socialist
Republics. As the depression increased in scope and
severity, many American businessmen and farmers over-
came their fear of the Bolshevik bogeyman in the belief
that there was a vast new market in Russia for their
products. Between December, 1932, and November, 1933,
Roosevelt sounded out the Russians on reestablishment
of diplomatic relations, which had been suspended for
fifteen years. On November 16 the two nations agreed
to restore relations. The Russians promised to restrict
their propaganda in the United States and to guarantee
religious freedom for Americans in the Soviet Union.
Russia's debt to the United States was left to future
discussion. President Roosevelt, however, got little of
what he wanted to gain. Russia and America certainly
did not stand together as a moral bulwark against
German and Japanese expansionism, and trade between
the Soviet Union and the United States did not amount
to a great deal. Propaganda was not greatly curbed, and
the debt was never settled. Since few Americans went
to the Soviet Union, the religious guarantee was of little
significance, and the hope that the Russians would
generally soften their attitude toward religion was un-
fulfilled. Yet recognition remedied the absurdity of the
two powers virtually ignoring one another and established a basis for discussion of disputes, even if it
seldom led to results. Both countries were able to gain

more intelligence about each other, for whatever that was worth. Most important, when the time came to build a wartime Soviet-American alliance in 1941, the machinery was available to arrange it, and some of the mutual ill will existing before 1933 had been cleared away. Recognition of Russia was not of monumental importance, but it was not insignificant either.

On balance the New Deal during its first year had great impact at home. It had dealt with an amazing range of issues and despite the ups and downs of 1933, had reversed the long-term downward fall of the economy. The average annual earnings of full-time employees rose from $1,002 in 1933 to $1,056 in 1934, the percentage of the unemployed declined from 24.9 to 21.7, and labor-union membership increased from 2,689,000 to 3,088,000. Bank assets mounted from $51,300,000,000 to $55,900,000,000, the value of construction from $5,300,000,000 to $6,600,000,000, the business-failure rate per 10,000 concerns dropped from 100 to 61, and corporate receipts jumped from $82,000,000,000 to $99,000,000,000. The index of gross production of crops decreased from 71 to 58, and farm-mortgage debt fell from $8,400,000,000 to $7,600,000,000. By all indicators the nation seemed to be climbing, albeit slowly, toward recovery. Moreover, innovative and fairly successful endeavors had been made to supply relief to the needy. Efforts to conserve natural resources and erect public works were going forward in high gear. As important as anything else, hope had dawned that "Happy Days Are Here Again."

It would be a mistake to conclude that this was all or mostly the doing of one man. Franklin D. Roosevelt was the leading spirit, but Hopkins, Ickes, Johnson, Morgenthau, Perkins, Wallace, and other high-level New Deal administrators played their parts. There were also the hundreds of bright young people and grizzled veterans of battles in the public interest who

flocked to Washington to contribute to the war against
depression, and their counterparts in regional government offices. Congress during the Hundred Days was
far from being a rubber stamp; much of the legislation
was born or amended in offices and committee rooms on
Capitol Hill. Neither can the states be overlooked, for
if there was a New Deal for the nation, there was also
a New Deal of the states. New York under Governor
Herbert Lehman extended or achieved the reforms begun under Roosevelt. Floyd Olson's Minnesota placed a
two-year moratorium on farm debts, which was widely
copied elsewhere, and experimented with cooperative
enterprises ranging from breweries to mortuaries. Alfred
Landon in Kansas successfully pioneered the state legislative council and ports of entry for collecting commercial motor-vehicle taxes. State and local governments
usually cooperated effectively with the myriad of new
and complicated federal programs and often were responsible for suggestions that led to their improved
operation. Not least was the cooperation and participation of individual citizens, private associations, and economic groups. Only during World War I had the
country previously been so united and effective in under-
taking concerted action in dealing with its problems. It
was an impressive year, 1933.

9

The Push for More, The Push for Different

THERE was no doubt that the Roosevelt Administration had accomplished a great deal in 1933. Roosevelt was riding the wild horses of the Right and the Left, however, and it was becoming plain by 1934 that they could not long gallop together in the same direction. Business's enthusiasm had cooled off. No longer were big-business interests pleading for a strong man in Washington. Things had improved sufficiently, and government intervention was no longer welcome. Yet for most Americans conditions by year's end had improved only enough to seem to require more improvement. Millions were still jobless, and most farmers and small merchants were barely holding on. Economic indicators inched upward until the spring of 1934, but then they reached a plateau where they would remain for a year. Pressure built among radicals, particularly on the Left, for more action.

Although the farm-strike movement was moribund, the search for satisfactory government programs continued among radical agrarians. The New Deal was likened to an anesthesia at a time when a remedy was clearly needed. In February, 1934, the *Wisconsin Dairyman's News* declared that "farmer and city worker must combine" politically to seek laws that would bring them an equitable return for their labor. A new organization, the Farmer-Labor Political Federation, crusaded among farmers, workingmen, and intellectuals for greater government control of the economy and increased popular control of the government. The group called for a new political party and had enlisted the support of Milo

Reno, the head of the Farm Holiday Association, and the interest of A. F. Whitney, president of the Brotherhood of Railway Trainmen. The F.L.P.F. backed the activities of the Minnesota Farmer-Labor party, which governed its state, the formation of the Wisconsin Progressive party in 1934, and third-party movements in California, Iowa, and South Dakota.

The goal of these groups was more drastic government action to raise farm and labor income. They could agree with Minnesota Governor Floyd Olson when he asserted in March, 1934, "I am a radical in the sense that I want a definite change in the system. I am not satisfied with tinkering, I am not satisfied with patching, I am not satisfied with hanging a laurel wreath on burglars and thieves and pirates and calling them code authorities or something else." Recognizing the strong sentiment among their followers for more radical national action, Philip La Follette and Robert La Follette, Jr., allowed the platform of their new Wisconsin Progressive party to proclaim that "Progressives in Wisconsin, cutting loose from all connections with the two old reactionary parties in this crisis, have founded a new national party." Senator Lynn J. Frazier, of North Dakota, and Mayor Fiorello LaGuardia, of New York, warned in October that a third party was inevitable if "reactionaries" continued to dominate the Democratic and Republican parties. In California novelist Upton Sinclair won the Democratic nomination for governor under the auspices of a self-created organization called End Poverty in California. He demanded the establishment of farm and industrial colonies for the unemployed that would produce not only for themselves but also for underpaid Americans elsewhere. Sinclair left no doubt that what he had in mind should be applied nationally. Raymond Haight, running as the gubernatorial nominee of the California Commonwealth and Progressive parties, also evangelized for Farmer-Laborite programs. And these people had po-

litical appeal. In the 1934 elections the Farmer-Laborites
retained control of Minnesota, and the Progressives
swept Wisconsin. Although Sinclair lost in California,
he and Haight, who polled 300,000 votes, attracted a
majority of the ballots for governor.

The year 1934 also saw the formation of the Southern
Tenant Farmers' Union, which strenuously sought relief
for the "landed proletariat." There were also Senator
Huey Long's Share-Our-Wealth movement, Father
Charles E. Coughlin's National Union for Social Justice,
and Dr. Francis E. Townsend's Old-Age Pension Group.
Under Norman Thomas the Socialist party reinvigorated
its efforts to establish a liberal-leftist front. Matters intensified in 1935. The Communists pressed for a popular
front of leftists and liberals. Organized labor, which
had been increasingly active in seeking heightened government action, showed some interest in the launching
of a new political party. At the 1935 convention of the
American Federation of Labor, thirteen new-party resolutions were offered by as many state federations and
international unions. The Farm Holiday Association
convention called for a national farmer-labor party, and
sentiment for such a move increased among members of
the National Farmers' Union. Radicals led by Senator
Homer Bone and Lewis Schwellenbach captured vir-
tual control of the Democratic party in Washington
state, and in Oregon the Grange and the state federation
of labor backed Peter Zimmerman's independent candidacy for governor in a special election in which he drew
one-third of the votes. The Share-Our-Wealth movement
under Louisiana's colorful Huey Long was making head-
way. Many people seemed to be responding to the man
who proclaimed that America under the New Deal was
"headed just as straight to hell as a martin ever went
to gourd." Indeed a secret poll indicated in 1935 that
Senator Long might receive up to 4,000,000 votes as the
head of a third-party ticket.

The import of all this was that the Roosevelt Administration increasingly felt pressed to act in order to
deflate discontent. The dissidents did not agree on what
should be done, but it was plain that they wanted more
economic controls and social reforms. Whether the dissidents were aiming at forming a new national party or
attempting to take control of the Democratic party,
the pressure for action was unrelenting, and the New
Deal responded. It endeavored to buy off some of the
radical leaders by giving them control of federal relief
programs in Minnesota, Wisconsin, and New York City.
Others it opposed strenuously, as with Upton Sinclair
and Huey Long. The administration also responded
with a more vigorous, liberal legislative program.

This led to a variety of federal action in 1934. The
Agricultural Adjustment Administration conducted crop
referenda among farmers to enlist their support of its
subsidy and crop-restriction programs. The Taylor Grazing Act of 1934 authorized setting aside eight million
acres of federal grasslands to be regulated by the Interior
Department with the cooperation of local stockmen's
associations in order to restore the grass and to keep out
unauthorized graziers. The Indian Reorganization Act
was passed in 1934 and offered reservation Indians some
self-government, improvement loans, protection against
encroachment on their lands, and additional employment in the Bureau of Indian Affairs. This and lesser
measures did not give Indians equal rights in American
society, but the New Deal provided them the opportunity to take a bigger step toward that goal than they
had received previously. The Roosevelt Administration
also took care to give Negroes a larger share of government benefits and even to listen to their complaints and
occasionally respond to them. This was an acceleration
of the slight forward movement of the 1920's, and
although it proved greatly insufficient to blacks and
Indians, it was a welcome development. Another trend

was also reflected in the New Deal's actions. That was to involve people more in government decisions, whether it be in the A.A.A. referenda, partial autonomy for Indian reservations, consultation of stockmen's associations, workingmen's balloting for bargaining agents, establishment of scores of advisory boards, or the drafting and operation of industrial codes. It gave people another way of expressing their views and gaining responses from government officials, and at the same time siphoned off a good deal of discontent. But many of the New Deal measures also encouraged interest-group activity at the expense of the general welfare and allowed the government unprecedented opportunities to manipulate the public.

Yet these were usually not the federal programs that were gaining the headlines in 1934 or by themselves having the greatest impact. The public wanted stricter control over high finance, and the President agreed with them to a large extent. The result was the Securities Exchange Act, which established the Securities and Exchange Commission to regulate stock-market practices, especially margin requirements, and to prevent misrepresentation in the sale of securities. Other important 1934 legislation included the establishment of the Federal Communications Commission to regulate the cable, radio, and telegraph industries, the creation of the Federal Housing Administration to insure private home loans, the Air Mail Act to place more stringent controls in federal air-mail contracts, and the Railroad Retirement Act to provide pensions for railway workers.

Of course, there were also the administration's and Congress's monetary experiments and a burgeoning of expenditures and deficit financing thanks mainly to the expansion of government services. Certainly there was grumbling as the national debt climbed from $22,500,000,000 to $27,000,000,000 between 1933 and 1934, which almost equaled the debt increase of the

entire Hoover Administration. President Roosevelt, however, felt keenly the pressure for even more government
action and appropriations. As he wrote to Colonel Edward House in May, 1934, "There will be many new
manifestations of the New Deal, even though the orthodox protest and the heathen roar! . . . We must keep the
sheer momentum from slacking up too much and I have
no intention of relinquishing the offensive in favor of
defensive tactics." The following month the President
announced that he would ask Congress in 1935 for an
immense program including housing, natural-resource
development, and social insurance.

Although the New Deal's actions kept the radical
movements at bay, they antagonized conservatives and
some moderates. By late 1933 the administration, because
of Roosevelt's monetary policies, had already lost the
services of several eminent financial advisers. Director
of the Budget Lewis Douglas resigned in August, 1934,
in protest over the severe unbalancing of the budget.
Businessmen were increasingly breaking away from the
New Deal coalition because of the administration's
monetary and fiscal policies, the N.R.A.'s interventions,
and the increase in regulatory legislation. The formation
of the American Liberty League in 1934 was the most
prominent sign of discontent on the Right. The organization included such corporate leaders as Irénée du
Pont, Alfred P. Sloan, Jr., of General Motors, E. T. Weir,
of Weirton Steel, and motion-picture producer Hal
Roach, as well as politicians such as Democrats Al Smith,
John W. Davis, and John Raskob, and Republicans
Nathan Miller and James W. Wadsworth, all of whom
had strong business connections. A.L.L.'s goals were to
"defend and uphold the Constitution," protect individual enterprise, and foster property rights. It asserted
that it intended not to oppose President Roosevelt but
to assist him to achieve those objectives. It was clear to
most people, however, that the organization was playing

the same game on the Right as the radical groups were playing on the Left: to influence the administration and if unsuccessful, to oppose it. As James Farley would later say, the American Liberty League "ought to be called the American Cellophane League" because "first, it's a du Pont product and second, you can see right through it."

One well-publicized New Deal measure in 1934 did little immediately either to antagonize or to please anyone. This was the Trade Agreements Act. During the spring of 1933 Secretary of State Cordell Hull had got Roosevelt's backing to submit a bill approving the negotiation of reciprocal trade agreements. The President had withdrawn it, however, for fear of complicating his relations with Congress. Hull was basically a free-trade man, but he knew that free trade stood no chance for advancement in the nationalistic economic world of the 1930's. He believed, however, that the United States could negotiate the reciprocal reduction of tariffs with other countries and thereby begin to dismantle international trade barriers. The white-haired gentleman from Tennessee labored to convince Roosevelt that America could neither profitably pursue an isolationist economic policy nor prosper in world trade with high tariffs. Only the policy of selective reduction of import duties on a quid pro quo basis would enlist maximum support in Congress and the country. It would also be the most effective approach to lowering trade walls at home and abroad. President Roosevelt was persuaded by 1934, and in March he requested reciprocal-tariff legislation. With the preponderance of Democratic strength in Congress, the measure was enacted by June. The new statute gave the executive the authority to reduce or increase import duties by as much as 50 percent for the products of nations that would give like treatment to American exports.

Hull's interpretation of the law is what became controversial. On the surface the government was authorized only to negotiate treaties with individual countries that would lead to the mutual reduction of tariffs. That Hull did, and with considerable success, for agreements were implemented with fourteen nations within a year and a half and with twenty-nine by 1945. What he did additionally was to apply the unconditional-most-favored-nation clause that had been lying around and only slightly used since the enactment of the Fordney-McCumber Act in 1922. That provision allowed Hull to extend the negotiated tariff reductions on specific imports to all other countries whose duties did not discriminate against the United States. The result was a lowering of American tariffs well beyond that contemplated by most officials and observers.

This infuriated not only high-tariff advocates but also Raymond Moley and George N. Peek, two of President Roosevelt's closest foreign-trade advisers. Moley and Peek did not oppose tariff reduction, but they wanted the unconditional-most-favored-nation principle to be applied only when other countries had granted trade concessions to the United States. Moley charged that Hull's approach jeopardized "the idea of a managed national economy" by extending tariff concessions without receiving a quid pro quo. Peek said that the secretary's policy contravened the purpose of the Trade Agreements Act, which was to expand overseas markets for American producers, not vastly to increase imports, too (which Hull wanted, for he believed it was essential for a healthy economy to strike a balance between imports and exports). Use of the unconditional-most-favored-nation clause was, Peek declared, "unilateral economic disarmament." Peek was both right and wrong. Congress had approved the Trade Agreements Act primarily to expand America's exports. Yet Hull was within his rights to exercise the unconditional-most-favored-nation principle to generate greater international trade. The controversy continued within the administration until the fall of 1935, when the Secretary of State, with strong support from Henry Wallace, finally won the President's full backing for his position. Peek then resigned. Since Moley's influence had been waning, this meant victory for Hull. Economic nationalists would continue to snipe at his policies, especially agricultural interests, which suffered from increased imports of foodstuffs. The harm was not too great, however, and the New Deal sought other ways to assuage farm grief.

The trade battle was somewhat more a triumph for principle than for economic recovery. The value of exports between 1933 and 1939 rose only from $1,700,000,000 to $3,200,000,000 and of imports from $1,400,000,000 to $2,300,000,000, well below 1929 levels. A balance of trade had obviously not been achieved. Moreover, the expansion of exports and imports cannot solely be attributed to Hull's policies, for devaluation of the dollar and improvements in national economies contributed to increased international trade. Nevertheless exports to countries that had negotiated trade agreements with the United States mounted faster than exports to other nations. Equally important was that the government's commitment to economic nationalism had been scrapped, thereby winning the United States some goodwill abroad and serving to America's advantage in the developing economic struggles with Fascist nations.

Whatever the arguments and pressures of 1934, the election results generally favored Roosevelt. All indicators showed that his personal popularity remained high. As a consequence of the November elections, only seven Republican governors held office, and Democrats increased their number of seats in the Senate to 69 and in the House to 319, contrary to the tradition that the party in power loses ground in a nonpresidential-year election. This was taken as overwhelming endorsement of the New Deal and particularly as approval for additional government action. The election of two third-

party governors, ten representatives, and two senators
seemed further to confirm the wisdom of the administration's continued lean to the Left. But Roosevelt was in
effect the issue, and Roosevelt was the victor. As Republican newspaper editor William Allen White said, "He
has been all but crowned by the people."

The expansion of government activity and power was
even greater during most of 1935 than in 1934. If Roosevelt could no longer ride the horses of both the Right
and the Left, he was still astride that of the Left. The
Progressive and Farmer-Labor parties' forces in Congress
had increased, and many of the new Democrats in the
House and Senate had been elected on platforms promising more government action, and some of them were
affiliated with the Farmer-Labor Political Federation.
The F.L.P.F. estimated that some forty to fifty representatives and senators would form the nucleus for a
radical legislative reshaping of government and the
economy. This legislative group in effect agreed upon
the need for what amounted to a farmer-labor-
progressive platform: heightened regulation of credit
and currency; higher gift and inheritance taxes; taxation of securities; lower farm- and home-loan interest;
additional farm refinancing; guarantees of farm profit
beyond the cost of production; maximum hours of work
and minimum wages in industry; guaranteed collective
bargaining; expanded public works; public ownership
of monopolies and natural resources; federal aid to education; government insurance to take care of the problems of illness, unemployment, and old age; and "no
foreign entanglements." This group, however loose-knit
it turned out to be, would find allies on individual issues
among the regular Democrats and Republicans in Congress, who themselves were often pressed by their constituents for greater federal action. Even Roosevelt's
willingness to do more did not match the temper of
Congress in 1935 or of his more radical aides who were

pressuring both "the Chief" and Congress. The results were to be himalayan.

Roosevelt began 1935 by asking Congress for legislation to continue and revise unemployment relief. Although what came out of the relief proposal was acceptable to liberals, the President's request was prompted by his conservative outlook on relief. "The federal government must and shall quit this business of relief," he asserted. Maximum employment, not government subsidization of the jobless, was his goal. Yet millions were unemployed, and Roosevelt did not intend to ignore them. He asked Congress to create a program that would provide public work at subsistence wages for 3,500,000 people. The other 1,500,000 on relief would have to be considered chronic cases and therefore left to local assistance and private charity.

The President was caught in the middle of sharp debate between conservatives who believed that the nearly five billion dollars for relief that he had requested was far too much and radicals who felt it was insufficient to do the job. The former contended that the dole would be less expensive but just as effective because the government would not have to supply materials and equipment for public works. The latter declared that too few people would be taken care of, that too great a burden would be placed on local agencies, and that Roosevelt's proposed "security wage" of about twelve dollars a week was too small to maintain human dignity. They wanted a larger federal program with work-relief recipients paid the prevailing wage in their particular sections of the country. After more than two months of argument, Congress gave in and passed the Emergency Relief Appropriation Act of 1935, which gave Roosevelt almost all he wanted. He got not only $4,800,000,000 but substantial discretionary power in spending it and in organizing relief administration. One drawback was that senior administrators in the new relief program were subject to confirmation by the Senate. This injected a considerable measure of partisan politics in the selection of high relief officials and guaranteed the appointment of a number of them who were unqualified or venal. This led to some waste, graft, and political intimidation in relief administration and consequently to occasional embarrassing scandals. Nevertheless the new relief agency, the Works Progress Administration, met the basic needs of large numbers of jobless.

Once Roosevelt got the new relief legislation, he had to make a big decision. Harold Ickes and Harry Hopkins battled strenuously for control of the appropriation, but the President chose Hopkins to administer the funds because he believed that his work-relief chief would be more effective in getting money to the needy. Ickes would undoubtedly have used the appropriation well in terms of building substantial and durable public works, and perhaps he would have been better than Hopkins in priming the economy. Roosevelt, however, considered mass relief a more pressing national problem than giving taxpayers their money's worth in construction projects.

Under Hopkins the Works Progress Administration not only pursued works projects in great numbers but expanded and developed the more imaginative programs of F.E.R.A. and C.W.A., its predecessor agencies. The W.P.A.'s Federal Theatre Project gave work to jobless playwrights, actors, directors, musicians, and other show people. Its plays, musicals, variety shows, and circuses were performed all over the country, thus boosting public interest in the thespian art. The government's willingness to allow theatrical experiments also encouraged professional and artistic improvement. During its lifespan some thirty million Americans attended performances sponsored by the Federal Theatre Project. Similar accomplishments were achieved by the W.P.A.'s Federal Art Project and Federal Writers' Project. Out-of-work artists and writers were enabled to ply their crafts.

Although a good deal of what they produced was mediocre, as was true of many of the theater productions, much was excellent. Public buildings were, as at no other time in American history, decorated with original art, and classes in a variety of art forms were offered to the public. The writers produced almost one thousand publications, including the well-received *Life in America* series. Thus, through these three projects, the W.P.A. provided appropriate work relief to artists, authors, musicians, and show people. The projects also had a significant impact on national culture, by broadening public appreciation of the arts, making them more respectable, and encouraging the development of new approaches and techniques.

The National Youth Administration was created to tend to the special problems of young people. As indicated earlier, they were among those most sorely affected by the depression, because they had few jobs to begin with and found it difficult to get the experience so often needed to qualify for work. Many young people also found it hard to complete their schooling. The N.Y.A., during its seven years of existence, provided part-time work for more than 2,000,000 high-school and college students and assisted another 2,600,000 youths with vocational training or work-relief jobs. Many of these positions were on W.P.A.-type projects, but large numbers of youth jobs were applied to staff programs that supported the operations of schools, colleges, and cultural agencies. The N.Y.A. was, therefore, a boon not only to young people but also to educational institutions.

Most of the federal work-relief recipients, however, were adult men and women of ordinary skills, and most of the work supplied them was in construction and the clerical chores related thereto. The Works Progress Administration contributed mightily to the reshaping of the face of America, which was shared in by the Public Works Administration and the Civilian Conservation Corps. The W.P.A. workers planted millions of trees, laid down tens of thousands of miles of streets and highways, and built thousands of other projects, including bridges, schools, hospitals, playgrounds, stadia, airports, golf courses, ski jumps, and even boat basins. The W.P.A. also operated traveling libraries, distributed vast amounts of surplus food to the needy, and inaugurated the hot-lunch program in schools all over America. All this was in addition to what was done through the art, theater, and writers' projects. Few were the communities not affected and benefited by W.P.A. activities. Thanks largely to Harry Hopkins and the inventive staff that he drew around himself, the problems of the unemployed were vigorously attacked, and huge amounts of federal money circulated in the struggle to revive the national economy.

Yet the work-relief program was not a complete success. Neither it nor state, local, and private agencies had sufficient funds to take care of all of the jobless. Consequently, several million needy Americans were left to shift for themselves. Another problem was that even those who received W.P.A. assistance received little in compensation for their work, as low as nineteen dollars monthly in some parts of the South. Then, too, because of the monumental nature of the relief problem and the necessity of securing Senate confirmation of senior W.P.A. officials, there was a regrettably high level of waste, inefficiency, and partisanship in the agency's operations. Yet the vast scope and long life of W.P.A., which continued into the early war years, indicated the biggest problem. Roosevelt and Hopkins had conceived W.P.A. as a program that would be terminated within a couple of years. By 1936, however, it seemed that millions of people would be permanently unemployed. In short, the nation's economy failed to generate sufficient jobs for all members of its laboring force. Many Americans thus appeared doomed to live forever on charity or at low wages on federal make-work projects.

Struggle as the New Deal did, it could not bring back the employment levels of the 1920's. The United States, until 1941, was to be plagued with wholesale unemployment and the need to administer a huge relief program. What the federal government could do, however, was fill some of the gaps in meeting the basic needs of the jobless and destitute. This idea is what lay behind President Roosevelt's request in January, 1935, that Congress establish a national social-security program. The proposal was the work of a Cabinet committee, and it looked like it. It was the result of numerous compromises and of fears that the states would oppose a bolder plan and that the Supreme Court would find a more thoroughgoing program unconstitutional. The New Deal's social-security bill called for (1) federal grants to help the states expand assistance to dependent mothers and children, the physically handicapped, and the needy aged, (2) a national insurance system, based on employee and employer contributions, that would pay old-age benefits to workers when they retired, and (3) a federal-state insurance system that would supply benefits to workers who had been laid off.

As with the emergency-relief bill, this legislation was attacked from both the Right and the Left. Conservatives asserted that the bill would be an unnecessary drain on business's recuperative powers and indeed a theft of the earnings of those citizens who could make their own way in society. Radicals contended, however, that the administration's plan was inadequate to meet the problems of the needy and the aged. The battle raged for months, and not until summer did Congress finally approve the legislation. What emerged was substantially what Roosevelt and his Cabinet committee had requested, since the opponents on the Right and the

Left largely canceled each other out. The Social Security Act of 1935 authorized federal funds to match state moneys in caring for dependent mothers and children, the handicapped, destitute persons over age sixty-five, and in operating public-health services for the indigent. Unemployment insurance was created, based mainly on employer funding, to assist workers who had lost their jobs, and old-age-and-survivors insurance was established to supply annuity benefits to workers who later retired and to their dependents in case of early death.

The act marked a significant departure in that the United States at last had an ongoing program to give benefits to the needy. Yet the law had numerous defects, many of which have marched down the corridors of time to the present. At the insistence of President Roosevelt and Treasury Secretary Morgenthau, provision for a government contribution to old-age-and-survivors insurance was deleted, thereby reducing the already modest benefits of the plan. Moreover, although employees and employers would begin compulsory O.A.S.I. contributions in 1937, no benefits would be paid until 1942, and those would be minuscule, because retirement payments were considerably dependent upon how much workers had earned. Only half of the nation's working force was covered anyway, since farmers, farm hands, and the self-employed, among others, were ineligible for participation. But there were other serious problems with O.A.S.I. Because the tax scale was uniform for all employees and employers, it did not take into account the ability to pay, and although the plan was sold as being only a 1-percent levy, provision was made to increase the rate over the years, so that within a generation O.A.S.I. would be the second biggest tax burden for most Americans. Furthermore, the vast pool of funds built up through O.A.S.I. taxes could not be used for any positive economic action, thus handicapping regeneration of the nation's business.

The cost of administering the program was unnecessarily boosted, since it took additional staff to collect and record employee-employer contributions beyond that which would have been required in paying straight pension benefits. The matching-fund aspects of the Social Security Act were similarly wasteful of federal and state staff and facilities, because of the extra record-keeping needed in a cooperative program contrasted to what would have been required in a wholly federal program. Moreover, the human impact of the federal-state matching programs was sad, for stipends were small, with, for example, the blind in New York City receiving in 1937 as little as five dollars weekly. Payments to the handicapped, aged destitute, and dependent mothers and children varied considerably over the nation because the states set the size of benefits. Some of the states were unbelievably stingy, and none could be called generous. The payments usually permitted their recipients to afford no more than the poorest quality shelter, food of the lowest nutritional value, and the shoddiest kind of clothing. Unemployment insurance posed similar problems, although the stipends were somewhat better. Moreover, those who registered for unemployment benefits did not have to meet the indignities of the means test or, as was usual with the aged destitute, sign over the titles to their real estate to the state.

It is obvious, in reviewing the Social Security Act, that the United States had learned little from the decades of European experience with social insurance. Certainly, the American plan was niggardly as well as economically mischievous. It was a jerry-built program that was to be too often administered cavalierly. Although the law marked a great turning point in America's acceptance of social responsibility, it did not compliment the nation's heart or intelligence, nor did it represent the country's ability to take care of its needy in an effective, dignified way.

Roosevelt proposed another important federal program to Congress in January, 1935, one that has stood the test of time well. That was rural electrification. Ninety percent of the nation's farms had no electricity in 1935, either because of the lack of power lines over the countryside or because where they were available, electricity was too expensive. As early as 1933 the administration showed interest in rural electrification and by 1934 initiated some small, scattered projects. Congress responded affirmatively to Roosevelt's 1935 request to earmark some of the moneys in the Emergency Relief Appropriation Act to fund bringing electricity to farm families. In May the President created the Rural Electrification Administration, headed by Morris Llewellyn Cooke, a veteran advocate of public-power development. Cooke undertook his responsibilities vigorously, pressing private electric firms to extend their power lines into farm areas and offering them low-interest federal loans to help finance the work. When the private companies refused to cooperate, Cooke fostered the formation of nonprofit cooperatives. Indeed private utility resistance was so stiff and widespread that in 1936 Congress countered by authorizing R.E.A. to give preference to nonprofit agencies in granting loans. The results of R.E.A.'s work were impressive. Electricity was found on 40 percent of the nation's farms by 1941 and on 90 percent by 1950, and thanks to reliance on nonprofit agencies for development and distribution, power rates were kept low. The flow of electricity to the farms revolutionized rural life. Not only did light begin to flood the home and barn, but electricity powered appliances that saved labor and permitted types of work that had been previously impossible. Electricity also enabled new industries to locate and operate in the countryside. The drawback of rural electrification was that it helped keep farm production high and thereby perpetuated agricultural surpluses.

Although the New Deal's intentions in sponsoring the Emergency Relief Appropriation Act, the Social Security Act, and R.E.A. may have been noble, certainly those programs were not radical. Roosevelt indeed considered the relief act a middle-of-the-road attempt at closing out the program and social security as a way to meet public pressure with a minimum of cost and federal involvement. In any event, radicals, whether of the native or Marxist variety, and even some liberals were neither greatly impressed nor satisfied with those two laws, nor did they view the establishment of R.E.A. as a major act. Moreover, there were evidences of Rooseveltian conservatism during early 1935 that dismayed them. Not only was the President not responding sufficiently to their many demands, but he had been saying nice things to and about business in an obvious attempt to regain some of its support for his administration. He had, to boot, occasionally backed employers in labor disputes, talked longingly of a balanced budget, and successfully opposed an amendment providing for payment of prevailing wages on work relief. Then, too, his veto of a veterans' bonus bill, however courageous politically, irritated those many radicals and liberals who were taken in by the quackery surrounding such raids on the treasury.

It was not so much that the President was a conservative, a liberal, or a radical. Roosevelt was Franklin on the spot. With each new government action, more businessmen abandoned him. Yet he was not doing enough to appease those who claimed to be standing at Armageddon and fighting for an ultraliberal Lord. Unable to satisfy both the Right and the Left and do his job as he saw it, Roosevelt would soon have to make a choice between them, at least temporarily. One thing was accomplished, however, before that time came. In an attempt to force the government to extend further protection to farm tenants, Jerome Frank, in the absence of Agricultural Adjustment Administrator Chester Davis,

ordered cotton planters to retain their tenants during
the period of their contracts with A.A.A. Davis soon
canceled the order and dismissed Frank and most of his
agrarian-reform allies in A.A.A. The President and Agriculture Secretary Wallace supported Davis, but Roosevelt was prompted to do something for the rural poor in
compensation. That was the establishment in April,
1935, of the Resettlement Administration under Rexford
Tugwell, the most prominent advocate of agrarian reform in the Department of Agriculture.

The Resettlement Administration was authorized to
assume control of the rural-rehabilitation program organized under F.E.R.A. and P.W.A.'s subsistence-homestead
operations. The homestead program was scrapped. Instead Tugwell promoted the creation of planned towns
that would be sited near major cities but yet surrounded
by countryside. The idea behind the "greenbelt" towns
was to provide an attractive and economically viable
alternative to life in the city or on the farm. R.A. built
greenbelt communities in the vicinity of Cincinnati,
Milwaukee, and Washington. The new towns operated
to take advantage of economic opportunities in the
nearby cities and yet afford the pleasantness of life in
the country and the benefits of completely planned communities. As such they were innovative and attractive,
but it soon became clear that few Americans could be
accommodated in small model communities, especially
with more pressing problems on hand. R.A.'s main
assignment, the resettlement of poor farmers on better
acreage with better equipment and tutelage on how to
use the land, fared even less well. The costs of supporting the program were prohibitive, in view of the enormous expense of finding good land and buying it,
screening candidates for resettlement, and then subsidizing their new life. Only 4,441 farm families were resettled during R.A.'s lifetime. Yet Tugwell's experiments
showed that the government was interested in dealing

with the grave problems of rural poverty and formed the basis for a later, more successful endeavor.

Two things in 1935 moved Roosevelt to decide what his course would be in the near future. One was a series of adverse Supreme Court decisions, and the other was the mounting, shrill criticism from conservatives and business. In 1934 the Court gave some evidence that it might approve the New Deal program. That year the justices upheld Minnesota's moratorium on mortgage payments and a New York law that provided for the fixing of milk prices. In the first case the latent power of the state in an "emergency" was involved, and in the second the Court expanded its conception of what could be done in the "public interest." Yet these were state statutes, and the vote on both was a narrow 5 to 4.

In January, 1935, the administration found that it was in trouble with the Supreme Court. Then, in *Panama Refining Co. v. Ryan,* the justices invalidated section 9 (c) of the National Industrial Recovery Act, which empowered the President to stop the interstate transportation of oil produced or stored in excess of state conservancy and price-boosting regulations. The Court reasoned in this 8-to-1 decision that section 9 (c) had not provided sufficient standards to guide or restrict the executive. In the Gold Cases, however, the Court, motivated largely out of fear of "the dislocation of the domestic economy," narrowly upheld Congress's nullification of the gold clause in public and private contracts.

Thus far neither the New Deal's pride nor its program had been seriously injured. That would change during May, however. Early that month five of the justices found the Railroad Retirement Pension Act unconstitutional. On May 27, "Black Monday," the Court unanimously invalidated the whole National Industrial Recovery Act, the Frazier-Lemke Farm Mortgage Act, and Roosevelt's removal of a member of the Federal Trade Commission. In *Schecter v. United States* the justices contended that the power delegated under the recovery law to make regulatory codes had been done without setting the legally necessary limits on either the President or industrial groups. As Justice Cardozo wrote, "This is delegation run riot." The mortgage statute, the Court next declared, violated the Fifth Amendment by authorizing the surrender of a mortgagee's property without just compensation. In *Humphrey's Executor v. United States* the justices held that the President's ouster power was confined to officers in the executive departments, not independent agencies such as the Federal Trade Commission.

Roosevelt had taken the Panama decision calmly and, of course, had willingly accepted the favorable verdict in the Gold Cases. The Supreme Court's May decisions, however, had dealt a blow to his prestige and his plans for the future. He was aware that the invalidated legislation had been sloppily drafted and therefore was an inviting target to the justices. Moreover, he had not favored the Frazier-Lemke Act and was sensitive to the fact that N.R.A. not only had lost its steam and impact but had become, under Hugh Johnson, an administrative nightmare. Yet substantial amounts of his power had been wiped out, and the implications for the future of the Court's actions were clear. Four of the justices—Pierce Butler, James McReynolds, George Sutherland, and Willis Van Devanter—were unalterably opposed to extension of the federal government's power over the economy, and two others, Owen Roberts and Chief Justice Charles Evans Hughes, were probably unwilling to go far in that direction. The remaining three—Louis Brandeis, Benjamin Cardozo, and Harlan Fiske Stone—were more liberal but obviously had minds of their own. It was a matter of simple arithmetic that led the President to conclude that he could not count on the justices for more favorable decisions. Although he might have been relieved to be out from under N.R.A. as such, still it seemed to Roosevelt that the Schecter case had turned the nation back to a "horse-and-buggy" interpretation of the Constitution on economic affairs. For the time being, he would stress that point to the country and hope for a turn for the better on the Court. He would also seek effective legislative ways to repair the damage done by the justices.

Also by May, 1935, business criticism of the New Deal reached a high pitch. The United States Chamber of Commerce denounced Roosevelt's program then, and that was the crowning blow after all the President believed he had done to assist and appease business. He was by then open to advice from the ultraliberals and radicals in the administration and Congress. And he needed advice, for it seemed that since January he had been drifting without a clear conception as to what direction his administration should take. The Supreme Court decisions of May 27 served as the catalyst. Now something had to be done, and quickly, to replace the legislation that had been struck down. The President had already been moved by progressive and farmer-labor arguments that he must respond more vigorously to America's human needs, but Black Monday galvanized him into action. In June, while Congress was on the verge of ending its session, Roosevelt demanded enactment of five "must" laws. These were social security, which had not yet been passed, the Wagner labor bill, a tax measure, and regulation of banking and of public-utility holding companies. Congress had its work cut out for it during that summer of the "Second Hundred Days."

The social-security bill was pushed through quickly. That was also true of the National Labor Relations Act, which was sponsored by Senator Robert F. Wagner, of New York. The Wagner bill provided for creation of a board to determine labor bargaining units and to keep management from violating the list of unfair labor practices specified in the bill. Neither Roosevelt nor Labor Secretary Perkins had supported the measure, yet in the middle of May the Senate, responding to organized labor's urgings, passed it overwhelmingly. That and the invalidation of N.R.A.'s labor provisions prompted the President to change his mind and bestow his blessing on Wagner's bill. Congress approved the bill late in June, and Roosevelt signed it into law on July 5.

The National Labor Relations Act gave labor unions a firm legal foundation, by recognizing their right to be bargaining agents for workingmen in labor-management disputes. It also legally defined unfair practices in labor relations, including employer-sponsorship of company unions, the refusal of management to negotiate with employee bargaining agents, and the firing of workers for trade-union membership. The National Labor Relations Board was created to certify labor's bargaining representatives and to sit in judgment on charges of unfair practices. The Wagner Act plainly opened the door wider to union organization of America's industrial workers; it gave workingmen the weapons necessary to raise wages, improve plant conditions, and protect themselves from employer harassment. It also put labor almost solidly in the New Deal's camp during the 1936 elections. What the law did not do was to curb abuse of its provisions by labor leaders or generate industrial peace. Yet the gains for workingmen were substantial and long overdue. Labor was now in a position really to combat business authoritarianism.

Roosevelt had earlier thrown his support to drastic regulation of utility holding companies. In June, 1935, however, he reinvigorated his efforts as it became clear that the power-and-light lobbyists were waging the fight of their lives against regulation. The battle centered on the provision inserted in the bill, at the President's insistence, that any utility holding company that could not justify its continuance would be dissolved by the

Securities and Exchange Commission after 1939. In June the Senate approved the "death-sentence" clause by only one vote. The House rejected it in July, however, by a seventy-vote majority, providing instead that S.E.C. would have to justify any dissolution order. Despite mounting evidence that the utility-company lobbyists were using extreme means, including the forging of names to protest telegrams and bribery, the House stood its ground. The administration was forced to compromise. Yet the resultant Public Utilities Holding Company Act, passed in August, was a stringent measure. The law abolished utility holding companies that had more than one company level between them and operating utility firms. Moreover S.E.C. was authorized to oversee the finances of holding companies and to initiate dissolution of any holding company that was not operating in the public interest. Thus were the nation's utility companies brought under effective public regulation.

Roosevelt had less of a victory in the Wealth Tax Act of 1935. Pressed by a variety of liberals and radicals, and perhaps feeling vindictive against business, he called for increased inheritance taxes, a levy on gifts, a graduated corporation-income impost, and a bigger bite out of large personal incomes. Although the President was initially strong in urging action, he flagged in the course of seeing the measure through Congress. It took strenuous work by Senator Robert La Follette, Jr., and his band of Progressives to force action that summer. And the opposition was heavy, for this was a bill that would reach into the pockets of every big-business man and investor in the country. They had the resources and the interest to struggle against this proposal of what they increasingly called the Raw Deal. Not only were many representatives and senators responsive to plutocratic cries of outrage, but some congressmen were deeply moved to save their own fortunes from federal tax collectors. Congress approved a pale copy of the original tax bill in August. The inheritance tax had been deleted, and instead the impost on gross estates was somewhat increased, as were federal levies on gifts, capital stocks, and large personal incomes. The graduated corporate-income tax was established, but at low rates. Altogether the Wealth Tax Act expanded revenue by only about $250,000,000, far from enough to balance the budget, and even less by way of redistributing either the nation's wealth or its tax burden. Nevertheless Congress had passed a tax for social as well as revenue purposes. Despite the law's mildness, most wealthy Americans were incensed by Roosevelt's support of it. He had drawn their unquenchable enmity, and not without reason, for there were more taxes to come.

The other major administration measure passed that summer was the Banking Act. Roosevelt played little more role in its enactment than tardily to endorse the proposal, which was the brainchild of Governor Marriner Eccles, of the Federal Reserve Board. Eccles's objective was centralization of the nation's banking and monetary system in the executive branch by giving the President greater and bankers less control of the Federal Reserve System. Starting in February, 1935, Eccles waged war almost alone in support of his proposal, against the staunch resistance of a vast array of private bankers and even administration elements. Then in June Roosevelt made the measure a "must" bill. Considering the stiff opposition, Eccles got more than he should have in the final measure. The Banking Act provided for a presidentially appointed Federal Reserve System Board of Governors. The new board's powers were greatly expanded. They included the right to approve the designation of the main officers of regional federal-reserve banks and the granting of more authority over rediscount rates, the reserve requirements of the system's regional banks, and open-market operations. The statute also eased the basis upon which federal-reserve banks could lend funds to member private banks and provided for almost universal membership in the system by requiring state banks to join by the middle of 1942 if they wanted to be protected under the federal deposit-insurance plan. The act fell short of what Eccles wanted, but it greatly forwarded government control of banking and monetary operations and thus contributed vitally to the stability of the nation's economy during the following generation.

The Second Hundred Days came to an end on August 27, with the adjournment of Congress. The impact of the legislation was great and would be felt for a long time to come. Congress and the executive branch had interacted in the ultraliberal atmosphere of 1935 to establish a national social-security system, lay the foundation for more equitable settlement of labor questions, break the stranglehold of public-utility companies, strengthen the nation's banking, credit, and currency system, and experiment with taxation as a social policy. There is no doubt that this represented a change from the policies of 1933 and 1934. Indeed the change seemed so clear that it was not long before observers formulated elaborate arguments distinguishing a First New Deal of 1933–1934 from a Second New Deal of the years following.

Certainly, the emphasis on planning in 1933 and 1934 was less evident later. The early dominant New Dealers urged that competition had to be subdued and by developing cooperation among large economic units with increased federal guidance. This philosophy was at work especially in the National Recovery Administration, the Agricultural Adjustment Administration, and the Tennessee Valley Authority. By 1935, however, the so-called neo-Brandeisians came into prominence in the New Deal with their ideas—updated from those of Justice Brandeis —of breaking up the economy into manageable units and reintroducing competition but with rules of fair play that would be enforced by a vigilant federal gov-

ernment. To a certain extent this is what happened.
Obviously, the New Deal planners were being subordi-
nated, and the neo-Brandeisians were gaining more
influence.

Other things were happening, however. The early
dominance of easterners, and especially conservatives,
was fading, and the newer breed of progressives from all
over the country was exercising greater influence.
Although many Progressives and Farmer-Laborites sympathized with parts of the neo-Brandeisian program, they
had plenty of ideas of their own, particularly in terms
of vesting more power in the federal government to
achieve the people's needs. If the neo-Brandeisians were
more consistent and more in agreement among themselves in their goals, the Progressives and Farmer-
Laborites commanded a far greater voter base. Yet,
despite their influence, neither the neo-Brandeisians nor
the Progressives nor any of the diverse political factions
in the United States alone represented the public will.
Consequently, President Roosevelt, as the focal point
of pressure, was besieged from the outset by a variety of
forces that demanded a wide range of actions. None of
these elements dominated public policy. For example,
in 1935 the neo-Brandeisians got what they wanted in
the Public Utility Holding Company Act, but they had
to have the assistance of other forces to see it enacted.
The Social Security Act was influenced by a wide range
of groups. The Wagner Act was basically the contribution of an uncompromising senator and of organized
labor. The tax law must be credited largely to Senator
La Follette, and Senator Huey Long was just as influential in aiding its passage as were the neo-Brandeisians.
Of course, the Banking Act attracted support from a
number of groups, especially the planners.

Then there was Roosevelt, the experimentalist of
experimentalists. In April, 1933, he told a press conference that as a political quarterback he never knew what

the play after next would be. "If the play makes ten yards, the succeeding play will be different from what it would have been if they had been thrown for a loss." He had no coherent ideology. His concern was to find the right combination of ideas and personalities to make his administration a success. He had no rigid conception of what his program goals should be except the pursuit of recovery, the provision of relief, and later the social-welfare reforms that the public demanded. And those were all to be accomplished within the framework of capitalism and representative democracy. The quarterback, to use Roosevelt's football metaphor, had to have a variety of plays and of players in order to win. With this in mind it becomes clear that some of the old plays had to be modified or abandoned and some of the veteran players sidelined. New plays and players gave the presidential quarterback more flexibility than ever, and they presented an even less consistent pattern than before. The so-called First New Deal had not been of a whole, mixing as it did a variety of conservative, moderate, liberal, and even radical ideas. If there was less of the conservative and more of the ultraliberal in the so-called Second New Deal, it was no less a mixture. It threw a number of new approaches in with the old ones, all of which did not add up to an overall program, much less an ideology.

Both of the supposed New Deals, however, did represent the diversity of thought and interest in American society, and logically so given the nature of the nation's political structure. Moreover, as President Roosevelt was the prime focus of pressure, so he was only *primus inter pares* in originating action in the government. The New Deal was not Roosevelt alone, for it included a large group of federal officials of different and changing ideas and abilities. It would also be folly to ignore Congress's contribution to the formulation of government policy. The administration frequently took its cues from members of Congress and was also subject to their sometimes independent, collective actions. Finally, it must be remembered that the national scene was fluid. The frequently arising new situations cried out for new approaches, just as earlier failures demanded fresh attempts at solving problems. The country's temper was changing, which the response of the Roosevelt Administration and Congress mirrored.

If there is any legitimate distinction between 1933–1934 and 1935–1936, it is in terms of the people wanting additional and more effective government action, even if it was somewhat different from that of the first two years of the New Deal. The subordination of planning and the increased interest in regulated competition was secondary to that. The long-term result would be a mélange of policies and programs that was so reflective of Roosevelt's pragmatism and the diversity of interests and influences in America during a time of great crisis.

10

A Breathing Spell and a Landslide

THE intense activity of the Second Hundred Days had borne other fruits than legislation. The pressures behind the President's "must" bills had irked many members of Congress with one another and with the White House. Moreover, the 1935 legislation had converted big business's dislike for the New Deal into alienation and even hatred. There were also rumbles of rebellion among conservative Democrats. Indeed by August rumors were circulating that former presidential nominees Alfred Smith and John W. Davis, Governors Albert Ritchie, of Maryland, and Eugene Talmadge, of Georgia, and former Secretary of State Bainbridge Colby were considering launching a "Jeffersonian Democratic" party to oppose the New Deal. It seemed time for Roosevelt to placate the forces on the Right, at least for the time being. Roy Howard, the head of the Scripps-Howard newspaper chain, wrote the President in late August that legitimate businessmen believed the New Deal was hostile to them. Howard suggested that business fears be allayed "through the granting of a breathing spell to industry, and a recess from further experimentation." Roosevelt replied defending his administration, but in a conciliatory fashion he added that his basic program to combat the depression "has now reached substantial completion, and the 'breathing spell' of which you speak is here—very decidedly so."

A presidential election year was coming up, and Roosevelt had done his bit to respond to the demands of progressives and ultraliberals. Now he was trying to whittle down opposition on the Right. This he planned to carry over into his policies in 1936. Moreover, Roosevelt was personally not inclined toward much more action, and he gradually acceded to Treasury Secretary Morgenthau's pleas to limit federal spending. Indeed early in 1936 the President urged the heads of emergency agencies to keep spending in line and reduced their allocations. Yet his maneuvers were not succeeding. Both the Left and the Right accelerated their attacks on him. The Gallup poll indicated in January that a bare half of the people was on the New Deal's side, and Roosevelt's foes increasingly spoke of their ability to defeat him. In seeking a new stratagem, he came up with the idea of doing little but of talking about it militantly. Thus he might woo both the Right and the Left.

The President's January message to Congress was a diverting performance. In an effort to put the United States in a favorable light he commented on the growth of dictatorships abroad and the possibility of war in other lands. Then he lashed out at "entrenched greed" and warned of attempts at home on the part of the "resplendent economic autocracy" to recapture power and enslave the people. Yet what Roosevelt outlined by way of a program was obviously a concession to business: A balanced budget was on the way, relief appropriations should soon be reduced, no new taxes should be needed. There was no word of legislation to expand the federal government's power.

This is what the President would have stuck with, except for two occurrences. One derived from the Supreme Court and the other from Congress. In January the Court struck down the Agricultural Adjustment Act in *United States v. Butler,* ruling that the processing taxes were unconstitutional because they were not levied for the general welfare but to regulate the activities of one class. The justices also directed the government to return the $200,000,000 in taxes collected from processors of farm products. Congress later added to the administration's financial plight by approving, over Roosevelt's veto, immediate bonus payments of almost $2,000,000,000 to veterans. Consequently, the White House felt forced to repair the damage through two pieces of legislation that it had not earlier expected to request.

The first bill was designed to rush aid to agriculture, which was both an economic and, in an election year, a political necessity. The vehicle was a measure that combined the Department of Agriculture's interest in furthering soil conservation with a new benefits program for farmers. This was the Soil Conservation and Domestic Allotment Act, which offered payments to farmers for substituting soil-enriching crops, such as soybeans and clover, for crops that impoverished the land. Because the main commodity surpluses were corn, cotton, tobacco, and wheat, which depleted the soil, the law would also ostensibly work to control agricultural production. Despite a flurry of charges of "communism," "regimentation," and "unconstitutional," Congress, also looking toward the upcoming election, approved the measure rapidly.

The administration's other pressing need was to meet the drain on the treasury occasioned by the Butler decision and the passage of the veterans-bonus law. It was a Hobson's choice for Roosevelt, for he had to enter the election campaign with either a monumental deficit or increased taxes, neither of which would please the voters. He decided to ask for higher taxes, but not higher income taxes, which would damage his political appeal and reduce the mass-consumer purchasing power so essential to sustaining the modicum of economic recovery that had been achieved. What the Treasury Department recommended was a tax on undistributed corporate profits. That levy would do one of two things: (1) subject idle corporate funds to taxation or (2) force corporations to pass on their profits to investors, thereby freeing more money for economic circulation and increasing the income of the wealthy that was subject to the income tax. This tactic would increase federal revenues by an estimated $1,300,000,000 plus whatever taxes would be gained from new business generated by the heightened spending and investing of money. The revenue bill would further alienate the rich, but that was better politically for the New Deal than irritating ordinary citizens who could less well afford a tax boost and who controlled more voting power.

Roosevelt liked the idea of an undistributed corporation-profits tax and in March suggested it to Congress. The opposition stiffened as the bill was thrashed out in legislative committee rooms. It was argued that the tax would rob corporations of their reserves for times of economic decline and would force them into the clutches of bankers when they needed cash. The battle shifted back and forth for weeks. What finally emerged, in the Revenue Act of 1936, was a compromise that increased regular corporation taxes and placed a nominal tax on undistributed corporate profits. The enmity of big business toward the administration was, of course, intensified. Yet, although Roosevelt did not get all he wanted, economic activity was sparked, federal revenues were increased, the deficit was reduced, and the principle of the undistributed corporation-profits tax was established.

Only one other significant piece of legislation was enacted before the congressmen adjourned in June to prepare themselves for the elections. This was the Walsh-Healey Act, which originated with Labor Secretary Frances Perkins and was designed to fill some of the gaps left by the invalidation of the National Industrial Recovery Act. The new law applied N.R.A. standards of hours, wages, and working conditions to businesses having contracts with the federal government. As such it not only was a forerunner of the Fair Labor Standards

Act of 1938 but set a precedent for later requirements that government contractors not discriminate in hiring on grounds of race, religion, and national origins.

Altogether in 1936 the federal government's activity was not as dramatic or as important as during the preceding three years. Not only had there been a "breathing spell," but economic indicators showed that the country easily took in its stride this hiatus in New Deal dynamism. The average earnings of full-time employees in all economic sectors continued to creep upward, from $1,056 in 1934 to $1,164 in 1936. During those years the percentage of the unemployed dropped from 21.7 to 16.9, and for the first time since 1931 their number dipped below 10,000,000. Labor-union membership climbed from 3,088,000 to 3,989,000. Bank assets mounted from $55,900,000,000 to $66,800,000,000, the value of new construction rose from $6,700,000,000 to almost $10,300,000,000, and the business-failure rate per 10,000 firms dropped from 61 to 48. Corporation receipts increased from $99,000,000,000 to $126,000,000,000, and farm receipts rose from $6,800,000,000 to $8,700,000,000. Yet between 1934 and 1936, the national debt climbed from one new record high to another, from $27,000,000,000 to $33,800,000,000, and the number of federal civilian employees jumped from 698,649 to 867,432, which surpassed the previous peak during World War I.

Politically, there were both security and danger for the New Deal in these trends. On the one hand, they gave proof of a slowly continuing advance toward recovery; on the other hand, the evidence was overwhelming that the United States was still in dire economic trouble and that the great change in federal fiscal policies had not worked an economic miracle. It was clear by 1936 that the President's popularity was slipping somewhat. In January Elmo Roper's *Fortune* public-opinion survey showed that 60.8 percent of his sample favored Roosevelt's reelection. By April the figure stood at 60.1 and by July at 59. The Gallup poll in January recorded only 51 percent inclining toward Democratic senatorial candidates. By no means did the election seem a sure thing for Roosevelt and the Democrats.

Nevertheless the thunder on the Left was subsiding. The Communists were curtailing their attacks on President Roosevelt. The Socialists found that he had attracted much of their depression-inflated following. Indeed 1936 was a year of continuing defections from the Socialist party, not only of its rank-and-file but also of some of its New York leaders who helped found the American Labor party as a way to remain radical but yet support Roosevelt for reelection. The Farmer-Labor Political Federation had largely given way to a new organization that it had sponsored in 1935, the American Commonwealth Political Federation. The two groups called for the formation of a farmer-labor-intellectual party in 1936 based on the principle of "production for use instead of for profit." They did not expect to win the Presidency in 1936, but they did anticipate electing a large delegation to Congress. Their hopes were high well into 1936, but by the time their convention met in late May, they found that their plans to assemble a coalition of radicals for the forthcoming election campaign had failed. Socialists and Townsendites refused to cooperate; the Communists, who had been pointedly excluded from the convention, had launched their own united-front movement; sentiment for third-party action within the Farm Holiday Association had fallen off rapidly after the death of its leader, Milo Reno; and the Wisconsin Progressive and Minnesota Farmer-Laborite leadership had decided not to take a chance on jeopardizing Roosevelt's reelection. As Governor Floyd Olson said, a national farmer-labor presidential candidacy might draw enough votes from Roosevelt to lead to the election of a "fascist Republican." The convention consequently could do no more than urge support for sympathetic congressional nominees. Thus America's radicals seemed to have no choice but to embrace the President's campaign for reelection or to back the weak Socialist or Communist parties.

A new possibility soon presented itself, however. That was the Union party, which was hastily put together in June. Senator Huey Long, in 1935, had been considered a major threat to the two major parties, with his swashbuckling promises to guarantee every American a home, an automobile, a minimum annual wage of $2,500, and an old-age pension. His program had had considerable appeal to many of the poor and the jobless. When the Louisianan was assassinated in September, 1935, it was a matter more of relief than of sorrow to national Democratic leaders. Yet Long's Share-Our-Wealth movement was kept alive, if only barely, by its chief organizer, the Reverend Gerald L. K. Smith, who was able to arouse some rabble by invoking Long's memory and stirring up religious and racial hatred. This gave Smith the organizational basis for an alliance with another angry man of God, Father Charles E. Coughlin. The Michigan priest had gained prominence by his skillful use of the radio in commenting on political and religious affairs and his early role as a defender of Roosevelt's policies. By 1935, however, Coughlin had broken with the President and developed his own organization, the National Union for Social Justice. What his group promised was jobs for all at "a just and living annual wage," nationalization of banking, utilities, and natural resources, a fair profit for agriculture, protection of unions, and rigid control of currency and credit through a federal central bank. There was, too, the occasional flavor of anti-Semitism in Coughlin's statements. Also among the political *nouveau riche* was Dr. Francis E. Townsend, who argued that an old-age pension of two hundred dollars per month would not only take care of the needs of the elderly but also put enough money into circulation to bring back national prosperity. His old-age-pension movement claimed to have the support of millions of Americans. If Townsend was not a bigot, he was just ambitious and radical enough to support a new political party. The fourth ingredient in the Union party was a veteran agrarian leader, Congressman William Lemke, of North Dakota, who served as the party's nominee for President. Lemke had become increasingly dissatisfied with the New Deal's policies, which he believed did not go far enough to assist farmers or to bring money, credit, and banking to heel.

Coughlin brought these four dissident elements together in the Union party. The party's platform was, on the face of it, a reasonable farmer-labor document. It called for control of money and credit through a government central bank, federal refinancing of farm and home mortgages, a guaranteed annual wage, guaranteed cost of production plus a profit for farmers, a decent old-age-security program, disavowal of foreign entanglements, expanded public-works programs at the prevailing wage, and limitation through taxation of inheritances and annual net incomes. In any logical analysis the Union party seemed to have a good chance to scramble the American political scene. Townsend was a dignified and, on the whole, reasonable man who led a popular movement. Coughlin also headed a national movement and commanded a vast weekly radio audience. His status as a Catholic priest would supposedly appeal to many Americans. Smith and Lemke were less well known and had less support, but nevertheless it was possible that the extremely gullible and frustrated might follow Smith and that Lemke might appeal to the millions who sympathized with the farmer-labor approach. Yet the Union party was a superb example of a situation where the sum of the whole equaled less than its parts.

The ultraliberal *Nation* declared that the Union

party had combined "under one banner all the major crackpot movements America has seen in the past decade." *Common Sense,* the organ of the American Commonwealth Political Federation, described the party's leaders as "fascists," "demagogues," and "Jew-baiters." Socialist Norman Thomas asserted that it was "a union of two and a half Messiahs plus some neo-Populists." It was clear from those comments that the party of Coughlin, Lemke, Smith, and Townsend would be too much to swallow for most of those to the left of Roosevelt. As it further turned out, many of Coughlin's admirers could not accept Smith's Protestant fundamentalism, nor could many of Smith's crowd stomach an alliance with a Catholic priest. Lemke's farmer-laborites were usually unable to accept the authoritarianism and clericalism of Coughlin and Smith, and they had grave reservations about their sincerity, or at least Smith's, on economic reform. As for Townsend, he always seemed uncomfortable with his Union party comrades, and his followers refused to allow the Townsend organization to endorse the party, largely because they were not eager to alter the American economic system except to provide security for the aged.

In short, the Union party was a grouping of contradictory programs and basically incompatible leaders. Most of their individual followings knew that and were repelled by it. Moreover, as much as many Americans might flirt with radical programs during the 1930's they were unlikely to vote for them, especially when Roosevelt had brought substantial relief and a modicum of recovery and reform. Shocked by the alliance of Coughlin, Lemke, Smith, and Townsend, the opposition to them rallied largely behind Roosevelt. It was plain that the great majority of Americans during the 1930's preferred to fight their political battles within the traditional two-party framework.

The chief opposition to Roosevelt and the New Deal

in the 1936 elections therefore was the Republican party. Yet this party was a collection of contradictions, too. They included those like former Pennsylvania Senator Joseph Grundy, who harked back to the laissez-faire system, Herbert Hoover, who wanted his own program given another chance, and William Allen White, who wanted to take the best of the New Deal, some of Hoover, and a large part of traditional progressivism in order to make what he thought would be a sound national program. And there were men like Senators Willam E. Borah and Gerald P. Nye who had their own brands of ultraliberal reconstruction for America. The party's self-confidence also varied from faction to faction and even from day to day. On the one hand, the Republicans had seen Roosevelt's popularity decline since 1935 to the point where they might have a chance to defeat him; on the other hand, they sensed his recuperative powers in politics, and they often doubted their ability to rise from the thrashings they had taken in 1932 and 1934.

Although there was no stampede for the Republican presidential nomination, several leaders were interested in gaining it. The most prominent contender for the nomination was Alfred M. Landon, the only Republican governor reelected in 1934. The forty-eight-year-old Kansan had been an able governor, bringing about reform and maintaining essential services while balancing his state's budget. Like the President, Landon was no ideologue. He was conservative in fiscal matters, moderate on state services and labor, and liberal on agriculture, civil rights, and conservation. He had twice bolted his party, once to work for Theodore Roosevelt's Progressive party and later, in 1924, to help manage William Allen White's gubernatorial campaign against the Ku Klux Klan. Landon had also made a name for himself in fighting to limit the power of utility interests and major oil companies. Unlike Franklin Roosevelt, he was not a charismatic figure. He was sometimes fumble-fingered in public speaking and never electrifying, and neither in dress nor in appearance did he stand out in a crowd. What set him apart was that he had been politically successful when few Republicans had been, and he had a record of accomplishment that might appeal to a variety of voters.

Among the other active competitors for the Republican nomination was another former Bull Mooser, the flamboyant publisher of the Chicago *Daily News,* Colonel Frank Knox, His political position could be described as consisting of a jigger of progressivism, a cupful of Hooverism, and two cupfuls of anti–New Deal spleen. Then there was the veteran Idaho senator, William Borah, who offered a variety of economic reforms, none of which had been acceptable to either the Hoover Administration or the New Deal. Arthur H. Vandenberg, who had been reelected to the Senate from Michigan in 1934, made it clear that he would accept the nomination on the basis of a program that leaned more toward Hoover than Roosevelt. There were also a half-dozen favorite sons and Herbert Hoover himself, who everyone believed would be happy to have another chance to run for President.

Employing an excellent publicity campaign and doing nothing to offend any major Republican faction, Landon remained the leading contender for the nomination. When the Republican convention opened in Cleveland on June 9, 1936, however, it was plain that the party was far from harmonious. A battle among the various elements on the platform committee raged throughout the first three days of the convention, and indeed the proceedings were delayed a day before the committee came to agreement. The patchwork-quilt platform that finally emerged was only barely acceptable to most of the delegates. One thing that the great majority of Republicans could enthusiastically agree upon

was its fierce indictment of the New Deal as an administration that had "dishonored American traditions and
flagrantly betrayed the pledges upon which the Democratic party sought and received public support." The
platform favored protecting the Supreme Court as the
bulwark of constitutional rights against legislative and
executive "encroachment." Exalting "free enterprise,
private competition, and equality of opportunity," the
document promised the removal of hindrances to business's ability to expand and therefore to provide jobs
for the unemployed. Until that was accomplished, there
would be federal grants to permit the states, and them
alone, to administer relief. The Republicans called for
old-age pensions, financed by a special tax on a "pay-as-
you-go" basis, and state unemployment-insurance programs. Labor was to be guaranteed the rights of organization and collective bargaining, and farmers were
promised a many-faceted program to increase sales of
agricultural commodities, encourage soil conservation
and crop diversification, and meet their financial needs.
The Republicans pledged effective regulation of business
practices in the public interest and restoration of the
merit system in federal civil service, which had been
"virtually destroyed by New Deal spoilsmen." The party
also demanded a balanced budget, a flexible tariff, sound
national currency, and equal opportunity and safety for
Negroes. The platform plainly took the Republicans to
the left of their 1932 position.

The convention then turned to nominations. Much
maneuvering had gone on in an effort to form a coalition against Landon, but it was beached on the shoals of
disagreement as to who would be nominated in his
place. There was also a rising fear that if Landon were
defeated, Hoover would be chosen instead, which none
of the avowed candidates for the nomination wanted.
Unable to agree upon an alternative to the Kansas governor, most of his rivals surrendered just before the

voting began. On the first ballot Landon received 984 votes to 19 for Borah. Afterward a serious problem arose from the fact that Landon and his allies had not agreed on a vice-presidential nominee. The governor inclined toward a dissident Democrat, particularly Lewis Douglas, but found that unacceptable to his advisers. Therefore, he largely left the matter of a running mate in his associates' hands. They decided on Vandenberg, but by the time they reached him, he had declared himself unavailable. Landon's aides then turned to Frank Knox, who was unanimously nominated for Vice-President.

The Democrats had few of the problems that the Republicans had. They knew who their nominees would be for President and Vice-President, and their platform would largely be dictated by the White House. Yet the Democrats had qualms. The polls did not give them enough of an edge to feel that they could win without a struggle, and there was constant worry early in 1936 that a third party might come along that would eat disastrously into their support. Then, too, the continued talk of prominent conservative Democrats refusing to back Roosevelt was bothersome. There was certainly no doubt that the Republicans would be excellently financed by outraged business, banking, and industrial interests. It was also possible that the more the economy improved, the less voters would feel that they needed the New Deal. For the Democrats the fight was not to be in their convention, but apparently in the following election.

The Democratic national convention met in Philadelphia late in June. The draft platform, which had been prepared in the White House, was altered only slightly by the resolutions committee. It easily won the approval of the delegates. The document blamed the Republicans for twelve years of "surrender to the dictatorship of the privileged few," a period that had left America "sorely stricken in body, mind, and spirit." The Democratic party prided itself on having restored the people "to the places of authority" and reviving in the people "the hope which they had almost lost." The party promised to continue its drive "to end the activities of malefactors of great wealth." The consumer was promised fair value for what he bought. Rural electrification would be extended, as would the government's housing programs. Labor, agriculture, and legitimate business would remain protected and prosper. Unemployment relief would be granted where needed, antitrust laws would be vigorously enforced, and the civil-service merit system would be extended. The budget would be balanced and the national debt reduced as soon as possible. In brief, the Democratic platform was a pledge, lovingly embroidered with shibboleths, to continue the pragmatic spirit of the New Deal in dealing with the nation's problems.

Conservative Democrats had given President Roosevelt only token opposition in the primary elections. His nomination by acclamation in the convention was no more than a formality, and John Nance Garner was renominated for Vice-President. The convention's high point was Roosevelt's acceptance speech before 100,000 people in Philadelphia's Franklin Field. Although he made some conciliatory gestures toward business, most striking was his indictment of the "economic royalists" who wanted a "new industrial dictatorship" established in America. Roosevelt also roused the crowd with his assertion that "this generation has a rendezvous with destiny," a destiny to do great things. That was a rendezvous he intended to keep.

The platforms had been adopted and the nominees chosen. Now came the campaigns. The Democratic and Republican campaigns were cut from quite different fabrics, for the depression had wrought great changes in the two parties. The Republicans had lost much of their Negro, labor, and agricultural support and even some small-business backing. Moreover, the shift in urban political loyalties to the Democrats, first clearly seen in 1928, had been accelerated during the 1930's. Although the Republicans could still draw on the coffers of the wealthy for campaign funds, they had lost federal patronage and had few state and local resources at their command. Also they had lost greatly in public prestige. The Republican party had only added the support of so-called Jeffersonian Democrats like Alfred Smith and John W. Davis and had reconstructed its leadership so that it reflected Main Street more than Wall Street. With all this in mind, Governor Landon planned a strenuous campaign to restore the party at least to national respectability.

Landon, Knox, and the new Republican national chairman, John D. M. Hamilton, made national speaking tours. They endeavored, with some success, to put new life into the party's shriveled state and local organizations. Often the leadership took to the radio, and almost daily they held press conferences. They flooded the nation with political advertising and rallied their key supporters to speak out publicly. Landon's campaign emphasized his positive and progressive viewpoints. He was the first major-party presidential nominee to appeal directly to black voters. He forthrightly denounced racial prejudice and religious bigotry. He contradicted one of his leading backers, publisher William Randolph Hearst, by condemning a loyalty oath for teachers. He was enthusiastic for conservation, drought relief, and aid to tenant farmers, indeed aid to all farmers. Landon stressed that labor had nothing to fear from him and that unemployment relief and old-age pensions would be given to the needy. He promised to balance the federal budget. That would not be done, however, by depriving any American of the assistance he needed, but by "cutting out waste and extravagance" and the political use of public funds. He also offered "hardworking, pains-

taking, commonsense administration" that would eschew
constitutional shortcuts and the perpetuation of a government so big and powerful that it threatened democracy in America. Furthermore, by operating a well-
administered, soundly financed government and by
avoiding what he charged were Roosevelt's divisive tactics,
Landon declared that the government could foster legitimate and speedy business expansion and thereby provide the economic growth necessary to attain recovery and
full employment.

Landon's generally reasonable campaign was, however,
offset by the shrill charges of Knox, Hamilton, Hoover,
and other Republicans and the Jeffersonian Democrats
that the New Deal was leading the nation down the path
toward dictatorship. They also accused the Roosevelt
Administration of unconstitutional behavior and the
erosion of the people's character. These charges were
seldom relieved by constructive discussion of how the
Republicans would put the country back on its feet
again or avoid the New Deal's excesses. Even Landon in
the last days of the campaign indulged increasingly in
negative criticism of the administration. The overall
impression was that there were two Republican parties
in the field, one requesting an opportunity to run the
New Deal right, the other waging a crusade against any
form of the New Deal.

The Democratic effort rested more on organization
than on the campaigning of its national ticket. Although
the administration's forces had only about nine million
dollars in campaign funds, compared to fourteen million
for the Republicans, it was used effectively in publicizing
the Democratic ticket, its accomplishments, and its
promises. Far more important was the vastly superior
manpower available to the administration's campaign
forces. Thanks to being in power in Washington and
in most places over the country, the Democrats had an
unusually large group of appointed and elected officials

who knew what to do to retain their jobs. These office-holders feverishly plunged into the business of telling voters the good news of the New Deal. National Committee Chairman James Farley again did a masterful job of gearing party groups and officeholders to the exigencies of the campaign. Indeed many civil servants and relief workers helped the party, although some of them were under pressure to do so. The Democrats also used auxiliary groups to rouse the voters. These organizations included Labor's Non-Partisan League, the Roosevelt Agricultural Committee, the Progressive National Committee to appeal to independent and Republican liberals, and the Good Neighbor League to attract intellectuals, Negroes, religious leaders, and women. Such groups mirrored the diverse elements in the coalition that Roosevelt had put together since 1932. Their effectiveness demonstrated that the coalition was not a myth.

Roosevelt himself, of course, was the keystone of the Democratic campaign. He was a leader who could make the people feel that he knew their problems, hopes, and aspirations and, equally important, that he intended to do something about them. He was no Jeremiah, for he believed that problems could be solved, if not in one way, then in another. He recognized that he could be guilty of sins of omission (sins of commission were exclusively reserved for his opponents), but he appeared willing to make up for them. His sense of humor made him seem human, and it nicely balanced his aristocratic accent and manners. He had also found a scapegoat in big business and the Republicans for the depression, and it was a believable scapegoat the way he pictured it.

Roosevelt contented himself with "nonpolitical" tours and overseeing political strategy-making until late September. Even then his campaigning before the election did not range widely, for he gave only a handful of speeches. In them he chiefly reiterated the New Deal's record and renewed his pledge to serve as the champion of the forgotten man and the enemy of the "forces of selfishness." The President also occasionally twitted Governor Landon for promising to lower federal spending and yet to continue a large-scale program of government services. As Roosevelt said, "You cannot be an old-guard Republican in the east, and a New Deal Republican in the west. You cannot promise to repeal taxes before one audience and promise to spend more of the taxpayers' money before another audience."

If Roosevelt's aim at his chief opponent's apparent campaign inconsistency was accurate, so Landon in late October was on target when he pointed out that the President had not specified what he was going to do if reelected. On issue after issue, the Kansas governor asked, "What is the President going to do?" and answered correctly, "No one can be sure." It was clear to him—since he got no response from the chief executive—that Roosevelt was asking the voters to issue a blank check to the New Deal. Especially pregnant with meaning was Landon's question as to whether the President would try to change the Constitution to authorize what he was doing, "or will he attempt to get around the Constitution by tampering with the Supreme Court?" With that the Republican nominee had lifted the curtain on the major issue of 1937.

Of course, Landon's probing questions made no difference. Roosevelt's popularity had been shooting upward since September, and the Kansan knew that he was fighting a losing campaign. The election results were even worse than the most pessimistic Republican had envisioned. Plainly the President symbolized what the great majority of Americans wanted. Roosevelt polled 27,752,000 votes to 16,680,000 for Landon, who carried the electoral votes of only Maine and Vermont. It was one of the biggest election landslides in American history. Not only were the Republicans buried, but William Lemke and the Union party received only 882,000 votes, and Norman Thomas and Earl Browder, running respectively for the Socialist and Communist parties, attracted far fewer votes than in 1932. The Wisconsin Progressives and Minnesota Farmer-Laborites again won their states, but partly by virtue of stressing their cooperation with President Roosevelt. The Democrats further extended their great majority in Congress, as the number of Republican representatives dropped from 103 to 89 and of senators from 25 to 16. The New Deal could understandably conclude that it had won a popular mandate for continuation of its policies.

11

A Mandate for What?

THE electorate had overwhelmingly approved the New Deal, but for what was the election victory a mandate? At most, the voters had called for more Rooseveltian experimentalism in seeking recovery, relief, and reform. How the President would go about these things was largely a mystery, for he had outlined no program for future action. In effect, as Governor Landon had suggested, Roosevelt had been issued a blank check. The two related questions to be raised were for what he would ask in trying to cash it and whether his requests would be honored.

President Roosevelt believed that the people had given him approval to extend government operations further in their behalf. In his inaugural address on January 20, 1937, Roosevelt asserted that the country could not afford to heed the voices of comfort, opportunism, and timidity. America must take the road forward. "I see one-third of a nation ill-housed, ill-clad, ill-nourished." These needs, he declared, had to be met, for their existence offended the nation's "common ideals."

In late 1936 and early 1937 administration officials and their congressional allies were preparing legislative proposals to raise standards of living in the United States. Especially prominent were measures to set national standards for maximum work hours and minimum wages and to expand public housing. The people had been stirred by Roosevelt's inaugural address and expected him to spotlight a wide-ranging number of legislative proposals aimed at improving the nation's quality of life. Few anticipated what he was to emphasize early in 1937 in his program—judicial reorganization.

Roosevelt had become increasingly irritated with the Supreme Court's invalidation of New Deal measures. Moreover, he had not had the opportunity to appoint new justices and saw no possibility to do so in the near future. He believed that the country's ability to right-order itself would remain too low unless changes were made in the Court. Early 1937, he concluded, was the time to act, directly after his overwhelming reelection and while the Democrats had more than a three-to-one majority in Congress. The President formulated his plans to restructure the Supreme Court in secrecy. Indeed it was not until the morning before he sent his special judiciary message to Congress, February 5, that legislative leaders were informed of his intentions. In the message Roosevelt asked for legislation that would authorize him to name additional justices, up to a maximum of six, in the event that already sitting justices served beyond the age of seventy years and six months. He requested the same power in the lower federal courts, with a maximum of forty-four new appointments. This plan, he said, would keep the courts in step with the times through a "systematic addition of younger blood" and would allow the judiciary to keep up with its work load.

Roosevelt's proposal for judicial reorganization created the greatest controversy of the decade, and it proved to be his biggest political mistake. He not only underestimated the public's veneration for the Supreme Court but had overestimated his strength on Capitol Hill. He erred in not consulting congressional leaders, many of whom were outraged by his obvious lack of confidence in them. Moreover, his timing was flawed, for 1937 was the sesquicentennial of the Constitutional Convention, and many of the widespread celebrations that were planned were easily converted into defense meetings for the Court. What the President had succeeded in doing was to create a coalition against his proposal consisting of those who considered the Supreme Court the last line of defense against the New Deal, those who approved of the New Deal but refused to alter the judicial system, those who favored Court reform but believed Roosevelt's plan unwise, and those in Congress who were irked by the President's failure to consult them. Furthermore, to many Americans, the proposition that a judge over age seventy could not function in the public interest seemed specious, especially since two of the oldest justices, Brandeis and Cardozo, were those most sympathetic to Roosevelt's programs.

Everything went awry for Roosevelt on the judicial-reorganization bill. Congressional Republicans generally kept quiet, letting the Democrats fight it out among themselves. Justice Van Devanter's resignation in May gave support to the contention that the President would soon be able to appoint enough of his own men to change the Court's character. Moreover, the Supreme Court's decisions swung toward approval of reform legislation. The justices upheld the Washington state minimum-wage law in March, the Wagner Act in April, and the Social Security Act in May. Consequently, it was doubtful by May that the White House commanded enough votes to pass the judicial-reorganization bill, yet the administration persisted in the hope that the tide might change in Roosevelt's favor. Another blow came in July, however, with the death of Joseph T. Robinson, the Senate majority leader and Roosevelt's champion on the Court issue in the upper chamber. With Robinson's removal, the court-reorganization forces immediately collapsed, and the bill was recommitted on July 22.

The President later asserted that although he lost the battle over judicial reorganization, he won the war. At best, that is only partially true. The threat to the Supreme Court in his reorganization proposal probably softened opposition on the bench to administration measures. Indeed from 1937 on the justices were to sustain all of the New Deal's economic legislation. Yet the new trend was also probably supported by the fact that the measures coming before the Court were generally better drafted than had been true in 1935 and 1936. Moreover, in making their decisions some justices might have been impressed by the popular support registered for the New Deal in the 1936 elections. It is also said that by going on the offensive, Roosevelt heightened pressure on the older justices to resign, a problematical conclusion at best. Nevertheless by 1940 Brandeis, Butler, Cardozo, Sutherland, and Van Devanter had retired. Thus, Roosevelt was able to appoint a majority to the Supreme Court.

Yet even if the President won the war, he paid a high price. There were serious defections from the Roosevelt coalition among both citizens and members of Congress. Many liberal Republicans and independents who had gone along with him in the past now came to distrust him. Moreover, his support among Democrats declined, partly because of the prestige he lost in being defeated on judicial reorganization and partly because deep wounds had been inflicted in the bitter fight which would never completely heal. The President had pushed too far and too hard. He would never again command the confidence among the middle class or even congressional Democratic leadership that he had before 1937. The results of this were readily seen in what happened to the rest of Roosevelt's legislative program in 1937. By trying to alter the balance between the executive and judicial branches, he lost his opportunity to launch a massive new program of economic and social reform. As historian William E. Leuchtenburg has observed, "The new court might be willing to uphold new laws, but an angry and divided Congress would pass few of them for the justices to consider."

Contributing to that anger and division was the rash of labor troubles that erupted during 1937. Despite the protection offered by the National Industrial Recovery and Wagner acts, the American Federation of Labor did little to recruit unskilled and semiskilled workers. Nevertheless some labor leaders, such as John L. Lewis of the United Mine Workers, pressed for unions composed of all workers in a given industry. When in 1935 the A.F.L. refused to accelerate its efforts or to grant better than second-class status to such industrial unions, leaders from the garment, textile, and typographical unions joined Lewis in forming the Committee for Industrial Organization to foster unionization of unskilled and semiskilled workers. A.F.L. leadership retaliated in 1936 by suspending their unions from the national organization. In turn, the suspended unions established the independent Congress of Industrial Organizations and initiated large-scale recruitment of industrial union members and increased labor pressure upon the Roosevelt Administration for economic reforms and labor benefits. C.I.O.'s vigorous participation in the 1936 election campaign in behalf of Roosevelt unsettled many conservatives and moderates, but that was as a light spring rain compared to what was to come.

It became clear in 1937 that the C.I.O. was firmly dedicated to unionizing unskilled and semiskilled workers. The first big battle was over the organization of workers at General Motors. The employees used the new tactic of the "sit-down" strike, occupying a plant for six weeks in order to gain General Motors' recognition of their union, the United Automobile Workers. Using traditional union tactics and the threat of the sit-down strike, C.I.O. affiliates made further advances by the end of 1937 in organizing the automobile, steel, rubber, electrical, textile, and farm-implements industries. This gigantic C.I.O. drive was largely responsible for increasing the number of labor-union members in the United

States from four million in 1936 to seven million in 1937. This was only the beginning, too, for by 1944 that number had doubled. More important, the C.I.O. as a result of its organizing, bargaining, and political activities had contributed hugely—perhaps more than any other force in America—to the improvement of job security, wages, and working conditions.

The rapid growth of unions and their spread throughout industry disturbed many middle- and upper-class Americans who saw their profits and status being jeopardized by the rise of a force that could fight effectively for a better share of the nation's wealth. They were further antagonized by the use of labor tactics that unsettled the economy's tranquillity. The number of work stoppages because of labor-management disputes had increased almost steadily between 1930 and 1936, from 637 to 2,172, but in 1937 they rose to 4,740. Moreover, although both workers and civil authorities usually disciplined themselves, there was enough violence involved in industrial disputes to scare many citizens into thinking that America was on the verge of wholesale disorder. Certainly, those who were better off in society usually took sit-down strikes as a form of violence, against property, if not persons, by alienating it from use by its owners.

Roosevelt was caught in the middle of all this. He refused to interfere, contending that labor, management, and the public would learn much from this season of struggle. Those lessons, he believed, would teach moderate ways of gaining industrial stability and equity. His was probably the statesmanlike approach, but it drew widespread condemnation. Business often charged that Roosevelt failed to do his duty by not restraining the more vigorous union activities, especially sit-down strikes. C.I.O. President John L. Lewis dramatically criticized him, saying, "It ill behooves one who has supped at labor's table . . . to curse with equal fervor and fine impartiality both labor and its adversaries when they become locked in deadly embrace." Labor and progressives had a further complaint, against Roosevelt's policy of reducing federal expenditures by paring the number of relief recipients and public-works employees after the 1936 elections. And Republicans and conservatives, far from being pleased with the President's attempts to balance the budget, declared that the reductions proved that Roosevelt had used relief and public-works appropriations to help gain reelection.

It all added up to further political trouble for the administration, for industrial strife supplied another reason for conservatives to oppose Roosevelt and made liberals and moderates less tractable. By the summer of 1937 an informal coalition of Republicans and conservative Democrats emerged in Congress. Its aim was, as Democratic Senator Josiah Bailey, of North Carolina, averred, to make a stand for "Constitutional Representative Government as opposed to mass Democracy," or, according to Republican Senator Vandenberg, to avoid losing "America to the mobs or to the Fascists." Although the composition and effectiveness of this coalition varied from time to time, it became an important force in Congress and seriously hampered the domestic programs of both Presidents Roosevelt and Harry S. Truman. The growing independence of congressional liberals and progressives added further to the New Deal's problems.

The consequences were often seen in the work of the House and the Senate. For example, liberals had been trying for years to obtain authorization for a massive program of public housing. Senator Robert Wagner, who was the congressional leader of this movement, introduced in February, 1937, a measure calling for one billion dollars in long-term federal loans for financing self-amortizing housing to be built by a United States housing authority. To Wagner's dismay, the President delayed endorsing the bill and instead subjected it to a round of analysis by interested federal agencies. Roosevelt's and Treasury Secretary Morgenthau's attempt to finance public housing largely with federal grants, which would greatly reduce the amount of housing that could be built, was staunchly opposed by labor, public-housing experts, and, of course, Wagner. In July the President decided to support the bill, largely to appease its powerful backers. The Wagner-Steagall Housing Act was passed in August, but only after a strenuous congressional battle that led to the appropriation for housing loans being halved to $500,000,000. It was plain by summer that the White House had few strings on either the more liberal or the more conservative elements on Capitol Hill.

It is worth noting in passing that the Wagner-Steagall Housing Act worked no miracles. Indeed by the beginning of 1941 only 350 housing projects were completed or in progress. The measure, however, did commit the government to try to clear away slums and to erect adequate housing for the lower economic class. For better or worse, public housing was an established federal program, one that would grow considerably in size and remain controversial. Over the decades it provided improved shelter for millions of citizens. But it also too often failed to supply as many new housing units as the old ones it replaced, thereby uprooting hundreds of thousands of Americans from inadequate homes and forcing them to live in worse. More often than not, social planning for the new housing complexes was poor, the location no improvement, the architecture appalling, and the quality of construction open to serious criticism. What was wrong was not so much the intentions behind federally sponsored housing as the fact that the program was usually carried out with inadequate thought.

If President Roosevelt did not get what he wanted from Congress in the housing act, he got most of what he requested in the Farm Tenancy Act of 1937, which was acceptable to most congressional factions. This legislation provided for loans to sharecroppers, tenants, and other agricultural workers to help them buy farms of their own and to farmers who needed rehabilitation. The measure also authorized the creation of some decent camps for migratory workers and established the Farm Security Administration to replace the fumbling Resettlement Administration. F.S.A. distributed over one billion dollars by 1942. If the new agency did not revolutionize rural life in America, it did assist tens of thousands of tenants to obtain their own farms and relieved the plight of migratory farm laborers. The great majority of F.S.A.'s loans were repaid, which testified further to its success and, of course, gratified the watchdogs of the national purse in both Congress and the treasury. What F.S.A. did it did well, but it was not financed well enough to do a thoroughgoing job of easing rural poverty.

Beyond the housing and farm-tenancy acts, Congress in 1937 enacted no other significant domestic legislation. Roosevelt failed to gain passage of a number of "must" items. The two most important among these were proposals to regulate labor's wages and hours and to reorganize the executive branch. After Congress adjourned in late August, the President decided to call a special session. In this five-week session, which met in November and December, he hoped that the legislators would be more responsive. They certainly had plenty of grist. Roosevelt again requested executive reorganization and a law to establish standards for minimum wages and maximum hours of work. He also asked for a new agricultural price-support program to help maintain farmers' purchasing power, liberalization of Federal Housing Authority requirements to stimulate more privately built housing, and a regional planning act creating "seven little T.V.A.'s." He got none of what he wanted, thereby suffering even a bigger rebuff than he had during Congress's first session in 1937.

Meanwhile another problem forced its way into the picture, one that caught both the public and the administration unawares. That was the recession of 1937–1938. Fissures began to appear in the economy in August. By December *The New York Times* business index fell to its 1935 level, dropping from 110 to 85. Two million people lost their jobs, and the stock market suffered a minor panic. Business inventories mounted. Widespread wage cuts were reported, farm income dipped, and relief rolls expanded, although the amount of relief available was insufficient to handle all those in need. There were two prime causes of the recession. First, business had not made the most of its opportunities to expand, partly because it was reluctant to take chances and partly because it lacked confidence in the government. If capital went "on strike" against the New Deal, as many observers charged, it was equally true that business had been made gun-shy by seven years of depression. Second, federal policies contributed. The administration's recent concern to avert inflation and to bring expenditures more in line with revenue led to severe cuts in relief and public-works allocations. And not only did Washington reduce its efforts to prime the pump, but the collection of some two billion dollars in social-security taxes drew off a considerable amount of money in economic circulation. Neither business nor state and local governments were willing or felt able to fill the gap.

This economic setback led to a grand debate within the administration and over the country as to what to do. While the words flew, however, almost everyone to the left and right of the President agreed that Roosevelt was largely to blame for the new economic crisis. He had invited reprobation, since he had often and grandly taken credit for whatever recovery had been

achieved since he took office. His critics remembered
well his 1935 statement that "yes, we are on our way
back—not just by pure chance, not by a mere turn of
a wheel in a cycle; we are coming back soundly because
we planned it that way." Few commentators failed to
remind him of those words. If his reputation for political infallibility had been badly tarnished during the
Court fight, so the recession robbed the President of his
claim to economic infallibility.

Worse was that Franklin Roosevelt really had no
answer to the recession. Aides like Treasury Secretary
Morgenthau pressed him to cut federal expenditures
and seek a balanced budget in order to retrieve business confidence and stimulate investment. Others like
Marriner Eccles and Harry Hopkins asked the President
to prime the pump with heightened relief and public-
works spending. Still others urged going beyond additional expenditures. Leon Henderson, of W.P.A., Assistant
Attorney General Robert Jackson, and Interior Secretary Ickes contended that the artificial price structure maintained by monopolies as well as monopolies
themselves had to be broken up. Some businessmen and
former National Recovery Administrator Donald Rich-
berg demanded planning along N.R.A. lines. Roosevelt
listened to all of them but seemed a prisoner to lassitude.
His requests to Congress for farm subsidies and the
spurring of more private housing construction marked
the limit of his positive thinking, and they were not
approved. He told his Cabinet, "Everything will work
out all right if we just sit tight and keep quiet." Morgenthau was obviously the winner in late 1937.

The economy did not respond to inaction. Yet the
President's public statements still revealed indecision.
In his January 3, 1938, message to Congress, Roosevelt
promised to deal with the monopoly issue. The next
day, however, he told the press that he favored some
sort of a new N.R.A. Later he affirmed Henry Morgen-

thau's statement that he was "just treading water . . . to see what happens this spring." The old verve was missing, and Roosevelt was unable to disguise his indecisiveness. He was suffering both from not knowing what to do and from battle fatigue. His self-confidence had been severely jarred by congressional intransigence, adverse reaction to industrial strife, and the recession. Furthermore, as shall be seen later, his ventures in foreign policy toward the end of 1937 had met with largely hostile reaction. The New Deal's Napoleon was, for the time being, afflicted with timidity.

Yet Roosevelt had to go on. He was committed to bills left over from 1937, and with his approval, new proposals were wending their way from the executive agencies to Congress. Although not an antirecession program, all this constituted a considerable set of positive recommendations for legislative action in 1938. Thus, in January and February Roosevelt requested a new farm price-support law, maintenance of W.P.A. appropriations, expansion of the F.H.A., executive reorganization, and minimum wages–maximum hours legislation.

The Soil Conservation and Domestic Allotments Act of 1936 had failed to support agricultural income adequately, largely because of lack of cooperation from farmers. Congress and the White House were met with a variety of proposals for action, including new versions of the McNary-Haugen scheme as well as Agriculture Secretary Henry A. Wallace's ever-normal granary plan to buy surpluses in high-yield years and to market them in years of low farm production. Legislators readily agreed that something had to be done about agriculture, but because no faction was dominant in Congress, the predictable result was a compromise measure. The agricultural-adjustment bill was the first important law passed in 1938, and it was rushed through the House of Representatives. The Senate was a different story, however, for it was delayed in acting by a filibuster over the

Wagner–Van Nuys antilynching bill until February 21. Roosevelt felt on the spot. With his support the antilynching bill might become law, for the House had already approved it, and the measure's sponsors in the Senate were optimistic. Yet if he backed the bill, whether it was enacted or not, the resultant ire of southern members of Congress might jeopardize his entire 1938 legislative program. The President's decision was to let Senators Wagner and Van Nuys do what they could, sensing that they would probably fail without his support. Fail they did, and Negroes lost their best chance to that time to secure federal sanctions against the crime of lynching. All Roosevelt lost was time, for the antilynching forces did not significantly blame him for his aloofness, and the southern congressional group was considerably appeased.

The antilynching bill disposed of, the Senate acted promptly to pass the new farm measure. The Agricultural Adjustment Act of 1938 authorized the payment of subsidies to those corn, wheat, cotton, tobacco, and rice growers who restricted their acreage and who used prescribed soil-conservation practices. Loans were also provided for surplus corps to be stored, as Secretary Wallace wanted, for sale on the market during years of low production. The act also approved crop insurance for wheat, the buying of farm surpluses for relief distribution, and research to facilitate better commodity marketing. Although the new agricultural measure helped support farm income and made soil conservation a permanent federal program, it failed to balance production and demand. Farm surpluses continued to grow. Only the coming of World War II, with its insatiable demand for agricultural commodities, prevented collapse of America's farm economy.

The bill to liberalize the Federal Housing Administration's operations was enacted in March, 1938. That and a change in the agency's leadership stimulated the investment of private funds in home construction and contributed somewhat to combating the effects of recession. In June, with only partial White House support, the Food and Drug Administration secured legislation providing for some federal control over the advertising of drugs. It was, however, no more than a start in the direction of regulating the widespread deception of the public by the drug business in its advertising and marketing practices. Congress also passed the Civil Aeronautics Act, which extended federal regulation over the continuously growing and controversial business of flying.

Far more important was the minimum wages–maximum hours legislation. This presidential proposal had been fought to a standstill in 1937 by entrepreneurs, who wanted no federal regulation, and by labor, which wanted more regulation than was provided for in the bill. Finally, after meeting some of labor's objections, but exempting domestic, farm, and maritime workers, Congress approved the measure in June. The Fair Labor Standards Act established the minimum wage for workers in interstate commerce at twenty-five cents an hour and was to be raised by 1945 to forty cents; the maximum workweek was set at forty-four hours, to be reduced to forty hours by 1940. The law also banned the employment of minors in nonagricultural work. Although the statute was shot through with exemptions, it effectively turned the tide against sweatshop conditions, which had been increasing since 1935, and outlawed most industrial child labor. Almost immediately, the wages of 300,000 workers were raised, and the workweek of 1,300,000 was shortened. Millions of other laborers were benefited as the law was more efficiently enforced and later expanded in its provisions and the categories of workers covered.

Thus far Roosevelt had not devised an antirecession program, although the F.H.A. amendments and the labor-standards and agricultural acts tended to buttress the economy. Unemployment by March, 1938, stood at four million above the level of early 1937, and business and the stock market continued to wind down. Late in March administration liberals pressed the President further to increase government spending and to act against monopolies. Roosevelt decided in April to follow their advice on expenditures. He asked Congress for additional funds for relief agencies, public works, and public housing. The pressure on Congress to act, especially in an election year, was strong, and in June Roosevelt in effect got what he requested, $3,750,000,000 for relief and economic pump-priming.

Emboldened by Roosevelt's acceptance of a spending program, Robert Jackson, of the Justice Department, again urged the President to deal with monopolistic price practices. Jackson was successful, and late in April Roosevelt asked Congress to authorize an investigation of monopolistic tendencies in the economy. The result was the prompt creation of the Temporary National Economic Committee composed of members of Congress and administration officials. Although the T.N.E.C. probe produced a mountain of information about big-business practices during its eighteen-month lifetime, its work led to little action. Roosevelt at heart was not opposed to bigness in business as such, nor was there any commitment on the part of a congressional majority to do anything about what T.N.E.C. revealed. Yet the antitrust elements in the government were willing to take things into their own hands, and they were dedicated enough to do so regardless of what Roosevelt thought. In 1938 Thurman Arnold, the new assistant attorney general who headed the Justice Department's antitrust division, launched a drive that resulted in the largest number of prosecutions under the Sherman Act during one administration. Despite Arnold's vigorous application of the antitrust statute, the results at best only dented monopolistic practices. His crusade proved the law's basic ineffectiveness and showed that some other approach was needed to curb the harmful effects of big-business operations. Neither the nation nor its government, however, was ready for action that would drastically alter its economic structure. In fact, because of mammoth governmental support of business during World War II, large corporations expanded their domination of the economy, although they were forced to become more amenable to federal regulation and advice. The Roosevelt Administration in effect confirmed the corporations' economic hegemony while working to make it more palatable to the public and to guarantee the people's share in the dividends of the interaction between business and government. For a generation after T.N.E.C. and Thurman Arnold, few people seriously questioned the system.

The year 1938 was not entirely one of legislative success for President Roosevelt. Republicans and conservative Democrats joined with such liberals as Marriner Eccles and Harry Hopkins to support elimination of the undistributed-profits tax as a way to encourage economic activity. The resulting Revenue Act of 1938 almost emasculated the undistributed-profits tax and gave other tax concessions to corporations and the rich. Roosevelt had threatened to veto the bill if the undistributed-profits levy was dropped; that alone saved what little remained of the tax. As it was, the President indicated his disfavor of the new law by letting it go into effect without his signature.

The great blow to Roosevelt in 1938 was the defeat of his executive-reorganization plan, which asked for little more than had similar proposals of Harding and Hoover. The measure encompassed expansion of the White House staff, extension of the merit system in the civil service, substitution of a federal personnel director for the Civil Service Commission, establishment of Cabinet-level de-

partments of public works and social welfare, consolidation of independent agencies with executive departments, and the strengthening of government accounting
and auditing. Opposition to the proposal in 1937 had
been quiet. In 1938, however, reorganization was widely
viewed as an attempt to subvert "constitutional government." As with the judicial-reorganization proposal of
the preceding year, the President had miscalculated
badly. Americans were becoming increasingly sensitive
to the rise of dictatorships abroad and were determined
not to lay the foundations for authoritarianism in the
United States. Some of these people feared that Roosevelt would use increased executive power to entrench
himself in office; others did not fear Roosevelt, but expressed concern that some future President might use
expanded executive power to establish a dictatorship.
Of course, many Republicans and the growing band of
antiadministration Democrats opposed executive reorganization just because it was sponsored by Roosevelt.
Many other congressmen believed that the measure
would, for no good reason, transfer some of the legislative branch's prerogatives to the President. Other legislators feared that the effectiveness of the independent
agencies would be reduced if they lost their independent status. In short, the many individual facets of Roosevelt's executive-reorganization proposal expanded the
number of opponents just as much as they gave rise to
the charge that the sum of the parts made it into a
"dictator bill." Whatever the reasons, or their validity,
the House of Representatives recommitted the proposal
in April, 1938, by a vote of 204 to 196. The President's
prestige was further damaged. He had considerably lost
influence in the Senate in 1937; now it was clear that he
could not count on the huge Democratic majority in
the House.

Plainly, the nation was returning to politics as usual.
The President could no longer expect the extraordinary

cooperation he had received before 1937. As it was, however, the 1938 session of Congress had been fairly cooperative. Despite Roosevelt's defeat on executive reorganization and, in effect, on the Revenue Act, and the
dilution of other measures, he had obtained a new comprehensive farm act, the Fair Labor Standards Act,
authorization for T.N.E.C., and the F.H.A. amendments.
None was revolutionary, but the President had not proposed anything revolutionary. In retrospect 1938 appears
a satisfactory legislative year for the White House. Roosevelt did not see it that way, however. He was determined
to obtain a more pliable Congress; in trying to do so,
he made another great political miscalculation.

Roosevelt felt that Congress had betrayed the voters
who had elected it. He had been doing what he thought
the voters in 1936 had directed him to do. Congress had
been given the same mandate but had not taken it
seriously. The people wanted action, he believed, not
reaction. Therefore, the President undertook to purge
the Democratic party of reactionary elements in the 1938
elections. He had been tugged in this direction by his
son, James, Harry Hopkins, and Harold Ickes, who
wanted both greater party regularity and liberal control of the 1940 Democratic national convention. This
group and its allies took it upon themselves to lash out
against conservative Democrats and to support liberals
against them in primary elections. Initially, the President remained aloof from this. After the adjournment of
Congress, however, he committed himself publicly to
the campaign against his party's "Copperheads." He
followed this up with a tour in which he backed men
like Senators Alben Barkley, of Kentucky, and Elmer
Thomas, of Oklahoma, for renomination and opposed
Senators Walter George, of Georgia, "Cotton Ed" Smith,
of South Carolina, and Millard Tydings, of Maryland.
Barkley and Thomas were renominated, which they
probably would have been without Roosevelt's inter-

vention. In his attempts to defeat conservative Democrats, however, the President was largely frustrated, winning only against New York's John O'Connor, the chairman of the House Rules Committee.

Again Roosevelt had blundered. His targets were usually too strong. Moreover, his campaign was labeled a purge, which played into the hands of those who portrayed him as tending toward dictatorship. Indeed in August, 1938, the Gallup poll indicated that 50 percent of the people believed that Roosevelt's policies had increased the possibility of a dictatorship in America, compared with 37 percent the previous October. He also misjudged the country's political leanings. The tide of recession had turned by the summer of 1938. Many voters, however, blamed the President for the recession, and others were willing to seek more conservative ways to achieve recovery.

The 1938 elections demonstrated that Roosevelt had overestimated both liberal sentiment in the United States and his own personal appeal. The Republicans gained 14 governorships, 7 seats in the Senate, and almost doubled their number of House seats, rising from 89 to 164. They were again a force to be reckoned with. And that was not all, for the Minnesota Farmer-Laborites and the Wisconsin Progressives lost in their states. Of course, the Democrats still controlled most of the statehouses and held a large majority in Congress, but the New Dealers would never again have the support they had commanded during their first six years in office. The administration had had both too much and too little success. In going as far as it did in building a strong government, the New Deal had scared many voters and collided with the interests of others. Yet the administration, for all its efforts, had not reached the goal of recovery. Large numbers of Americans believed that it was time to try something else, although none wanted to jeopardize the economic gains of the past six years.

Something else did develop, which had economic as well as political ramifications, but the stimulus for it came from beyond the borders of the United States. President Roosevelt had done little about foreign relations during his first term in office. In 1933 he had bluntly rejected international economic cooperation and had shown little public concern for the rise of Adolf Hitler's National Socialist dictatorship in Germany or the doings of Fascist Italy and militarist Japan. The League of Nations was of no interest to the New Deal. The administration had tried to mend fences with Soviet Russia and Latin American nations, largely to expand trade, but the results failed to match expectations.

Roosevelt's most positive policy was directed toward Latin America, although he started off on the wrong foot. The President had resisted pressure to intervene in Cuba when the Machado dictatorship was overthrown in 1933, but he refused to recognize the government of Dr. Ramón Grau San Martín, and the Fulgencio Batista regime took over instead. From there on, however, it was New Deal policy to avoid interference in the domestic affairs of other American countries. Roosevelt and Secretary of State Cordell Hull outspokenly repudiated the right of United States armed intervention. In 1934 the administration withdrew the remaining marines in Haiti, and Congress repealed the Platt amendment, which had given the United States the right of military intervention in Cuba. That same year the Senate ratified an inter-American convention that bound its adherents to the statement that "no state has the right to intervene in the internal or external affairs of another." Other agreements were approved to submit western-hemisphere disputes to conciliation or arbitration, and steps were taken to encourage goodwill among the nations of the Americas. President Roosevelt's trip to Buenos Aires for the Inter-American Conference of 1936 was taken as further evidence of his intention to be the "good neighbor" he so frequently talked about. Especially noteworthy was the administration's fostering of better trade relations with Latin America under the terms of the Trade Agreements Act of 1934. This Good Neighbor Policy made for goodwill between the United States and other American states. Equally important, it also released the Roosevelt administration from much of the pressure to entangle the United States in Latin American matters.

Of course, Roosevelt was aware of what was going on beyond the western hemisphere. He was appalled by the reports of repression and brutality coming from Germany and maintained great suspicion of Japanese expansionism. He talked with his associates about ways to cope with these threats to world peace, but he knew his administration could do little. America's military strength was skeletal, and there was little interest in the country for developing a voice in world affairs. The United States and its people were also geographically isolated. No nation within three thousand miles posed any immediate threat to its security, and most Americans were little acquainted with even their immediate neighbors—Canada, Cuba, and Mexico. Moreover, few American leaders had any significant experience in foreign affairs, and the corps of professional diplomats was small and exercised little influence.

All these were the traditional elements that had hampered the development and execution of United States foreign policy. Because of them the nation had relied far more on idealism and enthusiasm than on knowledge and experience in the conduct of foreign affairs. Yet there were other, special factors that contributed significantly to America's reluctance to involve itself in foreign matters during the 1930's. The severity of the depression riveted the attention of the vast majority of Americans on domestic issues. The fact that it was an international depression drastically loosened trade ties with other countries, one result of which was the economic isolation of the United States to a greater extent than had been true for a generation. Furthermore, the rise of authoritarian governments and nationalism abroad caused further deterioration of America's weak political links with other nations. This was particularly seen in the lessening American interest in the League of Nations and international disarmament. Then, too, there was a hostile domestic reaction against the almost universal cancellation of the debts of foreign governments to the United States. This sentiment was formalized in 1934 with the passage of the Johnson Act, which forbade the making of American loans to foreign governments that had defaulted on their debt payments.

There were also a swiftly growing popular conviction that the United States had been duped into entering World War I and an increased resolve to avoid at all costs entering another war. This was fanned to white-hot fervor by the investigations of the Senate's Nye committee in 1934, which pinned the blame for America's entry into the world war on bankers and the "merchants of death," munitions manufacturers. Pacifist and noninterventionist sentiment was at such a high pitch that Congress, the following year, undertook to pass legislation to ensure America's neutrality in future wars. The imminence of armed conflict between Ethiopia and Italy further spurred the administration and Congress to act. What Roosevelt and Secretary Hull wanted was a measure that would allow the United States to stop the sale of weapons to an aggressor. Congress, however, thought that this meant taking sides in a war. Consequently, the Neutrality Act of 1935 forbade Americans to sell arms to any belligerent country. The law also prohibited American ships from carrying weapons to or for a belligerent state and authorized the President to warn United States citizens that they could travel only at their own risk on vessels of belligerents. Persons who manufactured, exported, or imported arms and munitions were required to register with the Secretary of State and to obtain licenses for each of their export and import transactions. The Neutrality Act was a compromise, for it neither contained all the limitations proposed by strict noninterventionists nor gave Roosevelt the discretionary authority he desired on arms shipments to victims of aggression. The law was also an interim measure, valid only to the end of February, 1936, directed at preventing the President from acting as he saw fit while Congress was in adjournment.

When Italy invaded Ethiopia in October, 1935, Roosevelt immediately proclaimed America's neutrality and enforced the provisions of the Neutrality Act. He further announced that any kind of American trade with the two warring nations would be entirely at the risk of the businessmen involved. They could expect no protection from the government of the United States. Cordell Hull soon placed a "moral embargo" on shipments of all commodities to the belligerents in excess of normal exports. In taking their positions, the President and the Secretary of State supported the economic sanctions that the League of Nations placed upon Italy without getting the United States entangled in what Geneva was doing. Neither the League's sanctions nor Hull's "moral embargo" were really effective, however, for most nations were willing to let Italy do what it wanted in Ethiopia. When Congress met again in 1936, it resumed consideration of neutrality legislation. Roosevelt was often accused of flirting with the League and of attempting to favor Ethiopia against Italy, which contributed to the successful drive for extending the neutrality law. The new legislation continued the provisions of the original act and also forbade loans to belligerent powers.

The happenings of 1936 overseas further steeled the resolve of Americans to avoid foreign entanglement. Italy conquered Ethiopia, although only after a stiff fight. Hitler renounced the treaty of Versailles and marched his troops into the Rhineland in defiance of the treaty, which brought only whimpers in response from Germany's former conquerors. General Francisco Franco and his Nationalists plunged Spain into a state of bitter civil war. Germany and Italy pledged their collaboration in the defense of Europe against communism and in their policies toward Spain, which suggested future joint intervention in favor of Franco. Soon afterward, Germany and Japan signed an agreement to cooperate in the international containment of communism, to which Italy adhered in 1937, thus laying the foundation of the Axis alliance of World War II.

In reaction, American leaders at best could talk only generally of the desirability of peace and arms reduction. And, at that, they did not talk too often. During the 1936 election campaign Roosevelt made only one foreign-affairs speech and Landon two, none of which went much beyond platitudes that would accommodate the nation's noninterventionist feeling. That sentiment was dramatically measured. Public-opinion polls registered 71 percent for a national referendum to decide whether America could at any time go to war and 82 percent to prohibit the manufacture and sale of arms for profit. Seventy percent believed that the United States had erred in entering World War I, and 95 percent opposed the country's involvement in another world war.

The American antiwar feeling was so strong that when the Spanish civil war erupted, President Roosevelt applied the Neutrality Act to the conflict, even though it was an internal struggle. He also asked Congress to approve his action by amending the law to apply to

civil wars, which it did with alacrity in January, 1937.
What Roosevelt, and many others in the United States
and abroad, feared was that the Spanish conflict would
soon involve other countries and lead to a second world
war. He was right in the first respect, for Germany and
Italy gave open support to Franco's rebels, and Russia
assisted the Spanish Loyalists. Indeed people from all
over the world became involved in this staging area for
World War II, including hundreds of Americans, most
of whom fought for the Loyalists. The Spanish conflict
did not expand into another world war, however, for
no leading power was yet willing to go to war with
another, at least not over Spain. Yet in foreign affairs
the United States Government's biggest mistake of the
1930's may have been to apply the Neutrality Act to
Spain. With access to America's financiers and weapons'
suppliers, the Spanish Government would have had a
better chance to defeat Franco and to blunt or delay
further aggression by the forces of international fascism.
As it was, the Loyalists held out for almost three years,
thereby giving the world's anti-Fascist movement further
time for development.

American public opinion continued to be overwhelmingly noninterventionist in 1937. Japan's invasion of
China during the summer of 1937 seemed to confirm
the appropriateness of this course. In April Congress
had passed another neutrality act, which indefinitely
extended the provisions of the earlier legislation. The
statute additionally forbade Americans to travel on belligerent vessels and, for two years, allowed the President
discretionary power to prohibit the carrying of any commodities to or for a belligerent in an American ship.
Congress thereby eliminated most of the ways in which
private American citizens could involve the United States
in a foreign war. The legislators, however, had also indicated that the United States would do nothing to stop
aggressor nations, except to mutter "tsk-tsk," so long

as they did not violate American soil. Bolstering this impression were the administration's efforts to prevent Americans from visiting war zones and the increasing support being mustered on Capitol Hill for the constitutional amendment sponsored by Democratic Representative Louis Ludlow, of Indiana, that would require a national referendum before the United States could declare war, except in case of an attack on the United States.

The adverse reaction to Roosevelt's one positive 1937 statement on foreign affairs further illustrated America's determination to remain uninvolved. During a swing around the country to survey the effects of the economic recession, the President delivered an unexpected foreign-policy speech on October 5 in Chicago. There he condemned war and declared that the United States could not afford to proceed alone in an increasingly hostile world. He proposed that the peace-loving nations join together to "quarantine" warlike states before the contagion of aggression got out of hand. One of Roosevelt's aides, Samuel I. Rosenman, observed that "the reaction to the speech was quick and violent—and nearly unanimous. It was condemned as warmongering and saber-rattling." Judge Rosenman may have exaggerated, but there is no doubt that the American people were unprepared to tread the path indicated by the President. War-referendum forces grew, congressmen growled, and anti-interventionists took the quarantine speech as evidence of a major turn in Roosevelt's thinking. Promptly he turned back. He refused to tell a press conference precisely what he had in mind, saying that whatever it was, he was just·"looking for some way to peace; and by no means is it necessary that that way be contrary to the exercise of neutrality."

Roosevelt was more successful in his efforts to maintain the nation's defenses, particularly the navy, which he regarded as America's first line of defense. During his first term he used public-works funds for new naval construction, and between 1935 and 1939 the total number of Americans under arms rose slowly, from 251,799 to 334,473. The President asked for acceleration of the building of naval vessels in 1937. This request was met with a sizable outcry that he was plunging the United States into a naval armaments race with Great Britain and Japan. Yet he got most of what he wanted to enlarge the navy and keep it up-to-date. Roosevelt was also able to procure funds for a modest expansion of the army and naval air components. The point is that he could obtain outlays for defense because those nationalists who opposed American involvement abroad were willing to join with the small band of internationalists in Congress in order to construct a defense against possible external threats to American security. Moreover, Roosevelt was careful not to go too far in his requests, thereby keeping defense-minded anti-interventionists on his side.

The situation began to change slowly, almost imperceptibly, at the end of 1937. Despite the neutrality legislation, there was one place where the United States was vulnerable to incidents, and that was China. American trading vessels and warships were in Chinese waters. Indeed United States gunboats patrolled the Yangtse River to offer protection to American citizens and interests there. On December 12, Japanese warplanes sank one of the gunboats, the U.S.S. *Panay,* and attacked Standard Oil tankers on the river. The United States Government demanded compensation and an apology for the "indiscriminate bombings" of the American ships; Tokyo responded by sending its regrets and promising to pay a suitable indemnity. That exchange basically settled the incident as far as the two governments were concerned, but it did not end reaction in the United States.

The administration was sharply criticized for allowing American ships to operate in a war zone and even for antagonizing Japan by vigorously demanding redress. The backers of the Ludlow war-referendum amendment enlisted additional congressional support as it was rumored that some administration officials had discussed asking for a declaration of war against Japan. There was considerable debate as to why President Roosevelt had not invoked the Neutrality Act against China and Japan. (The answer is plain. Roosevelt knew that China relied almost entirely upon the United States for war materials, whereas Japan was superbly equipped to produce its own. He was determined not to cripple the Chinese in their struggle against the Japanese invaders, whom the administration believed would probably attack America in the future. The President justified not invoking the Neutrality Act on the ground that the Sino-Japanese conflict was an undeclared war and therefore did not technically come under the provisions of the legislation, even though the Italo-Ethiopian war had fallen in the same category.)

Despite the subsequent outcry against Roosevelt's policy in Asia, the noninterventionist bloc split on the *Panay* issue. There was sufficient suspicion of Japan in the United States for many people to make an exception to their noninterventionism in this case. Moreover, large numbers of nationalists rallied around the flag in the face of an overt assault on American vessels, and there were other Americans who were shocked by the incident into concluding that the United States could not ignore such an attack. The result was a considerable show of newspaper and magazine antagonism against the Japanese. To the administration's surprise, Republicans Alfred Landon, Frank Knox, and Henry Stimson came to Roosevelt's assistance, particularly condemning the movement toward the Ludlow amendment. With this kind of support and by exerting its own strenuous pressure, the White House early in 1938 secured the

defeat of consideration of the war-referendum measure
in the House by a vote of 209 to 188.

In a sense the heated national discussion of the *Panay*
incident and the Ludlow amendment marked the turning of the tide on foreign affairs. A boycott of Japanese
goods gained widespread acceptance, and many Americans contributed generously to relief in China and
Spain, and some filtered abroad to fight for those
nations' governments. Increasingly, magazines, newspapers, newsreels, and radio carried news and editorials
about foreign events. Much of the coverage and com-
mentary was anti-Japanese, anti-Nazi, anti-Fascist, and
anti-Franco, but even objective reporting made clear the
aggressive nature of the authoritarian powers. Novels,
short stories, and motion pictures also more frequently
dealt with the brutality of the dictatorships and their
threats to the lovers of peace. Almost no one called
for positive American action against aggressors, but the
sentiment for heightened national defense preparations
and private relief to the victims of war mounted as the
communications media gave more attention to Fascist
repression and imperialism.

From May, 1937, into 1939 the Gallup poll recorded
roughly a three-to-one sympathy for the Spanish Loyalists. The authoritarian nations were clearly distrusted,
as was evidenced by a March, 1938, poll showing that
Americans thought that either Germany, Italy, or Japan
was more likely than all other countries combined to
violate its treaty commitments. The percentage of
American opinion in favor of a war referendum declined
from 73 in October, 1937, to 64 by the end of December;
by August, 1938, 77 percent indicated that they were
willing to leave the question in the hands of Congress.
Sentiment for a bigger navy, army, and air force remained overwhelmingly high after 1935. By October,
1938, 94 percent disapproved of the repressive treatment
of Jews in Germany.

Make no mistake: The United States was not ready for any involvement overseas. It was, however, more willing to take steps to defend itself and to encourage, if timidly, the calming of world tensions. Roosevelt in 1938 again asked for larger appropriations for the military, especially the navy, and received them, although Congress refused to grant his request to fortify Guam. The President also wanted to sponsor an international conference to discuss ways to preserve peace but delayed proceeding with it at Neville Chamberlain's request. The British Prime Minister had made more definite plans for "a measure of appeasement" and wanted to see how they would work out. Roosevelt was not enchanted with appeasement—for example, the diplomatic recognition of Italy's possession of Ethiopia—but he was willing to see if Chamberlain could subdue the engines of war on the European continent. Adolf Hitler moved before the Prime Minister could act, for in a lightning move German forces occupied Austria in March. Americans were generally indignant, and Roosevelt allowed Secretary Hull to lash out at "international lawlessness" and inveigh against "isolationism" at home. The House of Representatives authorized an investigation of subversive activities because of the public's growing concern not only with Fascist infiltration but also with the purges in Russia. However, the resultant Committee on Un-American Activities, chaired by Representative Martin Dies, of Texas, took advantage of its authority chiefly to conduct a Red hunt.

Czechoslovakia was the focal point for American concern abroad in 1938, for, after annexing Austria, Hitler set his sights on that central European state. The issue ostensibly involved was the treatment of the German minority in Czechoslovakia, most of which lived in the Sudetenland, on the western edge of the country and on Germany's border. Hitler demanded that the Sudeten Germans be allowed self-determination, obviously so that Germany could incorporate the Sudetenland within its territorial boundaries. He made it plain that he was willing, if necessary, to detach the area by force, even at the risk of war with Czechoslovakia's allies, France and Great Britain. Prime Minister Chamberlain flew to Germany to dissuade the German leader from invading Czechoslovakia. Hitler insisted that Germany must have the Sudetenland. In September Chamberlain, with French support, forced the Czechs to agree to surrender the area, while Italy's Prime Minister Benito Mussolini, who was unprepared for a general European war, persuaded Hitler to accept the agreement. England and France were happy to accept the German chancellor's promise that "this is the last territorial claim I have to make in Europe" and relieved not to have to test their capacity for war against the Third Reich. As for the Czechs, they had lost not only the Sudetenland but also the elaborate defenses against Germany that they had constructed there. The price paid for what Chamberlain called "peace in our time," however, merely whetted the appetite of the Fascist dictatorships. Virtually stripped of its defenses, Czechoslovakia was occupied by Germany the following March, and Italy, following Hitler's example, invaded and conquered Albania in April. By the time Hitler ordered his legions into Poland on September 1, 1939, it was plain that the ultimate price, wholesale war in Europe, had to be paid.

There was little Roosevelt could do about the Czechoslovakian crisis. He and Secretary Hull indicated their concern and called for a peaceful settlement. But as the President said, "The Government of the United States has no political involvements in Europe, and will assume no obligations in the conduct of present negotiations." He knew that he had negligible influence on the European powers and, furthermore, that the American people were not ready for even official denunciation of what was happening in Europe. Yet the administration was willing to take several small steps forward on foreign policy. In August, 1938, Roosevelt, in a speech at Queen's University in Canada, asserted that the American people "will not stand idly by if domination of Canadian soil is threatened by any other empire."

The events of the Conference of American States in Lima, Peru, further indicated the administration's determination to defend the western hemisphere against foreign attacks. The United States urged its fellow American republics to advance beyond their 1936 pledge in Buenos Aires to consult with one another in case of an outside attack. Subsequently, in December, 1938, the American states unanimously adopted the Declaration of Lima, which condemned racial and religious prejudice everywhere and alien political activity in the Americas. The declaration also endorsed the use of appropriate measures to deal with threats to the peace, security, or territorial integrity of western-hemispheric nations. Although the Lima conference did not go as far as Secretary of State Hull wanted, the declaration constituted a sharp criticism of the Axis powers and served as the basis for developing collective security in the Americas.

Roosevelt also, for the first time, showed his teeth to Hitler. After the Nazi leader unveiled plans for accelerated German rearmament, the President responded by announcing in October, 1938, the allocation of an additional $300,000,000 for American defense. The wholesale terror and violence launched against Jews in Germany in November called forth sharp American reactions. Herbert Hoover, Harold Ickes, Alfred Landon, and prominent Catholic and Protestant clergymen joined in a national radio protest against these "inhuman actions." Roosevelt directed the American ambassador to return from Berlin for consultation and declared to a press conference that "I myself could scarcely believe that such things could occur in a twentieth-century civilization."

The administration also paid its respects to Tokyo. The Japanese had severely restricted the activities of foreign businesses in the occupied areas of China. Moreover, Japanese aerial bombs and artillery shells often sought out foreign churches, hospitals, and schools. The United States repeatedly protested. The Japanese gave apologies for the bombings and personal indignities, but it was clear that they intended to do what they wanted in China despite treaties and international conventions. In July, 1938, Secretary Hull stated that the United States "strongly opposed" the sale of aircraft to Japan, and most American airplane firms and exporters obeyed this "moral embargo." The government took a bolder and decidedly unneutral step in December when it extended a commercial credit of $25,000,000 to China for purchases in the United States.

By 1939 the Roosevelt Administration was seeking to gain more executive discretion in the application of the Neutrality Act, and consultations with anti-Fascist powers increased. On January 4, 1939, the President approached Congress to warn of the dangerous implications to the United States of aggression on other continents. Although he requested additional defense appropriations, he declared that other measures should be taken to blunt the possibility of foreign attack. "There are many methods short of war, but stronger and more effective than mere words, of bringing home to aggressor governments the aggregate sentiments of our own people." Specifically, he urged that America "avoid any action, or any lack of action, which will encourage, assist, or build up an aggressor."

The people of the United States were not yet willing to do more than express contempt for authoritarian brutality and reiterate their love of peace on earth.

President Roosevelt wanted to go beyond that, however, and indeed in small ways already had. He was shackled by public opinion and by Congress's obedient response to it. As historian Robert Divine has noted, "Frightened by the complex forces threatening the peace of the world, Americans sought to escape them by taking refuge in ironclad neutrality." That neutrality was, of course, not quite ironclad. Roosevelt used it both to cater to public opinion and to follow, as best he could, the foreign policy he wanted. The invoking of the Neutrality Act in the Italo-Ethiopian war tended to work against Italy, which was far more able than Ethiopia to procure the implements of war in America. Yet by applying the terms of the law to that conflict, the President offset the pressures from Italian-Americans and black Americans to favor one side or the other. Roosevelt genuinely feared that the Spanish civil war would develop into another world war, and this led him to invoke the Neutrality Act again. He became interested, as the Spanish struggle continued, in finding some formula to favor Loyalist forces, but without success. As in the Spanish situation, the administration had no significant ethnic-group pressure over the Sino-Japanese conflict. Indeed anti-Japanese sentiment in the United States allowed the administration to favor China, at least to the extent of not applying the Neutrality Act, of lending money to China, and of asking for a moral embargo on the sale of airplanes to Japan. Roosevelt also built up America's defenses and hemispheric solidarity against the Axis powers without incurring serious criticism. All this proved that strict neutrality was an illusion.

Each step along the path of aggression and repression taken by Nazi Germany, Fascist Italy, imperial Japan, and, yes, Communist Russia softened American neutrality. Moreover, as peoples fell victim to aggrandizement and brutality, the related ethnic and religious groups in the United States pressed for some action. Almost no Americans were ready to go to war over foreign crises. Increasingly, however, they wanted their country to prepare for defense and to speak out against authoritarianism. The United States slowly rearmed as a consequence and sought to strengthen its position with potential allies in Latin America, Europe, and Asia. By 1941 the Roosevelt Administration's policy was "all aid short of war" to those nations under attack by the Axis, even to the Soviet Union after Germany invaded it.

The roots of that policy lay in the period before the outbreak of World War II. The slackening in 1937 and 1938 of the New Deal's influence and imaginativeness in dealing with domestic problems coincided with the acceleration of authoritarianism and aggression in the world. President Roosevelt was aware that he had a new stage upon which to perform and was willing to use defense preparations as a way to reinvigorate the economy and to take attention from his failures at home. That was, of course, not his prime reason for focusing on international affairs, for he was deeply disturbed by the growing threats to world peace and civilization and to American security. He intended to persuade the public to perceive those threats and to act on his recommendations to cope with them. He took what actions he felt he could, even covertly, to meet the dangers from the unhappy developments abroad. The United States had a "rendezvous with destiny," and it was greater than even Franklin D. Roosevelt imagined. Not only would it give his administration the gift of economic recovery, thanks to the prosperity generated by war abroad and defense preparations at home, but it would drastically change the course of history for both the United States and the world.

12

State of the Union

THE depression was the most distressing experience visited upon the United States since the Civil War. Ten years of economic hardship and sharp political controversy left scars that were still seen a generation later in the mental and visceral responses of many Americans. The antagonisms occasioned by increasing involvement of the nation in foreign affairs exacerbated those reactions. There was much, for example, in the domestic and foreign programs of the John Kennedy and especially the Lyndon Johnson administrations that harked back to Franklin D. Roosevelt's policies. Although the Republicans of the 1950's and 1960's accepted the basic changes adopted during the New Deal years, they often did so grudgingly, and they frequently employed the rhetoric of Herbert Hoover and Alfred Landon to embroider their acceptance. The lingering concerns of depression and World War II contributed to the development of the much-discussed generation gap of the 1960's. The older generation, still captive to many of the issues of the Roosevelt era, had as much difficulty in understanding the outlook of those who came to awareness after 1960 as young people had in comprehending what had shaped the ideas of their elders.

Obviously America's response to the depression and to the emerging international problems of the late 1930's represented a change in the minds of the citizenry. The greatness of that change, however, was more relative than absolute. No fundamental change in American foreign policy had occurred by 1939. That was to wait upon the reaction of the United States to the outbreak of World War II and the nation's involvement in it. All the Roosevelt Administration did by 1939 was to bring America from the deep neutralist sentiment of the mid-1930's to an awareness that foreign events could not be ignored. Foreign-policy developments after 1939 would have a deep and far-ranging impact at home and abroad, but that is a later story.

The more germane question is, What were the results of the Roosevelt Administration's domestic policies? The New Deal had been experimental in its approach to the nation's grave problems. It had also been personal, for so much of what went on revolved around the strong personalities of Franklin Roosevelt and the people he chose to assist him, such as Harry Hopkins, Harold Ickes, Hugh Johnson, and Frances Perkins. The New Dealers were almost as imaginative as they were articulate. They also represented a variety of ideas, which meant that they and their allies on Capitol Hill were sometimes as much at war among themselves as they were with their critics over the land. Leaders in the administration and Congress early recognized the immediate problems and basic perplexities of the depression-stricken country, but they evolved no integrated program to meet those issues. This was partly because of the factionalism so evident in both the executive and the legislative branches and partly because the system of checks and balances in a nation of diverse ideas and interests worked against the development of a cohesive program. Yet if at any time in the history of the United States a majority could have been brought together for a logical, integrated program of reconstruction, this was it. Americans were eager for action and change in 1933, 1934, and 1935. Although they were not ready for radical change, as evidenced by the election returns of 1932, they were clearly willing in the next several years to go beyond what was achieved, and they had a President adept enough at leadership so that more could have been done and done more consistently.

Roosevelt, however, despite his great leadership ability, the people's confidence in him, and a huge majority in Congress, was unable to do more than he did. The failure to devise an overall program of national reconstruction must, therefore, be ascribed in part to his pragmatism and political opportunism. He could perceive the nation's immediate problems, but he could not formulate a profound plan to deal with them. Indeed Roosevelt did not seek one. His pragmatism led him to meet problems piecemeal, and his opportunism—reinforced by the nature of the American political system—forced him too often to keep one eye on the next election and therefore to cater to the interests of individual groups instead of to those of the country as a whole. The corps of officials in his administration mirrored his weaknesses, representing as they did a variety of interests, abilities, and ideas. Certainly, the President was seldom willing to risk his political popularity to champion any controversial program. Examples of this were his positions on the Silver Act and anti-lynching legislation and the many cases in which he allowed Congress to whittle down his recommendations without a fight. In the two instances where he displayed political courage, the veterans' bonus veto and judicial reorganization, the first was not likely to hurt him, and the second was rooted more in vanity than lion-heartedness.

Nevertheless Roosevelt's pragmatism and keen political sensitivity must be credited with achieving much that was accomplished by the New Deal. In its willingness to experiment, his administration was able to test a broad range of responses to the depression, and many of those responses proved successful at least as amelioratives. In catering to the interests of a large number of groups, the President was able to provide a wide range of satisfaction and to erect a political coalition that gave him, certainly through 1936, more than enough support to do so. If New Deal programs too often worked contradictorily, were sometimes foolish, and were occasionally administered poorly, that was the price of the administration's experimentalism, and it was a price that most Americans were willing to pay.

The basic goals of the Roosevelt Administration were relief, recovery, and reform. The New Deal's greatest success was in the area of relief. Employing a bewildering number of alphabetical agencies, the most prominent being the Federal Emergency Relief Administration, the Works Progress Administration, the Public Works Administration, and the Civilian Conservation Corps, and coordinating the work of state, local, and private organizations, the administration brought relief to most of the destitute and jobless. This endeavor was later supplemented by the provisions of the Social Security Act. Yet despite the scope and imaginativeness of the New Deal's relief program, not everyone was taken care of. There was never sufficient money available, and even those on relief seldom received enough to satisfy more than the most rudimentary needs.

The reforms fostered by the New Deal were many and far-reaching. Many of the deficiencies of the stock market, banking, and utilities were remedied. Organization and collective bargaining by labor unions was made vastly more effective under the National Industrial Recovery and Wagner acts. The federal government and the states assumed some ongoing responsibility, thanks to the Social Security Act, for the needs of the aged, dependent mothers and children, the handicapped, and the unemployed. Agricultural legislation and the Fair Labor Standards Act built a floor under the earnings of large numbers of farmers and workers. A variety of federal agencies, especially the W.P.A., P.W.A., and Tennessee Valley Authority, encouraged new and higher standards for public services. The Rural Electrification Administration effected a minor revolution by bringing electricity to rural areas. Negroes and Indians were given a fairer, though far from adequate, share of government services and benefits. The federal government considerably forwarded the conservation of natural resources. These reforms, and others, were not without their problems. As with social security, they often proved to be inadequate and cumbersome, and, as with the Fair Labor Standards Act, they frequently fell well short of covering all those who required protection. They sometimes worked at cross purposes, as with the various agricultural measures, which strove to limit production while expanding irrigation projects and otherwise providing farmers with means that could be used only to heighten production. In a nutshell the New Deal's reforms were scattered and sometimes contradictory. They represented, nevertheless, a greater amount of reform than had ever before been sought or achieved by government action in the United States. Moreover, the Roosevelt Administration, with the people's support, greatly encouraged and even forced substantial reform in state and local governments. If the federal government became America's most far-ranging enterprise during the 1930's, state and local government was only second to it, as they assumed a greater number of responsibilities and often expanded traditional operations in the service of their citizens.

The relief given to the needy during the New Deal period was substantial and reform significant. Far less effective, however, were the federal government's efforts to promote economic recovery. Understandably, the administration's prime objective was the return of prosperity, which was, after all, what the American people wanted. Relief was only a way to fill the gap until prosperity returned, and the New Deal's reform policies were devised in large part as methods of stimulating recovery. The results of the administration's recovery programs were far from substantial. In fact, they were dismal. Personal income in the United States stood at only $72,900,000,000 in 1939, compared with $85,800,000,000 in 1929, although the population had increased by more than 9,000,000. Almost 9,500,000 people, or 17.2 percent of the labor force, were still unemployed in 1939, about three-quarters of those out of work in 1933. One in every five Americans received some form of government relief in 1939, more than in 1936 and as many as in 1933. Of the world's major industrial nations, the United States in 1936 was the least advanced toward recovery and by 1939 was the only one still seriously affected by depression. There was no sign by 1939 that America on its own would soon retrieve prosperity. Indeed the Roosevelt Administration had concluded that the country would normally have at least 5,000,000 unemployed, and it had not formulated any new programs to spur recovery. When prosperity finally came, it was borne on the shield of Mars, not the escutcheon of the New Deal. It was plain by the end of the 1930's that the administration was stuck on dead center, neither receding toward classic economic doctrine nor reaching out to implement some new economic theory. The New Deal seemed content to split the differences between Herbert Hoover and the big-spending advice of British economist John Maynard Keynes and to wait to see what the future would bring.

Equally significant is that most Americans were also willing to settle for a modicum of recovery. Statistics could, after all, be turned upside down to show that national personal income had increased by over half between 1933 and 1939 and that the number of people with jobs had mounted by almost 20 percent. Furthermore, it seemed that the basic needs of most of the jobless and destitute were being met and that some of the worst deficiencies of the system had been remedied. The people wanted more, but like the administration, they were unwilling to do anything dramatic to achieve it for fear that they might lose what had been so arduously gained since Roosevelt took office. Lulled by the actual and claimed accomplishments of the administration, they, too, would wait to see what the future had in store.

Other matters of consequence, of course, came out of the New Deal period. Competition between Democrats and Republicans had become sharper, largely because of the greater number of intensely felt issues being debated. Epithets such as "Hoover's depression" or "Roosevelt's ruin," "reactionary" or "radical," "Fascist" or "Red" were tossed about without compunction. Class hatreds had risen to a high point, too, and Roosevelt's invectives against "economic royalists" and the "forces of greed" had contributed to it. As never before intellectuals and the working class set themselves against the entrepreneurial class, and farmers were lashing out at everyone— Wall Street, labor, intellectuals, and bureaucrats. Furthermore, the administration encouraged secrecy in government—although nothing like it would during World War II—as citizens, the press, and even the nation's elected representatives were sometimes told that what the executive branch was doing was none of their business. Even high administration officials complained that they were not adequately advised of what was going on. The President told Secretary of the Treasury Morgenthau, "Never let your left hand know what your right hand is doing." When Morgenthau asked, "Which hand am I, Mr. President?" Roosevelt replied, "My right hand, but I keep my left hand under the table." By 1938 Senator Sherman Minton, of Indiana, offered a bill, with some administration backing, to censor material that was "proved" false by the government and yet knowingly published. The bill got nowhere, but it reflected the tendency toward secrecy in some government quarters.

The New Dealers had no monopoly on arrogance in public office, but their self-righteousness was dangerous in a democracy as well as unnecessarily irritating. Too often, they were extremely sensitive to criticism and insensitive to responding constructively to criticism. There is much to Adolf Berle's observation about the neo-Brandeisian type, so prominent in the administration after 1934, who "has satisfied his lust for battle in mere punitive expeditions without having a clear picture of the result he intends to get; too often he has failed to recognize that the object is not winning a battle, but creating a socially workable result."

Another consequence of the New Deal was the alteration of federalism and the separation of powers. Although state functions and budgets grew rapidly, the states found themselves increasingly involved in joint programs in which the federal government imposed the goals and standards. Americans now more often looked to Washington instead of the state capital for action, and the states had relatively less power to preclude or offset the expanding range of federal operations. Similarly, the executive branch became the segment of the national government that initiated as well as implemented programs. Not only did Congress authorize more for the executive branch to do, but the legislators also delegated more of their decision-making powers. As Roosevelt's appointees took their places on the bench, the courts also became more responsive to executive initiative and influence. In short, the safeguards that had been written into the Constitution appeared to be withering away as the national executive branch became more powerful. By the end of the 1930's the states seemed to be largely clients of the federal government, and Congress chiefly an instrument to obstruct executive action, a role that the courts were less and less filling. Yet there appeared to be no other way to meet the popular approval for large-scale government operations. Congress could not administer its own legislation and had proved that it was not well enough organized to initiate and evaluate all government actions. The states had been unable to deal with the nation's economic crisis. Of course, the alterations in federalism and the separation of powers did not lead to the development of an authoritarian state in America. The continuance of the states as vassals of the national government rarely impaired and often enhanced the people's rights. Congress soon demonstrated that if it had largely lost the initiative in setting government policies, it could use its obstructive powers, for better or worse, to force compromises. By the 1950's the courts showed that they could act vigorously to uphold constitutional provisions against all comers.

It is clear that the New Deal brought neither political nor economic revolution to the United States. It is possible that it staved off violent revolution, however, considering the gravity of the economic crisis early in 1933. The Roosevelt Administration provided enough recovery, relief, and reform to regenerate confidence in the nation's political system and revive acceptance of the economic system. Although the New Deal satisfied few thinking people, it was, regardless of sharp and sometimes justified criticisms, accepted by the great majority of Americans, partly because the other political possibilities seemed far less attractive. Certainly, the New Deal and corresponding movements in the states demonstrated that government could move swiftly and positively in a crisis, even if erratically. What the New Deal brought about, perhaps without realizing it, was a large measure of state capitalism, which had been emerging as an element in American government since the turn of the century. By 1939 state capitalism's pattern was plainly seen in the operations of the federal government—that is, to provide for the needy, regulate and subsidize ailing segments of the economy, and coordinate the work of the various parts of government in these activities, and all within a framework allowing for a large degree of private enterprise and political freedom. With this the Roosevelt Administration salvaged the essentials of the old economic and political system and strengthened them with some new remedies and pain-killers.

In retrospect the New Deal does not seem the great change it appeared to be during the 1930's. It is more fairly described as a considerable acceleration of ongoing trends that clearly appeared before World War I. They were even sighted from time to time during the dozen years before Franklin Roosevelt became President. Warren Harding had favored reducing some federal activities, but he fully intended to add others. Although President Coolidge was largely content to administer what he had inherited, Herbert Hoover had great plans for using the national government to reinvigorate America's economy and life. His administration, although thrown off course by the depression, developed a more active federal government and advanced proposals for additional increments of power. If Franklin D. Roosevelt went well beyond what Hoover wanted, it must be remembered that President Hoover, by design and necessity, went considerably beyond his predecessors. The expansion of state and local activities and expenditures was also part of the continuing trend in the growth of government in America. State and local expenditures mounted from $1,100,000,000 in 1902 to $7,800,000,000 in 1927 to almost $10,000,000,000 by 1938. Moreover, the largest funding increases in state and local functions between 1927 and 1938 were for public welfare, the expenses of which expanded sevenfold, and health and natural resources, which doubled.

The growth of government, however, was only one of the many continuing trends in the United States during the interwar decades. The rate of population growth became even slower during the 1930's than the 1920's, thanks to restricted immigration and a lower birthrate, with the number of people in the continental United States increasing only from 105,711,000 in 1920 to 122,775,000 in 1930 to 131,669,000 in 1940. Negroes still poured out of the South to the North and West, which was one of the factors in the continued westward movement of the center of population. The proportion of women to men almost came into balance by 1940, as only 582,000 more males than females were counted. The number of Americans born abroad declined from 13,713,000 to 11,419,000 between 1920 and 1940, and the median age of the population continued to climb from 25.3 in 1920 to 29.0 in 1940. For the time being these trends had little impact, except that the relative increase in the number of aged contributed substantially to the pressure for social-security legislation. Yet the other population trends foreshadowed important changes, as more blacks resettled in areas where they had better opportunities to develop and be heard, as women outnumbered men, as the number of immigrants declined, and as the westward movement continued. It can be suggested that these trends were related to later movements for equal rights for Negroes and women, to a decrease in ethnic-group politics, and to a growing shift in political power from the eastern seaboard. Already of great significance was the dramatic rise in the proportion of city dwellers, which contributed hugely to Roosevelt's election majorities. The urban population mounted from 54,158,000 to 74,424,000 during the 1920's and 1930's, compared to an increase in rural folk of from 51,552,000 to 57,245,000.

The depression, of course, greatly slowed down the economy. Capital expenditures for manufacturing plants and equipment in 1939 stood at slightly more than half of what they had been in 1929, and the indexes of manufacturing production were almost exactly the same for the two years. Yet during the depression decade the

United States had retained and even somewhat expanded its capacity for production in leading industries. Although the nation by 1929 had developed its industrial productive capacity beyond what it could use, it was beginning to catch up by 1939. (Indeed within a few years America's industrial plant would be inadequate to the country's needs because of wartime demands.) By 1939 America's gross national product—that is, its total production of goods and services—surpassed the 1929 level, rising from $104,400,000,000 to $111,000,000,000 in terms of 1929 dollars. This was attributable in large part to the continued development of technology and labor productivity. The index of per man-hour productivity, extending a long-term trend, rose from 78.3 in 1920 to 97.5 in 1930 to 124.0 in 1940. New inventions and the extension of mechanical and assembly-line processes contributed immensely to the rising labor efficiency and expanded the number of new products for sale. Aluminum came into widespread use in home utensils and transportation equipment, because it combined strength with lightness and was rust-free. Continuing the change in fabrics, nylon came onto the market in ladies' stockings by 1939. Plastics were used in a wider range of products, and television programming appeared in 1939, although the war put it out of business for the time being. During the 1930's hybrid corn revolutionized the growing of that commodity. Every year saw a major improvement in aircraft design and manufacturing, as planes became larger and safer. The expansion of products was largely attributable to organized and particularly corporate research, as the trend in that direction was accelerated. By 1940 corporations were responsible for more than half of the patents issued, compared to slightly over one-quarter in 1920.

Despite the hazards of doing business, the lure of entrepreneurial activity remained high. There were

2,213,000 firms operating in 1929 and 2,116,000 in 1939. Equally noteworthy is that business became more stable after the worst of the depression had passed. The average annual number of business failures per 10,000 concerns for the period 1933–1939 was 64, contrasted to 136 for 1930–1932 and even 103 for 1921–1929. Concentration was still the rule, however, in business and industry, partly because the Roosevelt Administration alternated giving the patient stimulants and tranquilizers. The top 5 percent of corporations commanded 84.49 percent of the income of all American corporations in 1939, compared to 83.82 and 84.34 percent respectively in 1933 and 1929. A highly significant change in business during the 1930's was that government action and union pressure forced corporations to give workers a larger share of the profits. This was seen in the shift in the percentage of national income to employees from 60.5 during the period 1920–1929 to 66.8 during 1930–1939, a change that also helped put America's mass-production-consumption economy on a sounder basis.

There were, of course, other important labor changes. The postwar decade had seen a substantial reduction in weekly work hours. That advance was continued during the 1930's, at first because of workweek reductions to try to spread employment around and later because of union activities and New Deal legislation. Consequently, between 1929 and 1939 the average number of hours worked per week in factories declined from 44.2 to 37.7. The trend toward increased average hourly industrial wages, broken during the heart of the depression, also resumed, rising from $.51 in 1921 to $.57 in 1929 and rising to $.63 by 1939. Set beside reduced working hours, it meant that the average weekly paycheck of 1939 was $23.86, compared with $25.03 in 1929. Thanks to the lowering of the consumer price index, from 73.3 in 1929 to 59.4 in 1939, however, the American industrial worker's paycheck bought more. Another kind of improvement was revealed in the decline of work-injury frequency rates. The number of injuries per million man-hours worked decreased in factories from 24.2 in 1926 to 19.6 in 1932 to 14.9 in 1939. Clearly, the trend had begun during the 1920's, partly because of the industrial efficiency movement and the concern for reducing the financial losses involved in injury compensation. Workingmen, however, as the potential victims, were also keenly aware of the problem and added to the pressure for better protection against industrial accidents.

The trend toward more Americans earning their livings as professional, managerial, sales, and clerical personnel persisted, rising roughly from 29 to 31 percent of the labor force between 1930 and 1940, at the expense of the continued decline in farmers and farm workers. The number and percentage of working women also rose: 8,637,000 of America's 51,810,000 women worked in 1920, compared to 10,752,000 of 60,638,000 in 1930 and 12,574,000 of 65,608,000 in 1940. The caliber of positions available to women probably declined, however, as a result of the pressures to make room for jobless males, especially heads of families, during hard times. For example, few school systems employed married women, and often companies refused to hire the wives of their male workers.

The 1920's' trends for financial institutions also either continued through the 1930's or showed signs of resuming by 1940. The economic crisis accelerated the decline of the small bank and the concomitant growth of large banks. The number of banks in the United States had decreased from 30,909 to 24,273 between 1920 and 1930, but it shrank even more dramatically, to 15,076, by 1940. Banking assets had jumped from $53,100,000,000 in 1920 to $74,300,000,000 in 1930 and by 1940 had recovered from the depression to rise to $79,700,000,000. Because

of the disappearance of the weakest banks and the salutary effects of New Deal reforms, banking institutions
were more stable by 1939 than they had ever been in the
country's history. Americans were also still sold
on insurance. The value of life insurance in force
in 1939 amounted to $111,600,000,000, compared to
$102,100,000,000 ten years earlier. Moreover, a larger
variety of other insurance coverages was available and
selling well—for example, automobile and medical-
surgical insurance. Another trend affected the third
largest type of America's investment institutions, the
savings-and-loan associations. As with banks, their number declined steadily, though not as sharply. Savings-
and-loan assets, however, dropped from $8,800,000,000
in 1930 to a decade low of $5,600,000,000 in 1939. But
from there on, the resources of savings-and-loan associations would rise rapidly, thanks to their high interest
rates and the demands for funds to invest in housing.
It is clear from these data that Americans continued
to accept these three types of financial institutions.
Indeed New Deal stock-market and banking reforms
and regulations, as well as Federal Housing Administration loan guarantees and deposit insurance for banks
and savings-and-loan associations, strengthened them
during the 1930's and made them more acceptable to
the public.

Postwar transportation trends also continued during
the 1930's as shippers and passengers sought more efficient and especially cheaper ways of transportation.
Railroads declined further. Between 1929 and 1939 rail-
road-freight tonnage and the number of passengers carried fell off by approximately one-third. The number
of rail-track miles operated was cut back from its peak
of 429,883 in 1930 to 405,975 in 1940. Thanks to its
inexpensiveness, ship traffic on inland lakes and rivers
held its own. The amount of freight carried, for example, on the Great Lakes increased from 138,574,000 tons

in 1929 to 145,216,000 tons in 1940. Oil pipelines sliced into railway revenues as their networks grew in length from 55,260 miles in 1921 to 85,796 in 1929 to 98,681 by 1939. Trucking and busing competed ever more successfully wth inland water carriers and especially railways. This was evidenced in the expansion between 1929 and 1939 of the number of registered trucks from 3,550,000 to 4,691,000 and of buses from 34,000 to 92,000. Both of these developments were facilitated, as were similar trends during the 1920's, by the extension of surfaced roads, which jumped from 694,000 to 1,367,000 miles between 1930 and 1940. Despite the economic difficulties of the 1930's, even automobile registrations grew from 23,035,000 to 27,466,000.

The most dramatic transportation development, of course, was in aviation, which had just begun to get off the ground as an industry during the late 1920's. Business concentration was at work here as the vicissitudes of depression and the mounting cost of equipment reduced the number of airline operators. The number of revenue miles flown in the United States, however, soared from 22,729,000 in 1929 to 82,925,000 in 1939. Between those years the number of passengers carried domestically rose from 162,000 to 1,735,000, and the amount of express and freight ton-miles rocketed from 70,000 to 2,713,000. They still had a way to go, but it was plain that airplanes would soon be a major factor in American transportation.

Agriculture remained the weakest spot in the national economy. Government programs had been fairly successful in providing relief to financially stricken farmers, but they had been far less effective in reducing surplus production. Indeed federal land-reclamation and farm-improvement programs had worked, along with advances in seeds, husbandry, and technology, actually to expand America's capacity for agricultural production. The long-term increase in farm acreage had not been reversed, for it stood at 1,059,582,000 in 1939, compared to

974,277,000 a decade earlier. The production index of
farm commodities rose from 91.4 to 93.2 between 1929
and 1939, and the amount of farm exports continued
to drop. Agricultural mechanization forged onward, with
the number of tractors, for example, mounting from
827,000 in 1929 to 1,445,000 in 1939. The farmers' financial burdens declined as both taxes and mortgage indebt-
edness dropped substantially. Agricultural cash receipts,
however, despite federal subsidy payments, had not fully
recovered, rising to only $8,600,000,000 in 1939, com-
pared to $11,300,000,000 in 1929. The value of farms
also lagged well behind, standing at almost
$48,000,000,000 in 1929 but only slightly over
$34,000,000,000 ten years later. By 1939 it was plain
that farmers were not even as well off as they had been
during the difficult 1920's. Agriculture's basic problem
of producing more than it could find markets for remained unsolved despite all the activity and concern of
the Roosevelt Administration and the farmers themselves. Only the great demands for agricultural goods
created by World War II would meet the problem, and
then only temporarily, for the next generation would
also fail to balance agricultural supply and demand.
Large numbers of farmers would therefore have to remain, in effect, welfare clients of the federal government.

Another problem that the United States failed to solve
by 1939 was that of foreign trade. Both exports and imports fell disastrously during the depression and had not
recovered by 1939. Moreover, the excess of exports over
imports remained. In fact, in 1939 exports, which
totaled $3,200,000,000 compared to $2,300,000,000 in
imports, were proportionately larger than they had been
in 1929, when exports and imports were, respectively,
worth $5,200,000,000 and $4,400,000,000. This imbalance,
which troubled trade relations with other countries,
would continue for another generation until American
adventures and aid commitments abroad more than

offset the excess of exports over imports. Another foreign-
trade trend of the 1920's and 1930's worth noting is the
shift in whom the United States sold to and bought
from. More than half of the nation's exports went to
Europe in 1922, but only about 40 percent by 1939, as
markets for America's goods developed rapidly in Africa,
Asia, and the western hemisphere. A similar, though
not so pronounced trend also occurred in the sources of
imports. All this contributed to the increasing interest
of the United States in economic and political happenings in areas of the world other than Europe.

Some ongoing developments were barely interrupted
and perhaps even spurred by the depression. Education
is an example of this. The proportion of the population
between ages five and seventeen that attended school
remained fairly constant, between 81 and 82 percent, from
1928 to 1934 and then slowly increased to a high of 85.3
percent by 1940. The number of high-school graduates
soared, from 597,000 who received diplomas in 1928 to
1,221,000 in 1940. It was clear by the 1930's that the goal
of supplying an eighth-grade education had been substantially achieved. The United States, in fact, was well
on its way to providing a high-school education to all,
for by 1940 the percentage of high-school graduates
among seventeen-year-olds was 50.8, compared to 29.0
in 1930 and 16.8 in 1920. This phenomenon was attributable to the increasingly high premium placed upon
schooling, rising state requirements for attendance, the
tight job market that discouraged would-be school leav-
ers, and the diversified, elective curriculum. A higher
proportion of students enrolled in courses in industrial
education, home economics, agriculture, and business
subjects, in no small part because the need to train for
jobs was heavy on the minds of students and their
advisers. School consolidation also continued, encouraged
by the demand for more efficiency in school administration and aided by greater ease of transportation in the

form of the school bus. Largely as a result of the replacement of small schools by large, the number of elementary and secondary schools declined from 274,769 in 1930 to 238,169 in 1940. Vastly increased state appropriations, which almost doubled during the decade, and even a modicum of federal support helped relieve the burden on local tax resources.

The changes in higher education were even more dramatic. Between 1930 and 1940 the number of colleges and universities grew from 1,409 to 1,708, faculty members increased from 82,000 to 147,000, and students rose from 1,101,000 to 1,494,000. Junior colleges alone increased from 277 with 56,000 students to 456 with 150,000 during the decade. The number of bachelor's degrees conferred mounted from 122,000 in 1930 to 186,000 in 1940. The growth in the number of graduate degrees awarded was not as spectacular as in the 1920's, but it was still remarkable. The master's degrees granted advanced from 14,969 to 26,731 and of doctor's from 2,299 to 3,290. Again the emphasis on educational advancement and the exigencies of the job market in America accounted for these increases, which went far beyond the low population growth of the decade.

Despite the lessened availability of funds for research during the 1930's, science continued to advance. Indicative of this was that nine Americans, all native-born, won Nobel prizes in the sciences, compared to three during the 1920's. Refugee scientists from Europe, such as Albert Einstein, Isador Rabi, and Otto Stern, by 1940 were already having a significant impact. Americans, both native-born and newcomers, were preparing the United States to take its place soon in the forefront of science. The changes in science and their technological applications were to have awesome results. Not only did they eventually lead to a remarkable development of America's ability to produce an easier and more prosperous way of life, but they vastly expanded the country's military capability, which had tremendous consequences at home and overseas during the following generation.

America's concern during the 1930's with solving its economic and social problems and serving the rising structure of government led to noteworthy progress in the social sciences. Federal and even state agencies were receptive to the advice of social scientists and especially interested in their newly developing fact-finding and analytical devices. Particularly influential on younger American economists, if not on their seniors and government, were the theories of John Maynard Keynes, which called for the scientific use of deficit spending and redistribution of income in order to revive economic activity during a depression. Sociologists found that there was rising interest in their researches and particularly in community studies, a sophisticated example of which was the work of Robert and Helen Lynd. Because of the efforts of scholars like Charles E. Merriam and Leonard D. White, public administration also came of age as an academic field. Political scientists as well as sociologists moved into the area of gauging public opinion, which was made both more respectable and more scientific by the labors of Hadley Cantril and George Gallup. Historians benefited handsomely in both research and job opportunities from the rapid development of public archives caused by the movement of the federal and many state governments to put their records in order.

The health advances of the 1920's continued during the depression decade. The years of life expectancy grew from 59.7 in 1930 to 62.9 by 1940. Both infant and maternal mortality rates dipped remarkably, from 64.6 per 1,000 live births to 47.0 and from 6.7 to 3.8 respectively. The death rates for typhoid and paratyphoid fever, diphtheria, whooping cough, and measles were more than cut in half, in fact to the point where those diseases were no longer great causes of death in the United States. Medicine also made large strides in the struggles against tuberculosis, influenza, pneumonia, gastritis, duodenitis, enteritis, and colitis. The death rates for cancer and heart disease climbed, though not enough to offset health advances in the other areas. The development of new treatments was responsible for much of the improvement in the care of the sick. Insulin was brought increasingly to bear in controlling diabetes, liver therapy made significant inroads on anemia, and nicotinic acid on pellagra. Sulfa derivatives, which came onto the market late in the 1930's, were of startling effectiveness in combating a number of diseases, including pneumonia and meningitis. Vitamin pills and injections came into common use in strengthening bodily resistance to a wide range of ills.

The increased availability of medical facilities and personnel (and improvements in their training) also contributed substantially to the advances in the health of Americans. Although the number of physicians per 100,000 population rose slightly, the proportion of nurses shot up by almost 25 percent during the 1930's. The number of beds in general hospitals per 1,000 population increased by one-sixth. As during the 1920's, people were increasingly willing to go to the hospital when they were sick. This was documented in the growth of the average daily census of hospital patients from 763,000 in 1930 to 1,026,000 in 1940. It was obvious, however, that many Americans still lacked adequate medical care. They simply could not pay for it, regardless of growing public health programs and private medical insurance plans. Unfortunately, this was a problem that neither the medical profession nor most politicians gave high priority to solving in the generation to come.

Racial minorities in particular received neither a proportionate share of health care nor of employment and educational opportunities. Yet some benefits filtered down to them; others they wrested for themselves. Blacks constituted the largest racial minority by far, with 12,866,000 counted in the 1940 census. The percentage of them in skilled and semiskilled occupations increased from 23.3 to 28.8 between 1930 and 1940, and the percentage of young Negroes attending school climbed from 60 to 64.4. Health improvements were reflected in the extension of black life expectancy from forty-eight to fifty-three years. The number of voters among Negroes increased, almost completely as a result of their continuing migration from the South to other parts of the country where the burdens of discrimination and segregation rested less heavily. Franklin D. Roosevelt's promise of a new deal for Americans took on special significance for Negroes. Efforts, however often unsuccessful, were made to give them a share of government assistance, and larger numbers of them entered federal service. The President and especially his wife, Eleanor, listened to and talked with black leaders. Outstanding Negro writers, such as Langston Hughes, Alain Locke, and Richard Wright, achieved a measure of national prominence. The National Association for the Advancement of Colored People reached a membership of fifty thousand by 1940. Moreover, Negroes developed a greater sense of pride and community as a result of Ethiopia's vigorous struggle against Italy in the war of 1935–1936, Jesse Owens's Olympic victories in Adolf Hitler's Berlin, and Joe Louis's pugilistic triumphs. The successful use of black boycotts to increase job opportunities in New York, St. Louis, Washington, and other cities also contributed. The significance of the developments of the 1930's lay not in what had been tangibly gained, for that was little, but as the overture to what was to come. It was clear that black leadership, aspirations, and skills were increasing. They were to be put to good use in wresting concessions from other Americans during the war.

The nation's 334,000 Indians had been given special attention by the federal government during the 1930's, with attendant increases in education, economic status, health, and self-government. Whatever had been done, and it was monumental compared with past treatment of Indians, had not, however, given them the strength to do more than survive in a still highly discriminatory society. The several million Mexican-Americans—nobody knew exactly how many there were—found themselves in a similarly unfavorable situation, except they received no federal protection. Segregated, largely uneducated, desperately poor, and lacking political power, they were in no position to strive successfully to better their lot. Neither the Indians nor the Mexican-Americans had attained the level of leadership and skills enjoyed by Negroes. Even hope for something better was seldom theirs.

There were also the minorities of Asian origins, which in 1940 consisted chiefly of the some 127,000 Japanese-Americans and 78,000 Chinese-Americans. As with other racial minorities, Americans of Oriental ancestry could not move freely in society. Segregation, discrimination, and economic disadvantages were common to their lives, although, as a result of their small numbers, yearning for education, and entrepreneurial abilities, many of them found niches for themselves in marginal enterprises. Because of the skills and stakes they had acquired, they were in a better position than Indians, Mexican-Americans, and even Negroes to exploit the opportunities for advancement that would arise, for the Chinese-Americans during World War II and for the Japanese-Americans afterward.

There were minorities other than racial, of course, but their needs did not seem pressing enough to command major attention. The twenty million American Catholics used the traditional methods of education, economic improvement, legal action, and especially political influence to progress toward equality. Although discrimination was occasionally evident, one could agree with Arnold and Caroline Rose that by 1940 "it was questionable whether Catholics could any longer be called a minority group." America's five million Jews had also found a substantial position in the nation's life. Drawing on a strong sense of group identity and on traditions of accomplishment and cooperation, they had been able to make much of the opportunities for advancement. By the 1930's Jews were found in prominent positions in business, law, the arts, science, literature, education, and even politics. Yet they still suffered to a certain extent from being ghettoized and from being barred from or admitted on a quota basis to many educational institutions, social groups, and public accommodations.

As has been noted, the numbers of Americans of foreign birth greatly declined between 1920 and 1940, largely as a result of the severe restrictions imposed on fresh immigration. Antagonisms between newcomers and natives was considerably diminished, chiefly because Americans of foreign birth had had an additional twenty years to adjust to the United States and for native Americans to adjust to them. Moreover, most of the new immigrants of the 1930's came from the middle and educated classes and found it easier to make their way and be accepted in the New World. The Roosevelt Administration had also relied heavily on the votes of naturalized citizens and their children and had responded in recognizing their claims to equality and opportunity.

Obviously, the social order had changed considerably since 1920. As a consequence, men of Jewish background, Henry Horner and Payne Ratner, could be elected governors of Illinois and Kansas, Fiorello LaGuardia could be chosen mayor of New York, Joseph Kennedy could serve as ambassador to the Court of St. James, and a black, William H. Hastie, could be appointed a federal judge. More important, the use of violence and insult against minorities had declined, and additional opportunities for advancement were available. The religious and ethnic minorities benefited the most from this, and by the 1940's their legitimate complaints would be few. The plight of the racial minorities was still monumental, but some of their people had broken through the walls of discrimination if not of segregation, and larger numbers would force their way through in the years to come. Blacks and Oriental Americans were on the verge of developing enough strength to demand and occasionally receive attention from the rest of the nation. For them, the road would be long and sometimes hazardous, but it would be traveled.

Culture also marched forward in the United States during the 1930's. Of course, most of the impact came from the popular culture conveyed by radio, motion pictures, and mass publishers. The number of radio stations grew from 618 to 765 between 1930 and 1940, and the number of families with radio sets more than doubled, from 12,000,000 to 28,000,000. Radio confirmed during the decade what it had strongly suggested by the end of the 1920's, that it was a low-quality medium of fantasy and entertainment, of soap operas, sports, adventure stories, comedies, popular music, often punctuated by commercial advertising. Little of its time was devoted to good music, educational, or informational programs. Mass publishing still had great appeal, whether in the form of detective, western, movie, or romance magazines and books. Yet popular reading tastes were improving a bit as indicated by the rapid takeoff in circulation of *Reader's Digest* and the new picture magazines *Life* and *Look*.

Motion pictures continued to be the favorite out-of-the-home form of entertainment. Despite the depression, attendance remained high, dipping from an average weekly audience of eighty million in 1929 to sixty million in 1932 and 1933, then averaging more than eighty

million weekly from 1935 through 1940. Movies with
sound tracks had become standard by 1930 and provided
an additional attraction to the customers, as did the
advent of Technicolor late in the 1930's. As with radio,
the main function of films was to provide mass entertainment and escapism, although occasionally a great
production or a great performance reached the screen.
Yet, in contrast with radio and popular publishing, the
motion pictures offered a higher standard of entertainment. *I Was a Fugitive from a Chain Gang* was clearly
superior to *Gangbusters,* as were the vehicles of the
Marx Brothers to *The Fibber McGee and Molly Show.*
When films were good, they were culturally good; when
radio was good, it was only mediocre.

Yet if popular culture was becoming more popular,
higher forms of culture were diversifying and becoming
somewhat more attractive to the public. Radio audiences
for operas and symphony concerts were slowly growing,
and motion-picture producers found that quality films
could draw crowds. Literature was still king, however,
as far as quality was concerned, and its princes and
princesses were to a considerable extent the same people
who had dominated American letters during the 1920's.
Although their fortunes varied and their themes sometimes changed, the names of Sinclair Lewis, Ernest
Hemingway, Edna St. Vincent Millay, F. Scott Fitzgerald, Eugene O'Neill, E. E. Cummings, John Dos
Passos, William Faulkner, and Edmund Wilson remained among the most prominent on the literary scene.
However, several new luminaries—for example, John
Steinbeck, James T. Farrell, Pearl Buck, Richard Wright,
and Thomas Wolfe—joined the top rank during the
1930's.

The three main themes of the decade's writers were
social protest, cultural nationalism, and anti-Fascism.
Explications of American life were typical of novelists
William Faulkner and Thomas Wolfe, short-story writer

and playwright William Saroyan, poet Robert Frost, and playwright Robert Sherwood. Cultural nationalism and regionalism also pervaded the works of many writers of social protest, including James T. Farrell and John Steinbeck. Social protest, plain but not simple, was the major theme in the novels of John Dos Passos, the plays of Elmer Rice, Lillian Hellman, Maxwell Anderson, Clifford Odets, and Sidney Howard, and the poems of Langston Hughes, Edna St. Vincent Millay, and Archibald MacLeish. It is understandable that the collapse of the nation's economy should spur the literary exploration of the American character and the reasons for economic chaos. Increasingly, though, writers would show their concern for the rise of Fascism in the world, as evidenced in Sinclair Lewis's *It Can't Happen Here* (1935), John Dos Passos's *Adventures of a Young Man* (1939), and Ernest Hemingway's *For Whom the Bell Tolls* (1940). Other authors, of course, were less topical. F. Scott Fitzgerald's *Tender Is the Night* (1934) escaped popularity during the decade, but it stands as a momentous psychological inquiry. Pearl Buck groped for universal themes in her novels on China. Thornton Wilder in his play *Our Town* (1938) skillfully combined an examination of social problems with human universals, symbolism, and fantasy. And the poems of E. E. Cummings soared through a variety of emotions and experiences. Despite the depression, the state of letters was strong and vital in the United States. That it had been recognized internationally was documented by the award of Nobel prizes for literature to Lewis, Buck, and O'Neill during the 1930's.

America's interest in art and music continued to rise, partly in response to the federal government's relief programs for artists and musicians. The modernism and experimentalism of the art of the 1920's took a back seat to realism. As in literature, social protest and cultural nationalism were the most frequent themes. The pillars of society were harpooned in the paintings and cartoons of such gifted artists as William Gropper and Ben Shahn. The leading cultural nationalists were Edward Hopper and Reginald Marsh, who were outstanding at catching the spirit of urban life in colors and figures that demanded attention and empathy. American society was also illuminated by Thomas Hart Benton, John Steuart Curry, and Grant Wood, the three foremost regionalist painters, whose works dramatically celebrated life in the Middle West. The paintings of Isabel Bishop, Morris Kantor, and Moses and Raphael Soyer successfully combined protest and the provincialism of New York City. Primitivism, works by untrained painters, also came into fashion, as seen in the popularity of Grandma Moses, Horace Pippin, and John Kane. The acclaim given the work of Margaret Bourke-White and Walker Evans showed that photography had been accepted as an art. Carl Milles represented an influential compromise between sculptural modernism and realism, and Alexander Calder began his long career of crafting mobiles. The migration of Marcel Breuer, Walter Gropius, and Richard Neutra to America gave architectural functionalism and starkness a strong boost. Perhaps the greatest and certainly the most controversial art in the United States, though, was done by the great revolutionary Mexican muralists José Orozco and Diego Rivera. In any event it was plain by 1940 that art in America was coming of age. The artists' platoon of the 1920's had grown to a battalion, and the quality and even popularity of their work were no longer in dispute. The United States stood on the threshold of a golden age of painting and sculpting. The skills, the temperament, and the audience had been found.

Less dramatic were the developments in serious music, which in America remained largely devoted to the products of other lands and other times. Its popularity and inventiveness were growing, however, as American orchestras, musicians, and conductors improved. Aaron Copland, George Gershwin, and Howard Hanson still dominated composing, but fresh talents were in evidence and would add to America's small musical capital. Roy Harris skillfully employed home scenes and folk tunes, as heard in "When Johnny Comes Marching Home" and "Folksong Symphony." Walter Piston held the banner high for neoclassical composition in his ballet "The Incredible Flutist." Polyphony was the hallmark of William Schuman, the youngest of America's composers of emerging prominence. Virgil Thomson's sophistication and playfulness, as seen in *Four Saints in Three Acts,* with libretto by Gertrude Stein, was an added asset among composers who often took themselves too seriously. Although no Sergei Prokofiev or Richard Strauss appeared on the American musical scene, it was obvious by the end of the 1930's that native composers were capable of respectable and imaginative work.

The social as well as the cultural trends of the 1920's generally extended through the 1930's. Urban-minded Americans forged ahead in their struggles with the countryside. The battles over Sunday closings of places of entertainment were largely rear-guard actions, and the older moralistic attitudes toward tobacco, liquor, dancing, and the like were eroding rapidly. Women, though they had a long way to travel to achieve equality, were treated less like chattels. The Ku Klux Klan had all but disappeared, although other agents of radical and religious prejudice remained in abundance. Large-scale advertising, radio, motion pictures, more standardized education, and greater ease of movement, thanks largely to motor vehicles, had further increased the materialistic aspirations and common culture of Americans. Clearly, the old mores were fast falling before the onslaughts of urbanism, modernism, mass media, and the mass-produc-

tion-consumption society. Those forces, not the church
or traditional rural values, were largely shaping people's
actions if not their pronouncements.

Depression had sharpened the people's economic interests. Economic security was now the dominant objective.
Americans insisted that society provide the basics of
food, clothing, and housing, for themselves as individuals, if not always for other folk. The keen concern for
economic security motivated the depression generation
above all else, as most people came to demand stable
employment as never before in their lives. This concern
could be seen even beyond the 1930's in the large number
of Americans seeking positions in government, teaching,
large corporations, and even the military. It was also
reflected in the continuing demands of labor for job
security and of farmers for government subsidies. This
did not mean that the goals of success and prosperity
had been abandoned; Americans wanted to achieve those
just as much as they had in 1929. During the 1930's,
however, security had been added to the people's prime
economic desires. The mass-production-consumption society constantly encouraged those interests. Appetites were
whetted by the fantastic array of available products and
particularly the ubiquitous advertising of them. Therefore, Americans were not sacrificing their desire for success and prosperity when they demanded security. They
now wanted all three. Furthermore, Americans, despite
economic catastrophe, still believed in progress. And
why not, for news came almost daily of technological
developments that promised a new and better materialistic world to come. Even at the depth of the depression,
the Century of Progress exposition of 1933–1934 in
Chicago pictured a time to come that would be vastly
more prosperous and comfortable than the present or
recent past. This theme was elaborated upon at the
enormously popular world's fairs in New York and
San Francisco toward the end of the decade. Thus, Amer-

ica's long-standing economic beliefs were kept buoyant.

Another subject of high interest during the 1930's was the federal government, which advanced rapidly as a factor in people's lives. Before 1929 the federal government, except in times of war, played a minuscule part in the lives of the great majority of Americans. By 1939 it had assumed a major role. Despite its shortcomings, most citizens looked upon the national government as the prime force that could set things right. Only a minority of Americans questioned its good intentions, its essential morality, or its ability to effect needed changes. Even most of the opposition contended that the government's flaws could be set right by a change of policy-making personnel. Few people envisioned a grand scaling-down of the federal government. Even fewer suggested that it could develop interests of its own that might not coincide with the people's best interests. In short, the great majority of Americans looked to government chiefly as a force that could heal wounds and alleviate suffering, a force that could help them achieve both security and success. Government's emergence was uncritically taken by most as a step further toward national progress. Threats of disruption from overseas fortified that conviction, for it appeared that in case of war only the federal government could protect the people, although Americans were not yet willing by 1939 to entrust government with a more positive role in foreign policy.

Thus the 1920's and 1930's, viewed in retrospect, stand as a transitional period in the history of the United States. Government came to the fore in ways unanticipated in 1920, although not yet with the strength gathered after 1939. The trends of racial and ethnic prejudice were slowly reversed, though far from overcome. Great advances were made in establishing an American culture and homogenizing the life of the people. Health care, education, and technology developed dramatically. The United States remained an en-

trepreneurial society based on concentration of ownership of the means of production, although more
attention—especially during the 1930's—was given to
spreading prosperity around and to providing economic
security, partly because of the requirements and results
of the revolutionary mass-production-consumption aspect
of the economy. Despite the depression, the two decades
had far more in common than they had separating
them.

By 1940 the United States stood on the threshold of
a new world, toward which it had been traveling since
World War. I. That new world was far from what had
been anticipated. Material progress after the coming of
World War II exceeded most Americans' expectations,
just as did involvement in foreign affairs. The impact
was tremendous both at home and abroad and is far
from fully understood yet. It is clear, however, that
the roots and shoots of events since 1939 developed
significantly during the generation between the two
world wars. Then modern America had truly been
coming of age.

Bibliographical Essay

VITAL to the documentation of trends in America between the world wars is *Historical Statistics of the United States, Colonial Times to 1957* (Washington, D.C.: U.S. Government Printing Office, 1960), produced by the United States Bureau of the Census. The third volume of Arthur M. Schlesinger, Jr., and Fred L. Israel, eds., *History of American Presidential Elections* (New York: Chelsea House and the McGraw-Hill Book Company, 1971), contains estimable essays and relevant documents on the elections of 1920, 1924, 1928, 1932, and 1936. David A. Shannon's *The Socialist Party of America: A History* (New York: The Macmillan Company, 1955) and Irving Howe and Lewis Coser's *The American Communist Party: A Critical History* (Boston: Beacon, 1957) are useful surveys. Overviews of particular topics for the 1920's and the 1930's are found in Robert A. Divine, *American Immigration Policy, 1924–1952* (New Haven, Conn.: Yale University Press, 1957), Theodore Saloutos and John D. Hicks, *Agricultural Discontent in the Middle West, 1900–1939* (Madison, Wis.: University of Wisconsin Press, 1951), Robert M. Miller, *American Protestantism and Social Issues, 1919–1939* (Chapel Hill, N.C.: University of North Carolina Press, 1958), Blake McKelvey, *The Emergence of Metropolitan America, 1915–1966* (New Brunswick, N.J.: Rutgers University Press, 1968), Barbara Rose, *American Art since 1900* (New York: Praeger Publishers, Inc., 1967), and a magnificent cultural catchall, Edmund Wilson, *The American Earthquake: A Documentary of the Twenties and Thirties* (Garden City, N.Y.: Doubleday & Company, Inc., 1958).

No single book concentrating on the 1920's is balanced and dispassionate. The best general works on the period are, however, John D. Hicks's liberal-oriented but fact-filled *Republican Ascendancy, 1921–1933* (New York: Harper & Row,

Publishers, 1960), William E. Leuchtenburg's stimulating book-length essay, *The Perils of Prosperity, 1914–1932* (Chicago: University of Chicago Press, 1958), and Arthur M. Schlesinger, Jr.'s partisan but fascinating *The Crisis of the Old Order, 1919–1933* (Boston: Houghton Mifflin Company, 1957). Frederick Lewis Allen's *Only Yesterday* (New York: Harper & Row, Publishers, 1931) is still worth reading, despite its eastern, middle-class, and urban biases. The essays in John Braeman, Robert H. Bremner, and David Brody, eds., *Change and Continuity in Twentieth-Century America: The 1920s* (Columbus, Ohio: Ohio State University Press, 1968), are informative and often provocative. Important to understanding the postwar period are Arthur S. Link's "What Happened to the Progressive Movement in the 1920s?" *American Historical Review*, Vol. LXIV (July, 1959), and Frederick J. Hoffman's *The 20's: American Writing in the Postwar Decade* (New York: The Viking Press, Inc., 1962).

Many perceptive insights on the troubles arising immediately after World War I are found in William M. Tuttle, Jr., *Race Riot: Chicago in the Red Summer of 1919* (New York: Atheneum Publishers, 1970), Robert K. Murray, *Red Scare: A Study in National Hysteria, 1919–1920* (Minneapolis: University of Minnesota Press, 1955), and William Preston, Jr., *Aliens and Dissenters: Federal Suppression of Radicals, 1903–1933* (Cambridge, Mass.: Harvard University Press, 1963). The standard work on the 1920 Republican and Democratic election campaigns is Wesley M. Bagby's *The Road to Normalcy* (Baltimore: Johns Hopkins University Press, 1962). Robert K. Murray's *The Harding Era: Warren G. Harding and His Administration* (Minneapolis: University of Minnesota Press, 1969) is detailed, admirably balanced, and scrupulously fair. See Donald R. McCoy, *Calvin Coolidge: The Quiet President* (New York: The Macmillan Company, 1967), for the Coolidge Administration. Burl Noggle's *Teapot Dome: Oil and Politics in the 1920s* (Baton Rouge, La.: Louisiana State University Press, 1962) is a judicious account of the great political scandal of the decade. Able biographies of two of the most important legislators of the 1920's are Richard Lowitt's *George W. Norris: The Persistence of a Progressive, 1913–1933* (Urbana, Ill.: University of Illinois Press, 1971) and Marian C. McKenna's *Borah* (Ann Arbor, Mich.: University of

Michigan Press, 1961). David Burner, *The Politics of Provincialism: The Democratic Party in Transition, 1919–1932* (New York: Alfred A. Knopf, Inc., 1968), and Kenneth MacKay, *The Progressive Movement of 1924* (New York: Columbia University Press, 1947), are worthy studies.

L. Ethan Ellis, *Republican Foreign Policy, 1921–1933* (New Brunswick, N.J.: Rutgers University Press, 1968), and Joan Hoff Wilson, *American Business and Foreign Policy, 1920–1933* (Lexington, Ky.: University of Kentucky Press, 1971), are useful surveys. Thomas H. Buckley's *The United States and the Washington Conference, 1921–1922* (Knoxville, Tenn.: University of Tennessee Press, 1970) is the best account of that event. A scholarly and readable inquiry into the Pact of Paris is Robert H. Ferrell's *Peace in Their Time: The Origins of the Kellogg-Briand Pact* (New Haven, Conn.: Yale University Press, 1952). William Appleman Williams, "The Legend of Isolationism in the 1920s," *Science and Society*, Vol. XVIII (Winter, 1954), is a provocative challenge to the standard interpretation of America's foreign policy during the decade. Other aspects of government policy are ably dealt with in Preston J. Hubbard, *Origins of the TVA: The Muscle Shoals Controversy, 1920–1932* (New York: W. W. Norton & Company, Inc., 1961), Donald C. Swain, *Federal Conservation Policy, 1921–1933* (Berkeley, Calif.: University of California Press, 1963), and Robert H. Zieger, *Republicans and Labor, 1919–1929* (Lexington, Ky.: University of Kentucky Press, 1969).

On social history, Yamato Ichihashi's *Japanese in the United States: A Critical Study of the Problems of the Japanese Immigrants and Their Children* (Stanford, Calif.: Stanford University Press, 1932) is still worth reading. The best available secondary material on black Americans during the 1920's is generally found in biographies. See particularly E. David Cronon's splendid *Black Moses: The Story of Marcus Garvey and the Universal Negro Improvement Association* (Madison, Wis.: University of Wisconsin Press, 1955) and the competent volumes by Francis L. Broderick, *W. E. B. DuBois, Negro Leader in a Time of Crisis* (Stanford, Calif.: Stanford University Press, 1959), and Elliott M. Rudwick, *W. E. B. DuBois, Propagandist of the Negro Protest* (Philadelphia: University of Pennsylvania Press, 1960). Also worth examining is the stimulating work by Gilbert Osofsky, *Harlem: The Making of a Ghetto, 1890–1930* (New York: Harper & Row, Publishers, 1966). Don S. Kirschner's *City and Country: Rural Responses to Urbanization in the 1920s* (Westport, Conn.: Greenwood, 1970) is a challenging inquiry that investigates rural adaptation to urban styles as well as the nature of rural-urban conflict.

Three of the most highly publicized social-political manifestations of the 1920's are interestingly dealt with in Ray Ginger's work on the evolution controversy, *Six Days or Forever?: Tennessee v. John Thomas Scopes* (Boston: Beacon, 1958), Francis Russell's *Tragedy at Dedham: The Story of the Sacco-Vanzetti Case* (New York: The McGraw-Hill Book Company, 1962), and Andrew Sinclair's *Prohibition: The Era of Excess* (Boston: Little, Brown and Company, 1962). David M. Chalmers's *Hooded Americanism: The History of the Ku Klux Klan* (Garden City, N.Y.: Doubleday & Company, Inc., 1965) is a good survey. Norman F. Furniss, *The Fundamentalist Controversy, 1918–1931* (New Haven, Conn.: Yale University Press, 1954), and William L. O'Neill, *Everyone Was Brave: The Rise and Fall of Feminism in America* (Chicago: Quadrangle Books, 1969), are excellent studies. A social history of some of the most disadvantaged industrial workers and their attempts to organize is Irving Bernstein's *The Lean Years: A History of the American Worker, 1920–1933* (Boston: Houghton Mifflin Company, 1960).

Three fine monographs illuminate the election of 1928: Vaughn D. Bornet's *Labor Politics in a Democratic Republic* (Washington, D.C.: Spartan, 1964), Edmund A. Moore's *A Catholic Runs for President* (New York: The Ronald Press Company, 1956), and Ruth C. Silva's *Rum, Religion, and Votes: 1928 Reexamined* (University Park, Pa.: Pennsylvania State University Press, 1962). Matthew and Hanna Josephson, *Al Smith: Hero of the Cities* (Boston: Houghton Mifflin Company, 1969), is the best biography of the 1928 Democratic presidential nominee.

The standard survey of economic history for the 1920's is still George Soule, *Prosperity Decade: From War to Depression, 1917–1929* (New York: Rinehart, 1947). John Kenneth Galbraith's *The Great Crash 1929* (Boston: Houghton Mifflin

Company, 1955) is a readable account, written from a liberal nationalist perspective. Herbert Hoover sets forth his views on economic, political, and social matters during the period 1921–1933 in his *Memoirs*, Vols. II and III (New York: The Macmillan Company, 1951–1952). Harris Gaylord Warren, *Herbert Hoover and the Great Depression* (New York: Oxford University Press, 1959), is something of a scholarly defense of President Hoover's administration and crammed with data. Somewhat more objective, and more critical, are Albert U. Romasco's *The Poverty of Abundance: Hoover, the Nation, the Depression* (New York: Oxford University Press, 1965) and Jordan A. Schwarz's *The Interregnum of Despair: Hoover, Congress, and the Depression* (Urbana, Ill.: University of Illinois Press, 1970). Also see Roger Daniels's fine *The Bonus March* (Westport, Conn.: Greenwood Publishing Corporation, 1971). Hoover's foreign policy is ably considered in Robert H. Ferrell, *American Diplomacy in the Great Depression: Hoover-Stimson Foreign Policy, 1929–1933* (New Haven, Conn.: Yale University Press, 1957), Alexander DeConde, *Herbert Hoover's Latin American Policy* (Stanford, Calif.: Stanford University Press, 1951), and Raymond G. O'Connor, *Perilous Equilibrium: The United States and the London Naval Conference of 1930* (Lawrence, Kans.: University of Kansas Press, 1962).

Roosevelt's path to the White House is superbly reconstructed in Frank Freidel's *Franklin D. Roosevelt: The Triumph* (Boston: Little, Brown and Company, 1956). The best balanced work on the New Deal period is William E. Leuchtenburg's *Franklin D. Roosevelt and the New Deal, 1932–1940* (New York: Harper & Row, Publishers, 1963). For significant pro– and anti–New Deal accounts, see James MacGregor Burns, *Roosevelt: The Lion and the Fox* (New York: Harcourt, Brace & World, Inc., 1956), and Edgar E. Robinson, *The Roosevelt Leadership, 1933–1945* (Philadelphia: J. B. Lippincott Company, 1955). Arthur M. Schlesinger, Jr.'s *The Coming of the New Deal* (Boston: Houghton Mifflin Company, 1958) and *The Politics of Upheaval* (Boston: Houghton Mifflin Company, 1960) deal with domestic politics and policies through 1936: although highly favorable toward Roosevelt, these two large volumes are essential to understanding the New Deal and its times. Helpful views of the administration and a plenitude of information about some of the key political figures of the period are found in T. Harry Williams's Pulitzer-prize winning *Huey Long* (New York: Alfred A. Knopf, Inc., 1969), Searle F. Charles's *Minister of Relief: Harry Hopkins and the Depression* (Syracuse, N.Y.: Syracuse University Press, 1963), J. Joseph Huthmacher's *Senator Robert F. Wagner and the Rise of Urban Liberalism* (New York: Atheneum Publishers, 1968), Donald R. McCoy's *Landon of Kansas* (Lincoln, Nebr.: University of Nebraska Press, 1966), C. David Tompkins's *Senator Arthur H. Vandenberg: The Evolution of a Modern Republican* (East Lansing, Mich.: Michigan State University Press, 1970), Edward L. and Frederick H. Schapsmeier's *Henry A. Wallace of Iowa: The Agrarian Years, 1910–1940* (Ames, Iowa: Iowa State University Press, 1968), and especially John M. Blum's admirable *From the Morgenthau Diaries: Years of Crisis, 1928–1938* (Boston: Houghton Mifflin Company, 1959).

A number of competent works deal with various themes of importance during the New Deal years. Broadus Mitchell's *Depression Decade: From New Era through New Deal, 1929–1941* (New York: Rinehart, 1947) remains the standard survey of economic history. The international depression and the responses of various nations to it are treated in a series of scholarly articles in *Journal of Contemporary History,* Vol. IV (October, 1969). Otis L. Graham, Jr., *An Encore for Reform: The Old Progressives and the New Deal* (New York: Oxford University Press, 1967), explores the reactions of surviving prewar Progressives to the New Dealers and the intellectual connections and differences between them. Herbert Stein's *The Fiscal Revolution in America* (Chicago: University of Chicago Press, 1969) contains perceptive comments on the changed use of federal money to achieve national economic goals. James T. Patterson, *The New Deal and the States: Federalism in Transition* (Princeton, N.J.: Princeton University Press, 1969), treats the changing relationship between the national and state governments. A sympathetic social history of labor is Irving Bernstein's *Turbulent Years: A History of the American Worker, 1933–1941* (Boston: Houghton Mifflin Company, 1970). The split in the ranks of organized labor is effectively dealt with in Walter Galenson, *The CIO Challenge to the AFL* (Cambridge, Mass.: Harvard

University Press, 1960). Sidney Fine's *Sit-down: The General Motors Strike of 1936-1937* (Ann Arbor, Mich.: University of Michigan Press, 1969) is a masterful case study.

Although not comprehensive, Raymond Wolters's *Negroes and the Great Depression: The Problem of Economic Recovery* (Westport, Conn.: Greenwood, 1970) is the best work on relations between black Americans and the federal government. William T. Hagan, *American Indians* (Chicago: University of Chicago Press, 1961), Rose Hum Lee, *The Chinese in the United States of America* (Hong Kong: University of Hong Kong, 1960), and Carey McWilliams, *North from Mexico* (Philadelphia: J. B. Lippincott Company, 1949), include sections on the situation of Indians, Chinese-Americans, and Mexican-Americans in the United States during the 1930's. The standard general social history of the period is Dixon Wecter's *The Age of the Great Depression, 1929-1941* (New York: The Macmillan Company, 1948). Studs Terkel's *Hard Times: An Oral History of the Great Depression* (New York: Pantheon Books, 1970) is a fascinating evocation of a broad range of the attitudes of the time. Arthur A. Ekirch, Jr.'s *Ideologies and Utopias: The Impact of the New Deal on American Thought* (Chicago: Quadrangle Books, 1969) provides insights into the intellectual history of the New Deal era. The most convenient source for poll data is *Public Opinion, 1935-1946* (Princeton, N.J.: Princeton University Press, 1951), a monumental compilation by Hadley Cantril and Mildred Strunk.

A large number of books deal with specific aspects of the New Deal. See especially Sidney Fine's splendid case study of an N.R.A. code, *The Automobile under the Blue Eagle* (Ann Arbor, Mich.: University of Michigan Press, 1963), and Ellis Hawley's remarkable untangling in *The New Deal and the Problem of Monopoly* (Princeton, N.J.: Princeton University Press, 1966). Also rewarding are Van L. Perkins, *Crisis in Agriculture: The Agricultural Adjustment Administration and the New Deal, 1933* (Berkeley, Calif.: University of California Press, 1969), John A. Salmond, *The Civilian Conservation Corps, 1933-1942* (Durham, N.C.: Duke University Press, 1967), Jane DeHart Mathews, *The Federal Theatre, 1935-1939* (Princeton, N.J.: Princeton University Press, 1967), Thomas K. McCraw, *TVA and the Power Fight,*

1933–1939 (Philadelphia: J. B. Lippincott Company, 1971),
John A. Brennan, *Silver and the First New Deal* (Reno, Nev.:
University of Nevada Press, 1969), Ralph F. de Bedts, *The
New Deal's SEC: The Formative Years* (New York: Columbia
University Press, 1964), Michael Parrish, *Securities Regulation
and the New Deal* (New Haven, Conn.: Yale University
Press, 1970), Arthur J. Altmeyer, *The Formative Years of
Social Security* (Madison, Wis.: University of Wisconsin Press,
1966), Paul K. Conkin, *Tomorrow a New World: The New
Deal Community Program* (Ithaca, N.Y.: Cornell University
Press, 1959), Sidney Baldwin, *Poverty and Politics: The Rise
and Decline of the Farm Security Administration* (Chapel
Hill, N.C.: University of North Carolina Press, 1968), and
Richard D. Polenberg, *Reorganizing Roosevelt's Government:
The Controversy over Executive Reorganization, 1936–1939*
(Cambridge, Mass.: Harvard University Press, 1966). A num-
ber of useful articles on the Roosevelt Administration's im-
pact on the West is included in *Pacific Historical Review*,
Vol. XXXVIII (August, 1969). Frank Freidel, *F.D.R. and the
South* (Baton Rouge, La.: Louisiana State University Press,
1965), is a perceptive book-length essay.

Among the many scholarly treatments of political attitudes
and reactions during the Roosevelt years are George Q. Flynn,
American Catholics and the Roosevelt Presidency, 1932–1936
(Lexington, Ky.: University of Kentucky Press, 1968), John
L. Shover, *Cornbelt Rebellion: The Farmers' Holiday Asso-
ciation* (Urbana, Ill.: University of Illinois Press, 1965),
Donald R. McCoy, *Angry Voices: Left-of-Center Politics in
the New Deal Era* (Lawrence, Kans.: University of Kansas
Press, 1958), David H. Bennett, *Demagogues in the Depression: American Radicals and the Union Party, 1932–1936*
(New Brunswick, N.J.: Rutgers University Press, 1969),
George Wolfskill, *The Revolt of the Conservatives: A History
of the American Liberty League, 1934–1940* (Boston: Houghton Mifflin Company, 1962), and James T. Patterson, *Congressional Conservatism and the New Deal: The Growth of
the Conservative Coalition in Congress, 1933–1939* (Lexington, Ky.: University of Kentucky Press, 1967).

Foreign policy during the 1930's has commanded a good
deal of attention from historians. Lloyd C. Gardner, *Economic
Aspects of New Deal Diplomacy* (Madison, Wis.: University

of Wisconsin Press, 1964) is a searching study. Standard is Bryce Wood's *The Making of the Good Neighbor Policy* (New York: Columbia University Press, 1961). Edward M. Bennett, *Recognition of Russia: An American Foreign Policy Dilemma* (Waltham, Mass.: Blaisdell, 1970), and Manny T. Koginos, *The Panay Incident* (Lafayette, Ind.: Purdue University Press, 1967), treat two key episodes. An able study of the politics surrounding the passage of neutrality legislation is Robert A. Divine's *The Illusion of Neutrality* (Chicago: University of Chicago Press, 1962). Manfred Jonas makes salutary distinctions among the various elements too often lumped under the pejorative term "isolationist" in *Isolationism in America, 1935–1941* (Ithaca, N.Y.: Cornell University Press, 1966). William L. Langer and S. Everett Gleason's interventionist-oriented *Challenge to Isolation, 1937–1940* (New York: Harper & Row, Publishers, 1952) and Donald F. Drummond's well-balanced *The Passing of American Neutrality* (Ann Arbor, Mich.: University of Michigan Press, 1955) deal with events leading to the increasing involvement of the United States in world affairs.

Index

Some other books published by Penguin
are described on the following pages.

The Pelican History of the United States

CONFLICT AND TRANSFORMATION
The United States, 1844–1877

William R. Brock

Although William R. Brock gives politics their due weight in this survey of the momentous period that encompassed the American Civil War, his unconventional approach sees political decisions in the context of society as a whole. He therefore interprets the Civil War as an ideological struggle between men who were responding to the deeper needs of their times. Economic influences are considered, but the emphasis is on the way in which convictions drove men to irreconcilable positions. William R. Brock is Professor of Modern History at the University of Glasgow.

The Pelican History of the United States

UNITY AND CULTURE
The United States, 1877–1900

H. Wayne Morgan

This is a survey of America's growth into an increasingly unified nation between 1877 and 1900. Expansion in agriculture and industry, the beginnings of American imperialism, the rise of the new moneyed classes, and the attempt to reconcile individual freedom with material progress are shown to be among the features of the unifying process. In his review of that process, Professor Morgan lays particular stress on the vital roles played by labor, politics, and science. Finally, turning to the cultural renaissance of those years, he finds in the arts ample evidence of the homogeneous American personality that was emerging. H. Wayne Morgan is Professor of History at the University of Texas.

The Pelican History of the United States

RISE TO GLOBALISM
American Foreign Policy, 1938–1970

Stephen E. Ambrose

This is a searching review of American foreign policy between 1938 and 1970. American involvement
in World War II, the Cold War, the Korean conflict,
the Berlin crisis, the invasion of Cuba, and the war
in Vietnam are among the events that Professor
Ambrose surveys as he relates them to the larger
themes of America's rise to, and maintenance of, her
enormous global power. Yet going far beneath these
vast currents, he looks at traits of the American character—economic aggressiveness, racism, fear of communism—and shows how they have helped shape
the nation's foreign policy. It is this probing beneath
the surface of history that makes *Rise to Globalism*
a uniquely valuable work. Stephen E. Ambrose is
Professor of History at the University of New
Orleans.